History of Black Business

The Coming of America's Largest Black-Owned Businesses

By Martin K. Hunt

and

Jacqueline E. Hunt

Library of Congress Catalog Card Number: 99-94225

Published by the Knowledge Express Company, Chicago, Illinois

Printed by R. R. Donnelley & Sons, Chicago, Illinois

ISBN 0-9665221-0-9

Table of Contents

DEDICATION 6

ACKNOWLEDGMENTS 7

PREFACE 9

INTRODUCTION 12

Section One: The History of Black Business 13

CHAPTER ONE: HISTORY OF BLACK BUSINESSES BEFORE 1970 14
    ADVENTURERS 18
    INVENTORS 23
    BLACK BANKERS AND INSURANCE COMPANY FOUNDERS 36

CHAPTER TWO: THE COMING OF AMERICA'S LARGEST BLACK-OWNED
    BUSINESSES: 43
    A Summary Note on Black Business' Foundation for Growth 43
    Factor Conditions 44
    Strategy 53
    Related and Supporting Industries 58
    Conclusion 64

Section Two: Location as a Determinant of Competitive Advantage 65

CHAPTER THREE: CHICAGO: A MODEL FOR BLACK BUSINESSES
IN A METROPOLIS 66
    Banks and Real Estate 72
    Manufacturing 73
    Journalism 74
    Insurance Companies 76
    Recreational and Service Establishments 78

CHAPTER FOUR: CASE: SUPREME LIBERTY LIFE INSURANCE
COMPANY 81

Section Three: Cases in the History of Black Business 99

CHAPTER FIVE: JOHNSON PUBLISHING COMPANY, INC. 100

CHAPTER SIX: TLC BEATRICE INTERNATIONAL 105

CHAPTER SEVEN: JOHNSON PRODUCTS 123

CHAPTER EIGHT: BLACK ENTERTAINMENT TELEVISION (BET) HOLDINGS, INC. 129

CHAPTER NINE: HARPO, INC. 139

CHAPTER TEN: MOTOWN 149

CHAPTER ELEVEN: NORTH CAROLINA MUTUAL INSURANCE COMPANY 163

CHAPTER TWELVE: CARVER FEDERAL SAVINGS BANK 177

CHAPTER THIRTEEN: H. J. RUSSELL & COMPANY 187

CHAPTER FOURTEEN: VIEW TO THE FUTURE 197

    Lessons Learned 199
    New Opportunities in America 201
    The Entrepreneur's Purpose 201
    The Possibilities are Boundless 202

Appendix 205
    Selected Contextual Milestones in Black Business History 206
    Number of Black Businesses, 1863-1998 222
    Glossary 224
    Publicly-Owned African-American-owned businesses 226
    Top Commercial and Industrial Companies in 1997 227
    Top Auto Dealerships in 1997 228
    Top Banks in 1997 229
    Top Insurance Companies in 1997 231
    Top Investment Banks in 1997 232
    Leading Black Entrepreneurs 1820-1865 233

Bibliography 234

DEDICATION

I would like to take this opportunity to remember the fallen entrepreneurs who were stricken down too soon. Good bye to Reginald Lewis who pioneered the art of the deal for African-Americans. Good bye to Wardell Lazard, founder of W.R. Lazard & Company.

Mr. Travers J. Bell, Jr., I dedicate this book to you for breaking down barriers with Daniels and Bell, the first African-American-owned investment bank to become a member of the New York Stock Exchange (NYSE). To the late Mr. Ron Brown, former Secretary of Commerce, I dedicate this book to you who inspired all those who desire to reach the highest level of government.

I dedicate this book to the organizations whose mission ensures the future of many African-American business leaders of tomorrow. They include, but are not limited to:

- the Urban League,
- the NAACP,
- our churches and places of worship,
- our Black fraternities, historically Black colleges,
- the Ivy League, our State colleges,
- Harvard Business School,
- and all of the other institutions that will educate and instill America's work ethic to venture for the betterment of all.

The men and women in this book have left far and distant stars for us to aim. The field of possibilities may just now be opening up. Let's go get them.

ACKNOWLEDGEMENTS

I offer much thanks and appreciation to my friends and family who have given me their thoughts in writing the **History of Black Business**. Thank you to my beloved wife, Jacqueline, who supported and encouraged me through four years of getting this dream to come to fruition and who has written many of the case studies. Thanks to my mother who never stopped pushing me to finish this book so that a collective knowledge of Black-owned businesses could be concisely communicated to a national audience. Thanks to my sisters, Janine and Karen, for their support. Thank you Karen for putting up with my antics while you helped me start this book and structure its content. Thanks to my brother and my father who have given me their input with insights and opinions. Thank you to my mother in law, mamita linda, for letting us stay with her, so that we could afford to work on this important venture. Thanks to my life long friends Henry Timothy Foxx III and Garikai Campbell who have always been supportive and consultative. Thank you to Kristi Cunningham for excellent suggestions and value-adding comments.

Thanks to my mentors who have provided for this effort. Thanks to Professor Michael Porter for his thought, leadership and inspiration. It was Professor Porter who initially inspired me to write this book. Thanks to Earl Graves for sharing his ideas on the subject of Black-owned business and for creating BLACK ENTERPRISE magazine to bring Black business news to mainstream America. Thank you to Cornel West for his encouragement on a flight from Boston to Newark early in my writing process. His work inspires many.

Lastly, I thank the academic institutions that have shaped my life's experiences: Media Friends School, McCollough Elementary, George Read Junior High, William Penn High School, Swarthmore College, and Harvard Business School. Thanks to the many teachers who have guided me and the coaches who instilled discipline in me. Thank you, God, for allowing me to complete this endeavor while holding down a full time job as a consultant and corporate strategist, as well as for giving me many ideas for prospects larger and greater.

I hope you all enjoy this efficacious account of our African-American-owned businesses and learn from its stories.

Martin K. Hunt

PREFACE

Our goal in attempting this venture was to explore the realm of Black-owned business and to relay that knowledge to the wider population. If the stories chronicled in this document create a dream in the heart of a child, we would find their value immeasurable. Our experience has been that there are few other written endeavors that cover the story of Black-owned business in America. Because of this, many times the history of Black business is lost. This book presents our view on Black-owned business after four years of research and study. Unlike anything ever published, this book characterizes the flavor of Black business in America and gives you a framework with which to view Black-owned businesses in the future.

Our effort has come about somewhat by accident. In Martin's second year at Harvard Business School, he was given the task of surveying African-American-owned business while working with a leading strategy professor, Michael Porter. What he expected to be an easy assignment seemed impossible. There was no comprehensive book, summary, or analytical framework with which to view Black-owned business. The materials that were available were old or in sections of books aimed at Civil Rights, Slavery, and the like.

The most prominent sources of information on Black business that have existed over the past twenty years include **BLACK ENTERPRISE**, *The Black Political Economy*, and the U.S. Census' Survey of Minority-Owned Businesses. **BLACK ENTERPRISE** is a magazine dedicated to tracking the progress of Black-owned business. *The Black Political Economy* tracks Black political and economic events and the U.S. Census of Minority-Owned Businesses tracks macro-economic trends. Together these sources provide a composite view of the status of Black business.

Using these major sources as well as primary sources spanning two centuries, we have constructed a view of Black business that unifies the fundamental issues facing them, and that gives a reference point from which to view Black-owned businesses in the future. Conceptually, we will walk you through a brief background of Black-owned business, which will increase the relevance of the historic cases presented in the later chapters.

Chapter One, A Summary Note on the History of Black Business before 1970, introduces the four main types of entrepreneurs that existed before 1970. It explains how and why African-American-owned businesses were barred from the opportunites available to majority firms. Overall, using examples, the chapter summarizes the types of Black businesses and the challenges they faced in the years before Civil Rights.

Chapter Two, The Coming of America's Largest Black Businesses: A Summary Note on the Black Business' Foundation for Growth, investigates the elements that have served as the base for entrepreneurial growth in the past, and will be the foundation for future growth. We have used an analogy to Professor Michael Porter's 'Diamond' framework to create a 'Black Diamond' framework to explain the forces of competitive advantage for African-American-owned firms. This framework presents a unified lens through which to view Black business in the past, present, and future. This chapter also includes case studies on some leading Black businesses of today.

Chapter Three, Location as a Determinant of Competitive Advantage, explores an application of the "Black Diamond" using the city of Chicago prior to 1970 as an example. During the late nineteenth and early twentieth centuries, cities like Chicago, Pittsburgh, Cleveland and Philadelphia were areas of large African-American migration, which, in turn, created large African-American markets on which Black firms capitalized. Chicago has been chosen as an excellent example of how the forces of the Black Diamond shaped cities to become prime areas for Black business growth. Chapter Four showcases Supreme Liberty Life Insurance Company as a business whose experience typified many other businesses created in Chicago and other Northern centers of migration during the late nineteenth and early twentieth centuries.

Chapters Five through Thirteen showcase the world's largest Black-owned industrial and commercial firms that are the keystones for understanding Black business. Chapter Fourteen, the conclusion, brings together all the previous chapters and presents a vision for the future of Black business. The bottom line of this endeavor is to answer some interesting questions about Black-owned business and to inspire additional work or criticisms that might drive more widespread knowledge on Black-owned business.

What were the largest Black-owned businesses in 1860, 1890, 1920, 1950,1980 and now? Which are the Black businesses over $100 million in sales on the **BLACK ENTERPRISE** (BE) 100 list? What are their stories? Can we expect many more Black companies to join the list of businesses over $100 million in sales? Where are they headed, and what are the emerging industries that will replace today's industry leaders? These are the questions that this document will answer and in the process relay lessons learned from the sucesss stories presented.

INTRODUCTION

America's largest Black-owned business revenues have seen tremendous growth in the past twenty years. The 100 largest African-American-owned businesses produced revenues of over $473.4 million in 1972. In 1997, the largest businesses produced revenues of over $10 billion. Any explanation for this tremendous growth must highlight the connection between many complex subjects: business strategy, African-American history, the Civil Rights Movement, access to capital for African-Americans, and others. This book will outline a history of Black business that gives the reader a unique panoramic view of its development. The recreational reader will find this survey of business refreshing and eye-opening. The scholarly reader will find this document an excellent source of new thought on Black business as well as a concise and efficacious historical summary.

It is our hope that this historical account and collection of cases will be of interest to the general public because it will add to the limited information available on Black business as well as inspire the entrepreneurs of tomorrow. The history of Black business has been excluded from most schools and textbooks, and thus eluded teachers, and executives. Therefore, by exploring cases in Black business, we can learn about what determines their competitiveness and enrich our view of African-American enterprise.

The case-based approach used in this book will uncover the forces that have affected America's largest Black-owned businesses. We start with businesses before 1970 and then go forward exploring Black businesses after 1970. The focus of this book is to build an understanding of the business environments that have promoted or discouraged the most successful Black businesses. By showcasing their case histories, we will uncover which factors were most conducive to building each case so that we can all learn from their experiences.

Section One: The History of Black Business

CHAPTER ONE: HISTORY OF BLACK BUSINESSES BEFORE 1970

Black businesses before 1970 laid the underpinnings for Black businesses today. Being aware of this will facilitate an understanding of the origin of Black entrepreneurship. Slaves, ex-slaves, craftsmen, and many of the nearly 60,000 free African-Americans in 1790 contributed in some way to Black business' past. [1] There were ship builders, fur traders, barbers, saloon owners, and city founders who were entrepreneurs prior to the Civil War. However, in assessing Black business before 1970, we will focus on four areas of entrepreneurship: adventurers with successful economic ventures, inventors, insurance company owners, and bankers.

Several things that characterize Black business history before 1970 are: (1) Slavery and our government's racially-biased laws and restrictions diminished the flame for initial Black business growth. (2) The one hundred largest Black-owned businesses had sales less than $473 million. [2] (3) Most successful Black businesses after Slavery catered primarily to African-American customers. These businesses included banks, insurance companies, and hair care and cosmetics products companies. (4) Many Black inventors saw their ideas initiate the building of successful companies but were blocked from owning them. (5) All Black businesses during this time were constrained by extreme racial prejudice.

Black business in America, since the country's inception, has been affected by the social, economic, and political climate of the time. Before the founding of America and before some states were even part of the U.S., there were Black entrepreneurs. Examples are: **Emanuel Bernoon,** who established the first oyster house in Providence, Rhode Island in 1739, San Francisco's **William Leidesdorff,** who in 1846 became perhaps the first African-American millionaire, and Chicago's founder, **Jean Baptiste Point DuSable**, who ran a trading business in the 1770s. However, from the beginning of African presence in America there have been legal restrictions imposed and strictly enforced that limited the educational, economic, and entrepreneurial potential of African-Americans. The repercussions of these restrictions kept them from becoming more powerful in the mainstream business world. Despite the Civil War, followed by the ending of Slavery in 1865, and America's Reconstruction period, Jim Crow laws, prejudice, discrimination, and segregation legally and systematically hindered the attempts of African-Americans to conduct business. Knowing the Supreme Court ruled segregation constitutional in 1896, and that it was not substantially dismantled until the Civil Rights Movement of the 1960's, it is plain to see why in the past African-Americans did not participate in America's major business transformations.

The U.S. Census reported that Black businesses rose from over 17,000 businesses in 1890 to over 70,000 in 1926. [3] This roughly 400% increase over a 36-year period is a testament to the existence and growth of Black enterprise. However, businesses that required large amounts of capital or transportation across state lines were all blocked by mainstream American attitudes and laws and thus made it impossible for African-Americans to systematically build large businesses. As a result, Black businesses were not monopolies on markets or giants in their industries. Generally, successful businesses run by African-Americans were small-scale "Mom and Pop" organizations that operated on the simple concept of supply and demand. In other words, an industrious and aggressive individual saw a need in his/her community and filled it. There were a countless number of Black caterers, barbers, undertakers, restaurant owners, pharmacists, manufacturers and storeowners who fit this bill.

Early successful Black businesspersons came from a varied lot. Some were slaves who had worked to buy their own freedom, others were freed by the death of their master or had run away, and some of the business people were born free. All of them had a tremendous struggle to achieve economic stability: many lifted themselves from the depths of poverty to the heights of wealth. Many African-Americans started businesses with nothing but the change in their pockets, a good idea, and a healthy dose of determination. Their business strategy was "hope for the best, keep your fingers crossed, take it as it comes, and when life hands you lemons, make lemonade". Many, such as those who settled in Kansas in 1879, created their own self-sufficient Black towns allowing them to gain real economic control of their resources. Examples of such towns are the Oklahoma towns of Boley and Langston, the towns of Rosewood, Florida, Allensworth, California, Dearfield, Colorado, Nicodemus, Kansas and a host of others. [4] Some of these early African-American entrepreneurs owned businesses in territories at America's frontier such as Louisiana (prior to and after its purchase from France in 1803), Chicago, and San Francisco, and as a result, became some of their territories richest citizens (see Appendix for a list of some of the wealthiest African-Americans prior to 1900). These rich African-American entrepreneurs formed part of a growing African-American bourgeoisie in existence during the 18th and 19th centuries, which helped support the creation and existence of increased numbers of Black-owned businesses. After the Civil War, "largely as a result of the cadres trained by fraternal organizations, churches, lodges and pioneer black businesses, the black bourgeoisie increased in size and became a conscious and more or less organized in structure and thought." [5]

After Slavery, a plethora of Black businesses were started in order to serve the Black community. Examples include free-Black friendly societies that pooled money, Black newspapers, beauty product firms, banks, realtors and insurance companies. Examples of various newspapers created around the country during the early 20th century are Carl J. Murphy's *Afro-American*, P. B. Young's *Journal and Guide*, Robert L. Vann's *Pittsburgh Courier* and Robert Abbott's *Chicago Defender*. Black realtors such as Phillip A. Payton Jr., president of the Afro-American Realty Company of New York City, played crucial roles in meeting the housing needs of African-American migrants from the South. These businesses of the late 19th and early 20th centuries became the base of Black economic institutions that fueled a persistent economic growth after the Civil Rights movement (Black-owned business rose from 163,000 in 1969 to over 600,00 in 1992). Today, businesses based on serving the Black community are still among the largest Black businesses. These include Earl Graves Limited, Johnson Publishing, BET, and others that run throughout the BE 100 list (see Appendix).

Prior to 1970, African-American adventurers, inventors, bankers and insurance executives developed African-American enterprise more than any other four types of entrepreneurs. These entrepreneurs were among the founders of our largest cities, founders of Black towns, and innovators of our most common technologies. Adventurers founded new cities and continually pushed the envelope of our nation's unjust laws relating to African-Americans. Inventors led the way for all businesses as they presented new and better ways of doing things. These African-Americans pushed to benefit personally from their inventions, but also added undeniable evidence of the value they added to society. Black banks were equally important to the development of Black business: descended from secret societies that aided free Africans in the most hostile of times, they created the possibility for capital acquisition necessary for founding a business. Especially after the 1890s, and after the failure of the government-founded Freedman's Bank, African-American banks became the base for African-American-owned businesses. Finally, insurance companies were created out of a need by the African-American community for burial and life insurance coverage, a service that was being denied to them by majority-owned firms. The insurance companies formed during the late 19th and early 20th centuries created executives who went on to mentor some of our most successful African-American entrepreneurs of today.

The four types of entrepreneurs outlined above add to the history and give a bird's eye view of the foundation of modern African-American entrepreneurship and wealth yesterday, today, and tomorrow.

ADVENTURERS

In this section, classic examples of the business acumen of individuals who built their businesses as adventurers will be presented by focusing on six business cases:

- Edwin C. Berry
- Paul Cuffee
- Barney Ford
- John Jones
- Francis and Fannie Moultrie
- William Whipper

A small business success story can be told in the person of Edwin C. Berry of Athens, Ohio. Mr. Berry was born in Oberlin, Ohio on December 10, 1854 and was the son of free parents. He received a formal education at Albany Enterprise Academy in Athens, Ohio until the age of sixteen, when his father died. After his father's death he worked in a brickyard to help support his family. Soon thereafter, in 1872, he began work in a restaurant where he apprenticed as a cook for five years and got the inspiration to start his own. With hard work, help from a friend, and savings of forty dollars, Berry was able to open his own restaurant in 1877. The business was successful from the beginning and in 1880 Berry was able to buy a lot for $1,300, and secured a loan of $2,000 to erect a building on it. In 1892, Berry decided to open a hotel. He erected a twenty-room hotel on property adjoining his restaurant. After a rocky start, the Hotel Berry became a smashing success due to the extraordinary service received by its patrons. Berry is reputed to have been the first hotelkeeper in the United States to put a needle, thread, buttons, and cologne as well as a clothes closet in each room. He was also the only African-American of the time in the country that operated a first class hotel patronized by Whites. In 1907 the hotel was appraised at $50,000 and brought in $25,000 to $35,000 annually. [6] By the time of his 1921 retirement, the hotel had expanded to fifty-five rooms and Berry had become the most successful Black hotel owner in the country. Berry died on March 12, 1931, leaving an estate of over $55,000 (over $6 million by today's standards).

One of the most colorful Black businessmen of early American history was Paul Cuffe. Cuffe was the seventh of ten children born to an ex-slave, Cuffe Slocum, and a Native American mother, Ruth Moses, on Cuttyhunk Island, MA in 1759. Cuffe spent most of his life in Westport, MA, a Quaker settlement in Southeastern Massachusetts. He had a great love for ships and taught himself to read and write in order to learn more about them. At sixteen he put his book knowledge to the test and set out as a common seaman on a whaling expedition. During the Revolutionary War, Cuffe made his living by artfully dodging the ships of the British blockade of New England, supplying much-needed cargo for New Englanders. After the war, Cuffe and his brother David built and acquired trading and whaling ships for their personal use. The money Cuffe made from trading ventures was used to purchase a $3,500 farm and to build a wharf and warehouse for his fleet. Over time, Cuffe amassed a fortune derived from whaling, coastal shipping, and trade with the Caribbean and Europe. He entered into partnership with two sons-in-law to sell goods from Europe, Asia, and the West Indies. Aside from his business savvy, it was Cuffe's deep interest in Africa and effort to colonize Sierra Leone, Christianize its inhabitants and settle Blacks from the U.S. in that country that brought him an international reputation. By his death in 1817, Paul Cuffe's fleet and other business investments were valued at $20,000. [7] Cuffe's shipping and business dynasty lasted throughout his life and for another generation.

Another success story is that of Barney Launcelot Ford (c.1824-1902).[8] After escaping Slavery in Virginia in 1848 by means of the Underground Railroad, he settled in Chicago, married, and taught himself to read and write. In 1848, gold was discovered in California and many adventurous souls decided to travel there and seek their fortune. Barney Ford was one of those fortune-seekers. He packed up his family and boarded a ship destined for California. However, California did not end up being the place where the Ford family got off. That place ended up being Nicaragua. In 1851, in Greytown, Nicaragua, Ford opened what became the very successful United States Hotel and Restaurant. However, the hotel was destroyed in a diplomatic dispute between England and the United States, and Ford was forced to start over. He went inland Nicaragua to Virgin Bay, where he operated first the Hotel William Walker and then the California Hotel. These two business ventures allowed Ford to accumulate more than $5,000 in savings. He took this money and returned to Chicago where he opened a livery stable that became part of the Underground Railroad. In 1860, Ford decided to head west again in search of fortune in the Colorado gold fields. Even though at this time Blacks in Colorado were prohibited by law to own land, he made two land claims that were stolen by White claim jumpers. Undaunted, Ford headed to Denver and soon became the owner of two hotels, a restaurant, and a barbershop. Aside from these successful ventures, Ford gave financial assistance and food, and found jobs for escaped and freed slaves who drifted into Colorado during the Civil War. By the Reconstruction era, Ford was worth over a quarter of a million dollars and was the first African-American to serve on a Colorado grand jury. Aside from helping former slaves Ford also used his money to establish schools for African-Americans. Ford and Henry O. Wagoner, an old friend from his times in Chicago, established the first adult education classes for African-Americans in Colorado. Other business ventures Ford was involved in included a restaurant he operated from 1867 to 1870, when it was destroyed by fire, and a series of additional restaurants in Denver after 1882. Although Ford absorbed major losses in the depression of the 1890's, he was able to rebuild his fortune as owner of two barbershops and residential properties. He passed away a rich man in 1902.

John Jones (1816-1879) made his money through the business of tailoring, which he learned through apprenticeship. Jones was born free in Greene City, North Carolina to a free biracial mother and a German father named Bromfield. His mother, fearing that Bromfield or his relatives might seek to enslave John, apprenticed him to a man named Sheppard, who taught him the business of tailoring. In 1841, equipped with life savings of $3.50, he moved to Alton, Illinois and then in 1845 moved to Chicago, where he opened a tailor's shop. Within five years, John Jones' tailoring was popular enough to afford him a new four-story business building, making Jones worth over $100,000 by 1871. His prosperous merchant tailoring establishment enabled him to expand his abolitionist and civil rights activities,   which included his home becoming a station on the Underground Railroad through which countless runaway slaves escaped to Canada.

Francis Moultrie was born in Charleston, South Carolina in 1842. He moved North after the Civil War and worked in catering houses in New York State while his wife, Fannie, operated a small catering business of her own out of their Yonkers home. When this small catering business began to generate a more than sufficient following, Moultrie quit his job with private families and worked with his wife at home. Their catering business turned out so well that in 1878 it became necessary for them to rent a store-space downtown. On the first day the store was open, there was not a single customer. Fortunately, this did not become the norm. Shortly after opening their store, the Moultrie's found the space to be too small. This prompted a second move to a larger and more centrally located position. By the turn of the century the business was generating $25,000 a year (roughly $3 million by today's standards) [9] .

William Whipper was born in Pennsylvania in 1805, the son of a White businessman and an African-American house servant. He was raised in his father's house and benefited from his father's benevolence. William was treated the same as his White half-brother—he was well cared for and well educated. When his father died in 1835, he left William a small Columbia, PA lumberyard, which William and a partner, Stephen Smith, built into a successful wholesale company which carried on extensive business both in Columbia and Philadelphia. The young Whipper had always been ambitious: in 1828, he started a laundry business, and in 1834, a grocery store. By the 1850's, Whipper's company owned twenty-seven railroad cars and Whipper had acquired $18,000 of bank stock. The building of the Columbia Bridge brought him an additional $9,000. In 1853 Whipper visited Canada and bought land on the Syndenham River in Ontario. Several of his relatives emigrated to Canada and Whipper was preparing to follow but the outbreak of the Civil War caused him to stay in the United States, during which time he aided the Union cause financially. Other business ventures included a Philadelphia lumber business he ran from 1865 on, in partnership with his nephew, James W. Purnell. By 1870, William Whipper's personal wealth was estimated to be over $108,000. [10] Active in the Underground Railroad, Whipper estimated that between 1847 and 1860 he spent $1000 per year aiding hundreds of fugitive slaves who passed through Columbia. After a successful life as business person and civil rights activist Whipper died on March 9, 1876.

INVENTORS

Many successful African-American businesspersons were inventors who manufactured and marketed their creations for profit. One example of this type of businessperson is James Forten, who in 1798 invented an innovative sail and owned a sail-making loft that made him over $300,000. Another example is Madame C. J. Walker who in 1905 created a business from her beauty-enhancing products, making her the first self-made female millionaire in America. Other examples are George Washington Carver, an agricultural chemist and botanist who developed over three hundred peanut products which inspired new industries all over the South between 1900 and 1930, and Andrew Jackson Beard, who invented an automatic railroad car coupler which revolutionized the railroad industry in the late nineteenth century. The two latter men earned in excess of $30,000 each for the fruits of their labors.

The first United States Patent Act in 1790 made it possible for **free** Black inventors to receive a patent. Slaves at this point were still legally barred from receiving patents for their inventions. (It is interesting to note here that slave masters could not receive patents for inventions created by the slave, by order of the attorney general in 1858. This meant essentially that after this ruling, a slave invention could not be protected by law nor be legally recognized in any way, even if the slave master wanted to take the credit). Some examples of inventors whose work followed the 1790 law are: [11]

Free Ante-Bellum (Pre-Civil War) Entrepreneurs	Ante-Bellum (Pre-Civil War) Emancipated Slave Entrepreneurs	Post-Civil War Entrepreneurs
Thomas L. Jennings	John Parker	Jan Matzeliger
George Peake	Henry Boyd	Andrew J. Beard
James Forten		A.C. Howard
Lewis Temple		Garrett Morgan
Norbert Rillieux		Granville T. Woods
		Madame C.J. Walker

Thomas L. Jennings (1791-1859), believed to have been the first African-American to receive a patent for an invention, operated a dry cleaning and tailoring business in New York City. He received the patent on March 3, 1821 for a specific dry cleaning process and used the income from his business to support his abolitionist activities. Jennings was also the founder and president of the Legal Rights Association.

George Peake (1722-1827) was the first permanent Black settler of Cleveland, living on the frontier before settling in Ohio in 1809. He was born in Maryland and was a British soldier in the French and Indian War. He invented a highly-prized labor-saving stone hand-mill that produced a better quality of ground meal and proved efficient for frontiersmen. The invention put him and his family among the wealthiest of northeastern Ohians.

James Forten (1766-1842) was born in Philadelphia to two free Black parents. He studied briefly at the school of Anthony Benezet, the famous Quaker abolitionist. After his father's death, he worked in a grocery store to support his mother, and at age fifteen, during the Revolutionary War, volunteered as a powder boy on a Philadelphia privateer. During the war he was taken captive by the British and was imprisoned for seven months. He spent a total of twelve months in Great Britain, after which he returned to the U.S. and was apprenticed to Robert Bridges, a sail maker. Forten became foreman of the sail lot in 1786, and later, when Bridges retired in 1798, became the owner of the sail-making shop. After becoming owner of the loft in 1798 he invented and patented a sail-handling device, which together with other ventures brought Forten's personal worth to an estimated $100,000 by 1832. James Forten used his profits to fund not only abolitionist activities but also women's rights and equal rights for Blacks.

Lewis Temple (1800-1854) was a New England blacksmith who revolutionized the whaling industry with the introduction of his toggle harpoon, known interchangeably as Temple's Toggle and Temple's Iron. The harpoon he designed locked itself into the flesh of the whale, preventing escape. Because Temple did not patent his design, it was widely copied (another maker produced 13,000 Temple Irons between 1848 and 1868). The harpoon soon came to be known as the "universal whale iron" and became the standard harpoon of the American whaling industry. If Temple would have patented and been the only one to manufacture his toggle harpoon, he would have been able to grow a much larger business than he did.

Temple was born in Richmond, Virginia and little is known about his early life. In 1829 he arrived in New Bedford, Massachusetts and by 1836, Temple was operating his own whalecraft shop on Coppin's Wharf as well as being active in the abolitionist movement. In 1845, Temple opened his own blacksmith shop, where he profited from the manufacturing and sales of his iron. In 1852 Temple was able to move to a larger blacksmith shop next to his home and in 1854 he contracted with a construction company to build a new and bigger brick blacksmith shop near the Steamboat Wharf. Unfortunately, this shop was never finished for Temple died that same year as a result of complications from an injury attained in a fall in the autumn of 1853.

Norbert Rillieux (1806-1894), inventor of a sugar refining device, was a free biracial rich New Orleans man (some sources claim he was an octoroon, others claim he was a quadroon). He was born on March 7, 1806 to Vincent Rillieux, a wealthy French engineer, planter and inventor, and Constance Vivant, a free African-American woman. Vincent adopted Rillieux and gave him his name, a practice not usual at the time. Young Rillieux was given the material and educational advantages of the "Colored Creole" (also known as the "Cordon Bleus", an allusion to a blue cord or slash worn by pre-Revolutionary French nobility). Although the situation of Creoles of color had deteriorated after the 1803 purchase of Louisiana from France by the United States, Rillieux was able to attend Catholic schools in New Orleans and later received an education in engineering in Paris at L'Ecole Centrale. At age 24, after graduation, Rillieux worked as an instructor of applied mechanics at his alma mater, becoming the youngest instructor at the school at that time and contributing many papers on steam technology to engineering journals. It was during this time that Rillieux started conceiving the idea for his first invention: a multiple effect vacuum evaporation system for sugar refining. The method then in use, called the "Jamaica Train" was slow and inefficient and the quality of the sugar could not be well controlled. Rillieux's invention used a number of physical principles to increase the efficiency of sugar refining, becoming used widespread throughout Louisiana sugar cane farms.

Rillieux returned to New Orleans in 1840 to perfect his invention and to arrange for testing. Initial tests revealed various problems so he made several design modifications that eventually resulted in the first model to receive a patent, in 1843. Rillieux worked further on improving the machinery and was awarded a patent for an even further improved model in 1846. With it, he revolutionized the sugar industry and amassed a considerable amount of wealth. Thousands of his evaporators were erected on plantations in Louisiana and the West Indies. The rate of sugar production dramatically increased and its price was significantly reduced, making white crystalline sugar, which beforehand had been a relative luxury and was only used on special occasions, a generally used product. Rillieux's invention made sugar so abundant and cheap that sugar refiners had to create new markets for the product. It was soon marketed as a common household item.

Rillieux had to contend with numerous imitators and patent pirates. Some of his plans were stolen and taken to Europe, leading to thousands of evaporators being manufactured by pirates and sold as genuine Rillieux evaporators. Since his invention increased the production capabilities of sugar to such a large degree, it unfortunately increased the demand for field slaves. Following Rillieux's invention, the price of field hands strong enough to work in the sugar cane fields rose to as much as $5,000, a tremendous amount of money for the time. Following the success of his evaporator, Rillieux turned his attention to developing a sewage disposal system for the city of New Orleans. He submitted his plans to the city and was turned down because of his race. The abolitionist movement was gaining momentum in New Orleans so city officials were afraid that if they accepted a project developed by a 'Negro', it would only work to fuel and strengthen the abolitionist movement further.

Several years later, a sewage disposal almost exactly like his was adopted by the city. This experience, as well as the prevailing discrimination and racism in the country at the time, led Rillieux to become highly disillusioned with living in New Orleans. The straw that broke the camel's back came in 1854, when a law was passed which required all Blacks to carry identification passes. It was that year that Rillieux finally decided to leave America and return to France, where he stayed for the rest of his life. Upon his return to Paris, Rillieux went back to his old school, L'Ecole Centrale, and resumed teaching, eventually being made headmaster of the school. He was very active in engineering research and engineering journals of the period are filled with his articles. Back in Paris, Rillieux developed an interest in Egyptology and made significant contributions to the deciphering of hieroglyphics. He continued an active career until his death in 1894. After his departure from the U.S., following the Civil War, Rillieux's evaporator played a significant role in the economic recovery of the state of Louisiana, but Rillieux was unfortunately unable to witness the true impact of his invention. The multiple-effect evaporator principle is now a basic process in the chemical industry and is widely used in other applications such as the production of soap, gelatin and glue. Rillieux was finally recognized, albeit posthumously, in 1934 with a plaque honoring his contributions to Louisiana's sugar industry being placed in the Louisiana State Museum in New Orleans.

Not all African-American inventors and businessmen of this time were born free; many that we know about were born slaves. One such person was John Parker (1827-1900). Parker was born in Norfolk, Virginia, the son of a White slaveowner and a slave mother. At age eight, he was sold to a slave agent in Richmond who in turn sold him to a slave caravan headed for Mobile, Alabama. In Mobile, Parker was purchased by a doctor who employed him as a household servant and where he was able to learn how to read and write. When he got older, Parker worked in furnaces and iron manufacturers in Mobile and as an apprentice acquired rudimentary knowledge of the trade of plasterer. He later apprenticed to a molder at a local iron foundry and became a competent molder. In 1843, Parker was transferred to a New Orleans foundry where he worked until he was able to purchase his freedom for $1,800 two years later (roughly $200,000 by today's standards). That same year, he moved to Cincinnati, where he stayed until 1850, when he moved to Ripley, Ohio. In Ripley he first opened a small general store and helped more than one thousand slaves to freedom through the Underground Railroad. In 1854, Parker established a foundry to produce special and general castings as well as his own inventions. One of these inventions was a tobacco screw press, which he patented in 1884. Parker's business came to be named the Parker Machine and Foundry Company and manufactured, among other things, slide engines and reapers. It survived until the end of World War I, and was still operating in 1981, although no longer under family ownership. Parker is among the limited number of Black inventors who obtained patents in the U.S. before 1900.

Another slave-born entrepereneur was Henry Boyd (1802-1886), a furniture manufacturer and inventor. Without a day's schooling in his life, Boyd was well read in history, geography, and was an excellent mathematician and businessman. Boyd created and held the patent for the Boyd bedstead: a strong, unique, and popular wooden bed frame, which was the staple of his bedstead factory in Cincinnati and is the nearest approach to the modern spring bed. Born a slave, at age eighteen Boyd was granted a general pass from his master which allowed him to move away to the Kenhawa salt works, where he worked day and night for double wages. With this money he was able to quickly buy his freedom. He went North to seek his fortune and over time was able to save enough money to buy his siblings' freedom and to start his own factory. After buying his freedom, he learned the trade of carpenter and joiner and moved to Cincinnati, Ohio, a free state. The journey left him with only $0.25 and although a free state, Ohio did not prove to be all Boyd had hoped for. Local racism made it difficult for him to find employment until one day, when he met an Englishman shopowner who decided to hire him. Within days he was promoted to portership of the English merchant's store. When his boss needed someone to build a warehouse, he asked Boyd to do it. He was given money to buy materials and was put in charge of the job. The merchant was very pleased, leading to Boyd's shift to carpentry. Boyd started building houses in Cincinnati and over time accumulated significant amounts of property. Boyd became wealthy in the furniture manufacturing business, employing large numbers of both White and Black men. He sold his bedsteads locally and to various areas West and South, many of those who bought from him not knowing they were patronizing a Black-owned business. After twenty-seven years of success and twice rebuilding his business because of arson, he was forced to retire due to the refusal of insurance companies to carry his fire insurance.

With the end of the Civil War and the passage of the Thirteenth and Fourteenth Amendments came the right for **all** Black inventors to obtain patents. Many Blacks took advantage of this new right. They patented inventions developed in the course of operating their own businesses like barbershops, catering concerns, dry goods stores, restaurants, and tailoring businesses. One of these businessmen, Jan Matzeliger (1852-1889), invented a shoe-lasting machine that helped bring the shoe construction industry further into the efficient world of mechanization. His machine made the arduous task of lasting shoes by hand obsolete. Matzeliger was born in Paramaribo, Surinam (South America) to a Dutch engineer father and a native Black mother. In 1855 he moved in with a paternal aunt and at age ten began apprenticeships in machine shops superintended by his father, an occupation which soon sparked his interest and talent in machinery. At age 19, in 1871, Matzeliger left Surinam to become a sailor aboard an East Indian ship. Two years later, at the end of the cruise, Matzeliger disembarked at Philadelphia, where for the next two years he worked at odd jobs around the city. In 1876, he left for New England, living first in Boston, eventually settling in Lynn, Massachusetts. In Lynn, Matzeliger found employment in a shoe factory operating, among other machines, a sole-sewing machine. During this time he also took the chance to self-educate himself by going to night school and studying during his free time. At first, most of his time was spent learning English, but as he mastered the language Matzeliger soon became absorbed in learning about scientific and practical works. By September of 1880, Matzeliger had finished manufacturing his first shoe lasting machine. A newer model of that took him the next four years to complete, mostly due to the problem he faced in obtaining the adequate financing for the job. He needed capital to secure a patent for his machine, to arrange demonstrations and to complete the finishing touches. Two men by the names of C. H. Delnow and M. S. Nichols agreed to support him financially at the cost of two-thirds ownership of his device. Matzeliger was finally granted the patent for his device on March 20, 1883, after which he continued to perfect it. During the first public operation of the machine in May of 1885, it made a record run of lasting seventy-five shoes. Finding themselves unable to properly finance the production of Matzeliger's invention, Delnow and Nichols sought additional capital from George A. Brown and Disney W. Winslow. The result of this association was the creation of the Consolidated Lasting Machine Company, which began to manufacture the machine. The machine could turn out from 150 to 700 pairs of shoes a day compared to a top of fifty by the manual method. The great demand created in the machine because of its efficiency led to The Consolidated Lasting Machine Company, which eventually bought Matzeliger's patents, to quickly expand. By the late 1890's it had merged with a number of smaller companies to form the United Shoe Machinery Corporation, and Matzeliger's machine became the basis for the multi-million dollar growth of the company. Matzeliger's mechanical genius was not limited to the lasting machine, he patented a number of items before his death and had several granted thereafter. He died of tuberculosis in 1889, without seeing profound impact of his invention on the shoe industry, or reaping the benefit of the financial legacy of the invention. Proper recognition for the machine came only posthumously with the awarding of the Gold Medal and Diploma at the Pan-American Exposition of 1901.

Other inventors/businessmen of that era are equally noteworthy. One is Andrew Jackson Beard (1849-1941) of Alabama, who, without any formal training in either engineering or metal working invented and patented a railroad car coupler (the "Jenny Coupler") in 1897. His railroad coupler automatically linked two carts such that no one would have to climb in between the two carts, a cause of many injuries and deaths in the railroad industry. Beard is the first African-American known to have received a patent for a coupling device for railroad cars. He filed the patent application in September 1897 and was granted the patent two months later. Beard's sold his patent rights for more than $50,000 to a New York company that same year.

Another example of an inventor is A.C. Howard from Philadelphia, Pennsylvania who created his own brand of shoe polish. Howard started his own business and began manufacturing and marketing his polish with only $180 saved from work as a rail road porter in Chicago. He began by selling his polish to railroad porters he knew and by 1929 was selling his polish in large orders to the U.S. government. His polish was used at Fortress Monroe, Fort Todd and Fort Hamilton. In 1900 he was awarded the first prize at the Paris exposition. In 1902 he had his own factory and sales of $20,000. In 1907 he received the first prize at the Jamestown exposition.

Garrett Morgan (1875-1963), inventor of the safety mask (a precursor of the modern day gas mask) and the automatic traffic signal, became general manager of two companies which were designed to manufacture and market his inventions. Morgan was born and raised on a farm in Paris, Kentucky to a slave-born mother who had been freed by the Emancipation Proclamation of 1863. At age 14, with only six years of schooling, Morgan moved to Cincinnati where he worked as a handyman for a wealthy landowner who hired a tutor to help him with his grammar. In 1895 he moved to Cleveland where he remained the rest of his life and patented his inventions. In 1907 Morgan started his first of several businesses repairing and selling sewing machines. The business prospered and in 1909 he opened his own tailoring shop with thirty-two employees to manufacture coats, suits and dresses. Four years later he started yet another business, this one called the G. A. Morgan Hair Refining Company where he made a hair-straightening formula. During the early 1910's Morgan had also started to work on his safety mask invention. His first appearance with the safety hood and smoke protector was in 1912, using the subsequent two years to perfect it. He was awarded a patent for the safety hood in 1914. After a 1916 life-saving performance in a waterworks tunnel where workmen had become trapped, manufacturers started producing and fire departments started using Morgan's invention widely. Morgan started traveling from state to state demonstrating and promoting his mask. In Southern states he would have to hire a White man to demonstrate the device while he passed as a Native American. When it became widely known that the mask's inventor was African-American, production and use of the mask was significantly curtailed. His mask, however, was widely used by American soldiers in the battlefield to protect them from deadly chlorine gas fumes during World War I.

On November 20, 1923 Morgan was awarded another patent for an important invention: the three-way automatic traffic signal. Morgan also received patents for this device in Canada and England. He later sold the patent rights to General Electric for $40,000. Other business ventures included his 1920 establishment, in response to the inadequate reporting on African-American affairs, of a weekly newspaper. The paper, the *Cleveland Call*, unfortunately only lasted until 1923. Morgan also served as a treasurer of the Cleveland Association of Colored Men until it merged with the NAACP, where he became a life long member, and ran unsuccessfully as an independent candidate for City Council in Cleveland in 1831. He died in 1963 after a long life of diverse and profitable businesses.

Still another inventor was Granville T. Woods (1856-1910), known as the "Black Edison", who invented telegraphic and electrical devices and ran a small electrical equipment factory in the 1880s. Born in Columbus, Ohio, he began work in a machine shop at age ten, spending his evenings attending school or receiving private instruction. At age sixteen, Woods went to Missouri and worked on railroads as a fireman and engineer. In 1876, Woods started working in a Springfield, Illinois steel mill and later in a machine shop in New York City, while studying electrical and mechanical engineering in the evenings. Between 1882 and 1884 Woods was an engineer on the Danville and Southern Railroad, after which he and his brother opened their own machine shop in Cincinnati. He lived in Cincinnati from 1884 to 1890, and then lived in New York City until his death. Between 1884 and 1907 Woods patented some thirty-five inventions that were vital to development of electrical and mechanical equipment. His first patent was a steam boiler furnace, followed by a telephone transmitter, an apparatus that transmitted messages by electricity. This transmitter ended up being assigned to the American Bell Telephone Company of Boston. In 1887, Woods patented an invention of a telephone system and apparatus devised for transmission of words and other sounds conducted by electricity. In 1892, Woods was faced with a suit where he was accused of stealing patents for an electric railway. The huge legal fees that this suit brought with it led to that, despite all the significant contributions to the world of telephone systems he had made, Woods died in poverty.

The most well known and financially successful Black businessperson of the early 20th century was not a man, but a woman. Before the Women's Movement and not long after the Civil War, Madame C. J. Walker started a Black hair-care company which was to make her the first self-made female millionaire of any race in the United States. At a time when women and Blacks alike shared relatively little power or influence in America, Madame Walker defied the odds. At the National Negro Business League in 1912, she quipped, "I am a woman who came from the cotton fields of the South. I was promoted from there to the washtub. Then I was promoted to the cook kitchen, and from there I promoted myself into the business of manufacturing hair goods and preparations". [12]   She had certainly come a long way.

Madame C. J. Walker was born Sarah Breedlove in 1867 near Delta, in Northeastern Louisiana. Walker was the daughter of two poor farmers and was orphaned at an early age, after which a married sister raised her. At age fourteen, while living in Vicksburg, Mississippi, she became a wife and at seventeen a mother; by age twenty, she was a widow. As a young widow, Walker moved to St. Louis, Missouri, where she supported herself as a washerwoman for $1.50 per week. As she aged her hair began to thin causing her to experiment with treatments to remedy her embarrassing problem. In 1905 she began perfecting a formula for hair, using a hot iron to straighten hair, and working on a skin cream. In 1906 she relocated to Denver, Colorado, where she began selling her hair products, and married Charles Joseph Walker. In Denver she started selling her products door-to-door and trained agents to help her in her business. Over time her business expanded by travels, demonstrations and lectures in the South and East. In 1908, Walker established a second office for her business in Pittsburgh, Pennsylvania. In 1910 she and her husband moved to Indianapolis in an effort to bolster her business in one of the country's largest manufacturing cities, and to begin national distribution. Walker built a plant to manufacture her products and hired around 3,000 people, most of which were women, to help her run her business. Walker's marriage soon ended in divorce as a result of conflict about how the company ought to be run, but her business had no such unhappy ending. With time came more hair products, cosmetics, and an aggressive and effective marketing strategy. Madame C. J. Walker offered beauty at the fingertips of Black women all over the country. Especially popular in Harlem, Madame Walker's products allowed Black women to achieve the look that characterized the day. Her fame spread to the Caribbean and then to Paris, where her style was adopted in the 1920's by the famous dancer Josephine Baker. Walker's popularity in Paris inspired a French company to manufacture a similar pomade which came to be known as the "Baker-Fix".

"Within a decade, Madame Walker's business was making half a million dollars a year in gross revenues, her factory payroll came to $200,000 a year, and she had 2,000 salespersons, known as agents". [13]   Before her death, Walker had become a self-made millionaire and one of the most successful business people of the early twentieth century. Madame Walker, who had "promoted herself" from washerwoman to businesswoman, spent the rest of her life supporting civil rights and practicing philanthropy. She was a liberal contributor to the NAACP, Colored YMCA of Indianapolis and the underprivileged of Indianapolis, and also maintained scholarships for women at Tuskegee Institute. While she bequeathed most of her estate and business to her daughter, her will also established a trust fund for an industrial and mission school in West Africa and provided bequests for Black orphans and retirement homes, Colored YWCA branches, and private secondary and collegiate institutions. She died in 1919 leaving her thriving business to her daughter and a legacy of hope, perseverance, and success to her people. Madame Walker and all other inventors laid the groundwork and spirit for Black business' future.

BLACK BANKERS AND INSURANCE COMPANY FOUNDERS

The history of African-American-owned banks and insurance companies provides a flavor for the context in which Black businesses lived, and provides a background for reading the case studies of the Supreme Liberty Life Insurance Company, North Carolina Mutual, and Carver Bank (chapters four, eleven, and twelve, respectively). Both Black banks and Black insurance companies will be examined to provide a context for these two important industries and, in doing so, will point out examples of the constraints that have faced African-American-owned businesses since the inception of our country.

Black-owned banks and insurance companies had their roots in fraternal orders, secret burial societies, and mutual aid societies that African-Americans created to pool their money for use in times of need. In 1790, there were over 60,000 free African-Americans out of a total United States population of over four million. Societies such as the Newport, Rhode Island African Free Society in 1780, the Free African Society of Philadelphia in 1787, and the South Carolina Brown Fellowship Society in 1790 provided financial resources for its members, aiding them to cope with the increasing overt racism and discrimination that came to characterize the harsh environment of Slavery. These societies continued to grow over the 18th and 19th centuries, totaling over 100 in Philadelphia alone, and amounting to several hundred throughout the country by 1849. Later in the 1800's, during Reconstruction, it was societies such as the Masons, Knights of the Pythias, and other fraternal societies that used their money to start banks, insurance companies, as well as many of the early African-American businesses.

Banks

Mutual Aid societies were not uncommon to early mainstream 18th century America. Only three banks in America were chartered prior to 1731. [14]   By 1816, there were still only a total of 250 banks in the United States, none of which were Black-owned. [15]   Despite numerous attempts, there were no officially incorporated Black-owned banks prior to the Civil War. Were it not for specific laws stopping them, a number of Black banks could have been founded at this time. Instead, there were African-American businesspeople who owned shares in banks, as well as, wealthy African-Americans who served as substitute banks by lending their money to individuals. An example of such an entrepreneur was Stephen Smith of Pennsylvania, who was one of the wealthiest Northern African-Americans during Slavery. He was a coal dealer, real estate investor, lumber merchant, and owner of shares in various banks. [16]

During the Civil War, the Union Army established banks for Black soldiers and freedmen such as the Free Labor Bank of New Orleans, and two military savings banks in Norfolk, Virginia and Beauport, South Carolina. [17] After the Civil War and during Reconstruction, the Freedman's Savings and Trust, established by the federal government, was created to provide a place for free African-Americans to put their money. After an initial success, the bank, not federally guaranteed, and not controlled nor operated at any level by African-Americans, became an economic travesty. It grew rapidly from its inception, setting up thirty-four branches in six years, and enjoyed relative success for a couple of years. However, as a result of money mismanagement and unusually high loans to White businessmen, when Freedman's Trust closed its doors in 1874 it had lost the money of over 61,000 depositors and had destroyed a large part of the African-American wealth base. Before its collapse, in a last ditch effort to restore confidence in African-American depositors, Frederick Douglas was appointed President of the bank. This tactic did nothing to improve the financial situation of the bank and Douglas ended up being used as a scapegoat for the bank's demise.

After this debacle, the traditional African-American mutual aid societies became increasingly successful at marshaling African-American resources, and a period of formation and incorporation of Black-owned banks and insurance companies began to take place. The True Reformers' Bank of Richmond, Virginia, chartered on March 2, 1888 (and opened in April of the same year), and the Capital Savings Bank of Washington, D.C., which opened in October of 1888, became the first two Black-created and Black-run banks in America. [18] More than twelve banks were chartered between 1888 and 1900, and seventy-five between 1900 and 1914. A total of one hundred and thirty-six Black banks were established between 1888 and 1929. After the Depression only eight remained. After World War I, the development of African-American banks was again in a stage of experimental growth as new banks formed and dissolved on a year by year basis.

In 1906, Black bankers founded a banking affiliate of Booker T. Washington's National Negro Business League called the National Negro Bankers Association. This association worked on the formation of a central Black bank, a task that never came to fruition. Clearly, the dream of a centralized Black bank, stock market, or any other national standardized financial institution was not feasible without the power of government backing, guaranteed and protected Civil Rights, equal protection under the law, and benefits of size and experience. As a result, the early African-American banks that persisted stayed relatively small, were concentrated in the South, and were related to fraternal orders. This was less so the case twenty years ago, when of the forty-five African-American banks in existence in 1975, nineteen had been founded in the South (eight of which had been founded between 1960 and 1975). Twenty-one of the thirty-eight banks in 1975 had been founded in the North and five in the West, all of which were founded after 1940. The number of African-American banks reached sixty-two at its highest point in 1913, but only those with the savvy to deal with racism and economic realities of running financial institutions survived. The Great Depression and the bank moretorium of 1933, left eight African-American banks, five of which were among the only forty-five banks operating by 1975.

Insurance Companies

Black insurance companies have a history quite similar to Black banks. Insurance companies grew out of the need for mutual aid among free Blacks. They were created from fraternal societies and religious orders that had previously served as insurance providers. In 1810, the African Insurance Company of Philadelphia became the first known Black insurance company established in the United States. Although it was never incorporated, it had capital stock in the amount of $5,000.

Because of laws and forces aligned against African-American insurers, there were no officially incorporated insurance companies until 1888. The Southern Aid Society of Richmond, Virginia, established in 1893, and **North Carolina Mutual Life Insurance Company** of Durham, North Carolina, established in 1898, were among the first officially incorporated insurance companies. The turn of the century precipitated an increase in the number of Black insurance companies and led to the subsequent founding of the National Insurance Association in 1921. North Carolina Mutual was the first Black-owned insurance company to attain $100 million in assets. **North Carolina Mutual Life Insurance Company** still exists and ranks number one on **BLACK ENTERPRISE**'s list of Black insurance companies (see list in Appendix).

Most of the major Black insurance companies that are in existence today were operating before 1960. All but three of the insurance companies in 1975 were established prior to 1960, eight between 1890 and 1909, seventeen between 1910 and 1939, thirteen between 1940 and 1959, with the remaining three between 1960 and 1975. Like with banks, most insurance companies saw their origins in the South. Of the 41 insurance companies in 1975, thirty-four were founded in the South (four in the North, and three in the West).

Caselette - Arthur G. Gaston, Sr.: Insurance Company and Bank Owner

A.G. Gaston was born on July 4, 1892 in Marenbo County, Alabama [1]. His mother moved to Birmingham to become a cook for A.B. and Minnie Loveman, the founders of an Alabama department store chain called Loveman's, and Gaston was educated at the Tuggle Institute located in one of Birmingham's finest African-American neighborhoods. The Tuggle Institute created the educational base that Gaston would use to become one of the nation's finest African-American entrepreneurs of the early 20th century.

Gaston saw many examples of Black entrepreneurs in Birmingham in the early 1900s. He worked for Oscar Adam's *Birmingham Reporter* and was exposed to other African-American entrepreneurs who were vital to the Birmingham community like Reverend T.W. Walker, Charles M. Harris, W.R. Pettiford, and T.C. Windham. [2] Like many other African-Americans, A.G. Gaston started his businesses by serving African-Americans who were denied products and services by the majority community.

He got his start in entrepreneurship while working at the Tennessee Coal and Iron Company during the 1910's and 1920's, bulding railroad cars. During this time, to earn extra income, Gaston loaned money to coworkers, charging them twenty-five cents on the dollar every two weeks. It was during Gaston's tenure at the Tennessee Coal an Iron Company that many Black-owned burial and insurance companies were formed in the South, encouraging Gaston to create his own. Modeling it on these examples, Gaston and his father-in-law, Abraham Lincoln Smith, created the Smith & Gaston Funeral Directors business. Open for business in 1930, it was incorporated as the Booker T. Washington Burial Insurance Company in 1932. Resigning from Tennesse Coal and Iron in 1930 in order to fully devote himself to his new endeavor, he created the company with the aim to provide a means for African-Americans to afford burial and funeral services (A.G. Gaston later sold BTW Insurance to his employees for $3.5 M in 1987).

BTW Insurance took off immediately and provided Gaston with the means to fund other ventures even as the Great Depression was ravaging other businesses (the number of African-American-owned retail stores in Birmingham declined from 200 in 1929 to 132 in 1935). [3] In 1939, Gaston's businesses were going so well that he found it hard to find enough qualified workers, so he founded the Booker T. Washington Business College in 1939. Gaston used his college as a hiring ground for his businesses. More importantly, graduates of his college were among the first to benefit from the Civil Rights

Movement that created laws to protect an African-American's right to work at majority firms.

Gaston founded other ventures after 1940 that added to his existing businesses which were among America's largest African-American-owned companies. Among A.G. Gaston's later business were: New Grace Cemeteries, Inc. which was purchased in 1947; the Gaston Motel where Martin Luther King stayed during the 1963 Birmingham demonstrations which opened in 1954; Vulcan Realty and Investment Company founded in 1955; Citizens Federal Savings and Loan Association founded in 1957; WENN and WAGG radio stations which were purchased in 1975, and A.G. Gaston Construction Company which opened in 1986.

(1) BE June 1992, BE March 1996

(2) African-American Business Leaders: A Biographical Dictionary, BE June 1992, BE March 1996

(3) African-American Business Leaders: A Biographical Dictionary

CONCLUSION

These businesses, banks, insurance companies, and inventor-initiated companies are only a few examples of Black businesses before 1970. The spectrum of early Black enterprise ranges from tiny to substantial and is varied with respect to industries. Owners and operators of successful businesses included people from all walks of life: slaves and free Blacks, southerners and northerners, men and women, and the educated and the illiterate. It is within this environment that the forces affecting today's Black businesses first came to be.

CHAPTER TWO: THE COMING OF AMERICA'S LARGEST BLACK-OWNED BUSINESSES:

A Summary Note on Black Business' Foundation for Growth

The 100 largest revenue producing Black-owned businesses have increased their size more than 2000% over the past two-and-a-half decades, yet any definitive framework to explain this growth has eluded us. Although there have always been Black-owned businesses, before 1970, education, access to capital, segregation, and the existence of few supporting industries limited their growth. Adam Smith's free market theory was only a theory for Blacks in the face of denied civil and ownership rights. Change came after the Civil Rights movement of the 1950's and 1960's, when the government began creating development programs, tax breaks, and procurement programs. These programs allowed a group of educated value creators to begin to establish companies and build competitive advantages by freeing the prevailing forces of the Black consumer dollar, creating coalitions with Fortune 500 companies, building interstate connections, and opening up access to capital.

As the historical barriers against Black-owned businesses were restrained, free market factors started playing a greater role in the development of businesses by African-Americans. On a national level, these factors can be summarized by using four national competitive forces: (1) the demands of customers, (2) factor conditions such as education and access to capital, (3) the strategies of firms, and (4) supporting industries. These four factors form the base of Strategist Michael Porter's "Diamond Framework" for assessing the competitiveness of locations. An outside, but ancillary force is our government. (The government's effect on African-American businesses has been negative for nearly 200 years and only somewhat possitive in the past thirty years.) For this chapter, an analogy to this framework is used to assess how the change in America's business environment has sparked growth in Black businesses from 1970 to the present.[1]

The Black Business Diamond

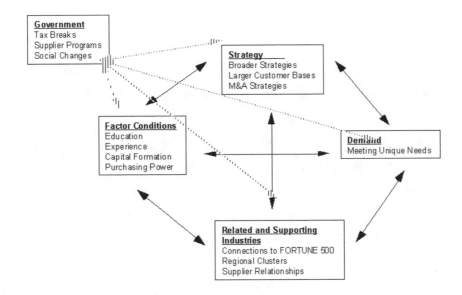

Factor Conditions

After 1970, increased opportunities in education, new job assignments, capital formation and purchasing power allowed for the increased growth of African-American-owned businesses. The total income of African-Americans rose from less than $300 billion in 1980 to over $500 billion in 1998.

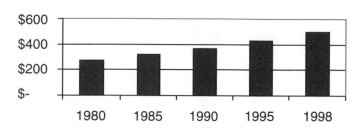

Source: US Census, Personal Income, 1998 estimated by the Knowledge Express
          Company.

This increase in income is particularly important to Black-owned firms because they are four times as likely as non-minority firms to have minority customers. [2]

Spurred by the Supreme Court's 1954 Brown v. the Board of Education decision, the number of college educated African-Americans has also increased dramatically. Between 1960 and 1980, the most popular African-American college major shifted from Education to Business Administration. Whereas in 1965, less than 300,000 African-Americans were enrolled in college, by 1980, 1,107,000 African Americans were enrolled in colleges across the nation. [3] The growth in educational credentials and work experience of potential entrepreneurs has driven Black-owned firms through a dramatic industry shift from traditional small-scale retail and personal services businesses to nontraditional fields such as manufacturing, construction, and business services.

Better educational credentials, coupled with an increasing income, have also led to better work experiences, which in turn have led to more successful African-American entrepreneurs, as many of these seasoned business people eventually go on to run their own businesses. For instance, the number of Black managers, which includes executives and administrators, grew by over **230%** between 1970 and 1990.

Percentage Among African-Americans

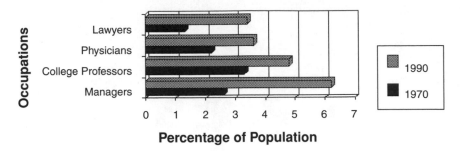

Source: The Wall Street Journal, February 21, 1995

This growth in African-American professionals has led to an increase in the appointment of senior executives at Fortune 500 companies. These business leaders will provide a large impact on the potential for large-scale entrepreneurship by African-Americans in the future. Two examples of such executives are Fannie Mae's CEO Franklin D. Raines, and Starwood Lodging's CEO Richard Naula (Richard Naula was previously a Senior Executive Vice President and CFO for the Disney Corporation). Other examples of senior African-American business leaders are:

Ken Chenault	COO, American Express.
Curtis Crawford	President of the Microelectronics Group of Lucent Technologies Inc.
Ann M. Fudge	Executive Vice President, Kraft Foods, Inc.
Michelle Hooper	President of the International Business Group of Caremark International.
Noel Hord	President and CEO of Nine West Group.
Thomas W. Jones	Chief Executive of the $120 Billion Smith Barney Asset Management.
George R. Lewis	President and CEO of Philip Morris Capital Corporation.
E. Stanley O'Neal	Executive Vice President of Merrill Lynch & Co.
Richard Parsons	Time Warner President and former Dime Bank Corp. CEO.
Barry Rand	Executive Vice President of Xerox Corporation.
Ray Robinson	AT & T President of Southern States.
Warren Shaw	President of the $28-billion Chancellor Capital Management.
Lloyd G. Trotter	President and CEO, General Electric's Electrical Distribution and Control.

| Lloyd D. Ward | President of Maytag Appliances and Executive Vice President, Maytag Corporation. |
| Carl Ware | President of Coca-Cola Africa. |

Many individual executives such as these have eventually left the corporate ranks to start their own businesses, as many undoubtedly still will do in the future.

In addition to the increase in appointment of seasoned executives and a rise in the number of African-Americans that have started new businesses, many wealthy African-Americans have used a portion of their personal wealth to acquire companies. This can be seen most clearly in the case of wealthy African-American sportsmen who have ventured into business after the end of their professional sports careers. Over the past twenty years, high salaries have given professional athletes access to large amounts of capital, thus allowing them to play an important role in the formation of large Black enterprise. Professional sports is among the highest paid professions, and many of these athletes prepare for their early age retirements by starting businesses with their fortunes. The BE100 and other lists of large Black-owned businesses have been riddled with former athletes at all levels. A few well-known examples are:

Magic Johnson started Magic Theaters (regularly ranking in the top 10 grossing movie houses), a state of the art theater with twelve screens in South Central Los Angeles; plans to open theaters in Atlanta, Detroit, Houston, New York City, and Washington DC through a 50-50 deal with Sony. (Magic also owns 5% of the Lakers, runs a sports-apparel company, and manages $50 million which he invests in inner-city supermarkets.) Johnson and **BLACK ENTERPRISE** publisher Earl Graves purchased Pepsi-Cola of Washington, DC, a soft-drink distributor facility, for $60 million. Johnson has built a $60 million a year business including concert promotions, a traveling performance team, and adult and children's basketball camps. In 1996 *Forbes* estimated his net worth was edging up to $100 million.
Drew Pearson, an ex- Pro Bowl football player, has a $58 million business selling brand sports gear.
Julius Erving, the Philadelphia Seventy Sixers great, is co-owner of the $357 million BE100 Philadelphia Bottling Co.
Gayle Sayers, a Chicago Bears Hall of Famer, owned Crest Computer which was number 48 on the BE100 list in 1990.
Laurence Taylor IPOed his firm, All-Pro, which licensed technology from Virtual Reality, Inc., raising $4.5 million. (The company's market value was $24.2 million in 1995.) (*Businessweek*, "L.T. Just Might Sack His Skeptics." January 30, 1995, pg. 84)

Brady Keys, Jr., a former All-Pro defensive back for the Pittsburgh Steelers, owned 24 Burger King and Kentucky Fried Chicken franchises.

Sidney Moncrief, a former Milwaukee Buck, was CEO of Sidney Moncrief Pontiac-Buick-GMC- Truck Inc. that has over $40 million in sales.

Mel Farr, a former All-Pro running back with the Detroit Lions, is President of a holding company, Mel Farr Automotive Group, which has over $503 million in sales.

Isaiah Thomas owned a stake in American Speedy Printing Centers (a $150 million company) and was part owner and manager of the Toronto Raptors, an NBA franchise basketball team. Also, in February 1997, Thomas formed a group to invest $1.5 million to buy 4.5 million shares of common stock of the basketball equipment company "Sure Shot". (USA Today, "Sure Shot Thomas." February 25, 1997, pg. B1) (Forbes, "Compounded interest are our favorite words." December 19, 1994, pg. 244)

Source: **BLACK ENTERPRISE** magazine (BE)

Drew Pearson is an interesting example of an athlete turned entrepreneur:

Caselette of a NFL Player Turned Businessman: Drew Pearson Companies

Drew Pearson's NFL career was cut short by a car accident in 1984. The liver injuries sustained during this accident ended Pearson's intentions of playing for another three to four years. Forced to shop around for a new career, Pearson found work with CBS as a color analyst for NFL games and later as a wide receiver coach for the Dallas Cowboys. When Pearson began to lose interest in these endeavors, and after relentless prodding from Kenneth Shead and Mike Russell, Pearson decided to go into business. Shead and Russell had the idea to start a marketing company and sell licensed sports items by reproducing corporate logos on head wear, T-shirts and other sports apparel. They started out selling their goods to high school sports teams. Their first major client was a professional soccer team, the Dallas Sidekicks.

Initially, financing was virtually impossible to secure. The business was run out of Shead's home, with only $100,000 they had been able to secure from four private investors. First year sales totaled $3 million, but Shead and Pearson had to go without salaries. It was by a stroke of luck and a hearty endorsement from an associate in the business that Drew Pearson Companies (DPC) landed a $5 million line of credit from Merchants Bank in Kansas City, Kansas.

Another obstacle faced and overcome in the early years was that of obtaining major licenses. "DPC won its first major license in 1986 with the U.S. Olympic Committee to supply all of its corporate sponsors for the 1988 Olympic Games in Korea." [4] Soon came hard-won licenses from Disney, the NFL, and MLB. "Today Drew Pearson Companies is the leading head wear licensee for Disney, generating around $20 million in sales (and paying about $2 million in royalties.)" [5] In the recent years, DPC has secured licenses with the NBA (1988), Walt Disney Children's Headwear (1990), and Warner Bros. (1992). "Last year, DPC landed its first major deal to do sweat shirts and T-shirts, as well as caps, when it was granted licenses to print the logos of NCAA teams." [6]

In 1992, DPC bought majority ownership in Minneapolis-based Fresh Caps Inc., one of its major distributors. This move, which cost DPC about $2 million, heightened the distribution power of the company, as well as giving it a producer of caps with a ready-made client base. DPC's main concern now and in the years to come is the establishment of brand equity. Larry Lundy, director of client services for Advantage Marketing Group, which represents DPC, says: "to support the next decade of growth DPC is going to have to aggressively and strategically market its trademark." [7]

In a time when Michael Jordan can affect a $2.2 billion stock swing, create $10 billion in value for his endorsement companies, and own a $250 million division of NIKE, Dr. J and Dave Bing can both own part of a top ten BE 100 business, Isaiah Thomas can own part of a $150 million business as well as a small part of his new NBA franchise team, Evander Holyfield can invest in a South African Coca Cola bottling company, or when Calvin Hill, (NBA Grant Hill's father) can own part of an NBA franchise, there is every reason to believe that these millionaires will continue to build and to own significant equity stakes of companies above $70 million in revenues in the future.

Demand

The **demand** for Black products, such as Black hair care and beauty products, barber shops, newspapers, insurance companies, banks, record companies, and funeral homes was met by hundreds of Black-owned businesses as early as the late 1800s. During this time, there were also businesses that served both Black and White consumers. However, violence, laws, and economic exclusion killed many potentially significant businesses that served a predominately White clientele. Businesses that catered to only the Black consumer demand, however, were those which were allowed to flourish, such as in the case of Madame C. J. Walker's hair care business of the early 1900s.

Still today, 30% of the largest Black-owned businesses continue to cater to Black customers. These firms are comprised of two major segments: ethnic products and ethnic communications. The ethnic products cluster includes firms like Soft Sheen, Pro-line, Luster Products, Johnson Products, and Cross Colours. Similarly, the communications segment includes firms like Johnson Publishing, BET, Burrell Communications Group, Essence Incorporated, InnerCity Broadcasting, and the Mingo Group. These firms focus on communication with African-American audiences. BET has brought cable directed at the Black audience. Johnson Publishing, Essence, and Earl Graves Limited have all added to the knowledge of African-American issues through magazine publications. The Mingo Group, and other African- American advertising firms such as UniWorld and Burrell Communications, have added to the awareness and importance of advertising directed at African-Americans. Many are expanding their expertise to broader markets like Burrell Communications, which just acquired a majority-owned advertising firm. Majority firms, however, are also venturing into this type of 'ethnic expertise' area such as the global ad firm DDB Needham, which created a joint venture with Spike Lee called SPIKE/ DDB. [8]

Caselette on an Ethnic Demand Communications Firm: InnerCity Broadcasting

Inner City Broadcasting is one of the staples of the ethnic demand communications cluster. Inner City Broadcasting Corporation's history began at a time when many African-Americans first began to build the largest Black-owned businesses of today. It began with a single AM radio station in 1972, and is now a multimedia mini-empire in possession of several successful FM stations, Harlem's Apollo Theater, and growing cable ventures. Its now-retired founder and chairperson, Percy E. Sutton, is largely responsible for its success.

Percy Ellis Sutton was born November 24, 1920, the youngest of fifteen children of a father born in to slavery. As a child he daydreamed of becoming a radio announcer. Sutton kept this childhood dream alive and well in the back of his head throughout his adolescence and early manhood, throughout college, three years in the U. S. Army Air Force during World War II, and law school. He kept it alive through work as an intelligence officer for the Air Force, through clerking for a New York attorney, and then working for the New York subway system. He kept it in mind through a ten-year stint as a self-employed lawyer, through his position as assemblyman for the New York State legislature (1964-1966), and through eleven years as the Manhattan borough president (1966-1977). After an unsuccessful bid to become New York's first Black mayor in 1977, Percy Sutton turned his full attentions to his childhood dream—a dream that, over the years, had changed in character and intensity. It was no longer suitable to Percy's eager and entrepreneurial mind to be a radio announcer, Percy wanted to own his own station.

The chance to do just that presented itself to Percy Sutton during his second term as Manhattan borough president. Harry Novick, owner of New York stations WLIB-AM and WLIB-FM, took Percy up on his passing offer to buy them. So in 1972, after years of searching for loans and investors, Sutton took the plunge into his fifty-year old sea of dreams. He, along with a menagerie of sixty-two investors, including singer Roberta Flack, and Malcolm X's widow, Betty Shabazz, purchased WLIB-AM for $1.9 million, with an option to buy its FM counterpart within two years. Sutton exercised that option, changed the call letters to WBLS-FM, and, within a five-year time span, watched WBLS-FM take the number one spot in New York City ratings with a "community-oriented, urban-contemporary" format.

Following a failed attempt at mayorship in 1977, Percy Sutton concentrated all of his energies on InnerCity Broadcasting. He bought five radio stations in less than six months, from late 1978 to early 1979. [9] InnerCity then turned the bulk of its attentions to a strategy of rapid diversification, and in 1981 Sutton purchased the world-famous Apollo Theater out of bankruptcy for $250,000. Percy intended not only to breathe life back into the dying piece of African-American history, but intended on turning it into a production facility to spark InnerCity's move into "television syndication, music recording, and artist management". [10] By 1982, InnerCity had landed one-third of what was being called one of the nation's most lucrative cable franchises in the New York borough of Queens. "That venture, shared with National Black Network and two individual investors, had an estimated value of about $150 million". [11] In that same year, InnerCity Broadcasting also landed the enviable title of **BLACK ENTERPRISE** magazine's 'Company of the Year', and bought a fifty percent interest in the Sheridan Broadcasting Network, a Virginia-based network with over 100 radio affiliates.

Throughout the decade of the eighties, InnerCity Broadcasting had its ups and downs, but managed to hold its ground as a force to reckon with in the Black business arena. In 1988 it ranked number twenty-eight on the **BLACK ENTERPRISE** Industrial/Service 100 list with $28 million in revenues. That same year its "two New York stations had combined operating income of $4.1 million on net revenue of $14.8 million. Estimated and measured ad revenue for the 1988 New York marketplace [was] $389 million". [12] Thus, InnerCity controlled a relatively substantial percentage of the market. But all was not wine and roses that year: InnerCity sold its stations in Detroit and Los Angeles, which were not doing particularly well, in a move they called a "redistribution of assets." These sales reportedly led to a decline in the company's net revenue from the early 1980's, when InnerCity had had revenues of almost $30 million.

The new decade of the nineties brought with it the seeds of change for InnerCity Broadcasting. After nearly twenty years, Percy Sutton turned over the chairmanship to his son, Pierre, so that he might concentrate on the company's cable television interests. Meanwhile, Pierre has taken InnerCity Broadcasting to over $50 million in revenues in 1998 and towards a bright and varied future.

Strategy

The ability to raise capital for business strategies of larger scope is another indicator of Black business growth. Overton, Fuller, and other entrepreneurs of the past used mergers and acquisitions to grow more than five decades ago (see Chapter Three). However, they were the exceptions to the rule. The concept of a merger, an acquisition, a venture capital-backed company, or 'going public' were rare words in the past, but today they are prerequisites for any serious considerations of being a large Black-owned business.

The corporate strategies of many large Black-owned businesses have used Mergers and Acquisitions (M&A) to create value. For example, the TLC Group led by Reginald Lewis acquired one company after the other before landing the now famous TLC Beatrice deal; Granite Broadcasting acquired many broadcasting companies; and TSG Ventures, a venture capital firm, acquired Envirotest and took it public while maintaining controlling interests in the company.

Some Black entrepreneurs have built their businesses from the ground up, like Oprah Winfrey's production company (see Chapter Nine) or Don King's hundred million-dollar business in the boxing and pay per view industries. Other firms such as Johnson Products, BET, and TLC Group have used the ability to raise capital to venture into new areas. Several firms have actually 'gone public' or ventured abroad with expansion money. Those firms that have gone public have afforded the owners a great deal of personal wealth such as Johnson Products, BET, Granite Broadcasting, and Envirotest. These strategies, fueled by access to capital and driven by the desire to add new capabilities or to enter new business areas have allowed Black-owned businesses to reach new industries and new international customers. Finally, some of the largest Black-owned firms have sold their business to majority owners. Examples of these are Johnson Products, which was sold to IVAX for $61 million, Technology Applications Inc., which was sold when its founder retired, Motown, which was sold to MCA, Inc, and Barden Communications which was sold to a larger majority-owned company. These transactions have afforded their owners a great deal of capital and thus the potential to start or buy new businesses.

Merger and Acquisition Strategies enabled by access to capital enabled many of the largest African-American firms to become large. A few examples are:

In November 1994, **Active Transportation Company** acquired **Jupiter Transportation Systems** with $240 million in revenues to create the largest Black-owned trucking concern (*FORTUNE*, May 15, 1995).	The 1989 **West Coast Beverage** sold out to a majority firm after 15 years on the BE100 list.
The BE100s #6 firm in 1995, **RMS Technologies**, traded equity for growth capital in 1995 (*BE*, January 1995).	In 1988, **Gary White** of Trans Jones/ Jones Transfer Company and **C. Everett** of City & Suburban bought companies and so entered the BE 100.
TLC Group bought **McCall Industries** in 1987. Then after selling McCall and buying Beatrice, TLC sold 12 Latin-American operations for $100 million, cutting its LBO debt. **TLC Beatrice** sold its French food distribution business for $573 million in 1997.	In 1995, **Brooks Sausage** sold Barden Communications and Network Communication for $100 million.
Berry Gordy sold **Motown** for $61 million in 1988. In 1997, Gordy sold a 50% stake of his two music publishing companies, **Jobete Music Publishing** and **Stone Diamond Music**, to EMI for $132 million.	**Johnson Products** was sold for $70 million in 1993.
In 1988, **Bruce Llewellyn** began buying companies. He now owns at least three BE100 companies totaling over $500 million.	**Advanced Consumer Marketing** grew 74% to $48 million by acquisition in 1989.

Publicly Traded African-American-owned Firms

BET Holdings Inc. (went private 1998)	**Carson, Inc.**
Envirotest (sold 1998)	**Granite Broadcasting**
American Shared Hospital Services	**Ault Inc.**
Broadway Financial Corp.	**Caraco Pharmaceutical Labs**
Chapman Holdings	**Carver Bancorp**
Pyrocap International	**United American Healthcare**

Source: **BLACK ENTERPRISE** magazine, Public Records.

Venture capital firms like the Black-owned TSG Ventures have specialized in providing capital to innovative companies such as the ones mentioned above. Since its creation by the Equitable in 1971 as Equico Capital Corporation, TSG Ventures has funded several BE 100 companies such as Reginald Lewis' first deal for McCall Pattern Company, Essence Communications, Earl G. Graves' EGG Dallas Broadcasting, and Envirotest. It is venture capital companies such as TSG which have added to the growth in Black-owned businesses. In anticipation of future businesses that will grow with venture capital money, entrepreneurs like Earl Graves, who formed the **BLACK ENTERPRISE**/Greenwich Street Fund with an expected capital base of $60 million, are forming venture capital funds of their own to fund the next generation of large African-American firms.

Caselette of a Venture Capital Investment: Envirotest

One of the most interesting buy-outs was one involving the firm Envirotest, because it placed a Black-owned business at the top of the new emissions control industry. Envirotest Systems Corporation organized in 1990 to buy a unit of United Technologies Corporation for approximately $51 million. Two years later, Envirotest acquired ETI, formerly known as Systems Control, Incorporated, from SD-Scicon Plc (a British subsidiary of Electronic Data Systems), for $83.5 million.

Today, Envirotest can call itself the leading provider of centralized vehicle emissions testing programs for states and municipalities. It operates ten of the sixteen contractor-operated centralized programs in North America, and in 1992 performed nearly two-thirds of the tests in these programs. Envirotest can also be touted as the most experienced operator in the industry and the only American provider of contractor-operated centralized testing services outside the United States.

Envirotest designs, constructs, and operates centralized vehicle emissions testing programs which are established in accordance with federal regulations to test motor vehicle emissions for compliance with air pollution standards. Historically, this business has generated stable and predictable revenues. On September 30, 1992, the company had a revenue backlog of approximately $375 million for contracts extending through 1999. Its sales have almost tripled in four years, from $53.3 million in 1992, to $124.5 million in 1996.

Envirotest anticipates significant growth in centralized emissions testing programs in the United States due to regulations adopted by the Environmental Protection Agency and anticipated increases in the market for contractor-operated centralized testing programs. The company strategy is to aggressively pursue new emissions testing program opportunities utilizing a marketing agreement with WorldCom Telecommunications, and growing through a joint venture with ARCO gas stations in Southern California. Envirotest was sold in October 1998 to Stone Rivet Inc. for $266.3 million and the assumption of $275 million in debt.

African-American entrepreneurs are still buying and selling businesses. In the past two years alone, several Black businessmen have attempted several historic financial deals: Frank Washington attempted a $2.2 billion deal with Viacom; Whitman Heffernan Rhein & Co. tried to build the largest Black-owned bank in U.S. history; and Capital Baseball, led by Robert Johnson, bid to acquire the first Black-owned baseball team. There is no reason to believe this trend will not continue.

Related and Supporting Industries

Increases in Black firm size, the initiative of several large companies, and some incentive from the government have allowed Black businesses to begin tapping the power of America's world-class industry clusters. FORTUNE 500 companies have connected with Black-owned firms in the auto dealership market, the defense industry, the financial services industry, and in supplier industries for companies like McDonalds and GM. These connections with large, world-class FORTUNE 500 companies have served to create internationally competitive Black-owned businesses.

Auto Dealerships

A prime example of these connections can be found in the auto dealership industry. The BE100 formed a separate list in 1987 to track African-American autodealership growth revenues, which now command over two-fifths of the BE100s sales revenues:

Growth of Top 100 Auto Dealerships vs. Top100 Industrial/Service Firms

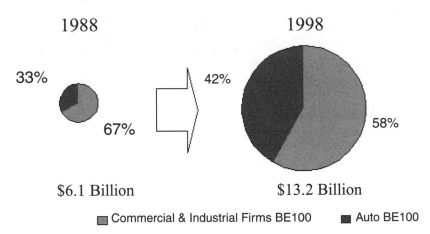

1988 — 33% / 67% — $6.1 Billion

1998 — 42% / 58% — $13.2 Billion

▨ Commercial & Industrial Firms BE100   ■ Auto BE100

Note: This is an analysis of the BE100s, 1988-1998. Sales are from 1987 and 1997 respectively. Professional services firms are not included (i.e. banks, insurance companies, money managers, etc.)

Auto dealers have had among the highest growth and revenues of all BE100 firms. This growth is increasing due to efforts of GM, Ford, and Chrysler to encourage African-Americans to purchase their dealerships. The BE100 list of Auto Dealers (see Appendix) is an example of the growth in major dealership-ownership over the past ten years.

Financial Firms

Like autodealerships, African-American financial firms have benefited from connections to supporting industries. Like all large financial firms, these African-American firms have links to other financial firms, investor groups, and pension funds. Through these links, dozens of leading African-American money managers are just now getting their start. Ray Baylock of Baylock & Partners, John Utendahl of Utendahl Partners, and Fred Terrell of Provender Capital are examples of this new generation of entrepreneurs starting financial services firms. An other example of such a money manager is thirty-five year old James Francis of Paradigm Asset Management, a firm with over $2 billion in assets. Paradigm started with $200 million in assets and had grown to over $200 billion after Francis bought the firm out in 1994 and sold 30% to a partner mutual fund. Under his direction and ownership, and through the decision to partner with a large mutual fund, Paradigm has come to rank among the top 20 institutional money managers.

Commercial and Industrial Companies

African-American-owned commercial and industrial companies have links with large companies such as GM, Ford, and Chrysler. For example, Dave Bing's Bing Steel was awarded a $32 million contract in 1995 by GM. Contracts like these indicate that Black-owned businesses will continue to build additional competitive advantages by tapping all of America's business clusters and networks just as all other businesses do. The influence of industry clusters and their related and supporting networks will no doubt continue its role in the development of strong businesses for African-Americans and all Americans alike. An important point to add is that since industry clusters tend to be located in metropolitan areas, Black-owned firms have also concentrated themselves in and around metropolitan areas. The following ten metropolitan areas for industry clusters are currently home to over one third of all Black-owned business revenues: New York, Los Angeles, Washington DC, Chicago, Houston, Atlanta, Philadelphia, Detroit, Baltimore, and Dallas.

Some of the new opportunities for joint partnerships between Black-owned firms and large American businesses are becoming apparent in the emerging South Africa, as Black entrepreneurs partner with large firms to make an entrance into the South African market. Coke, Pepsi, and many Fortune 500 companies have already begun. Graimark Inc., for example, has announced a multi-million dollar deal through a master franchise agreement to form the New South Africa Pizza Company with Domino's International. The deal is expected to generate $100 million in sales and 4,500 jobs in 164 stores. The first stores will open in Johannesburg and then focus on Greater Capetown, Greater Durban and the Geuteng Province including Pretoria. [13] Others who have announced their entrepreneurial plans in Africa are Pearcy Sutton, who intends to create a wireless communications network in Africa, and Robert Johnson who intends to expand BET's cable service to that continent. Entrepreneurial deals similar to these will become more common as the competitive advantages for Black-owned firms in America continue to develop.

Caselette on Entrepreneur: Earl G. Graves, Sr.

Building Connections between Fortune 500 Firms and African-American Entrepreneurs

For the past thirty years, Earl Gilbert Graves has been the preeminent promoter of connections between African-American entrepreneurs and America's largest companies. As the publisher of **BLACK ENTERPRISE** magazine, and through events he sponsors with Fortune 500 companies, Mr. Graves has promoted Black business since his magazine's inception in 1970 and has raised the awareness of Fortune 500 companies to Black business like no other.

The oldest of four children, Graves was born in 1935 to immigrant parents from the Caribbean island of Barbados. Graves expanded his business career by forming Earl G. Graves Limited after a series of other successes:

- graduating from Morgan State University in 1958,
- joining the Army and becoming a Green Beret,
- achieving the rank of Captain,
- working as a narcotics agent,
- becoming a manager of a real estate firm,
- working as a staffer for Robert Kennedy,
- and starting a consulting firm.

This series of successes foreshadowed Graves' greatest achievement: bringing the accomplishments of African-American entrepreneurs to the public through **BLACK ENTERPRISE**, the only major magazine dedicated to this goal. Graves also started America's largest Pepsi franchise, the Pepsi Bottling Company of Washington D.C. with $55.6 million a year in revenues.

Graves' interactions with large businesses and African-American entrepreneurs allow him to bring people together to do cooperative ventures. Some examples of these significant interactions are:

1. After his release from prison in 1991, South Africa's President, Nelson Mandela, sought out Earl Graves to better understand the forces that would encourage his country to develop a healthy Black entrepreneurial class. With that in mind,

Mandela sought to strengthen links to African-American entrepreneurs. Graves went on to form an impressive coalition to bring a $100 million Pepsi-Cola franchise to South Africa that included Percy Sutton, Shaquille O'Neal, Whitney Houston, Danny Glover and Motown Chairman, Clarence Avant. (Graves had had a relationship with Pepsi since 1990, when he and Earvin "Magic" Johnson teamed up to form the Pepsi-Cola of Washington, D.C., L.P.)

2. Earl Graves connected many businessmen to former Drexel Burnham Lambert CEO, Fredrick H. Joseph. One such connection allowed Reginald Lewis to meet informally with Joseph. Lewis completed his LBO of Beatrice with the backing of Drexel and Michael Milken less than a year after meeting with Joseph.

3. Graves' **BLACK ENTERPRISE** properly publicized Motown's value when Motown ran into trouble in 1991 and put Motown's CEO at that time, Jheryl Busby, in contact with key African-American businessmen that helped Motown refocus its strategy. Less than two years later, Motown was sold to PolyGram NV for $325 million.

4. In 1997, Graves formed a $60 million venture capital fund, **BLACK ENTERPRISE**/ Greenwich Street Corporate Growth Partners, with the Travelers Group to help finance the growth of mature businesses owned or managed by minorities. This fund will help African-American entrepreneurs grow into what will be the next generation of BE100 firms.

These are but a few examples of how Earl Graves has enhanced the trends that allow for the growth of Black businesses. Graves regularly sponsors events that have become "classics" that bring people together with Fortune 500 companies such as AXA/Equitable, NationsBank, and Pepsi. These events include, but are not limited to, BE's Entrepreneurs Conference, Golf and Tennis Challenge, Ski Challenge, and Kidpreneurs Program. Graves' alma mater, Morgan State University, renamed its business school the Earl G. Graves School of Business and Management, in honor of Graves' contributions to African-American enterprise and in honor of his efforts to help us recognize the value of African-American spending power and entrepreneurship. Earl Graves is also the author of "How to Succeed in Business Without Being White" a

New York Times and Wall Street Journal business best seller.

Entrepreneur, Black business promoter, and international leader, Earl Graves' influence will no doubt bring us the next generation of African-American entrepreneurs as they use the forces of the "Black Diamond" to reach new heights.

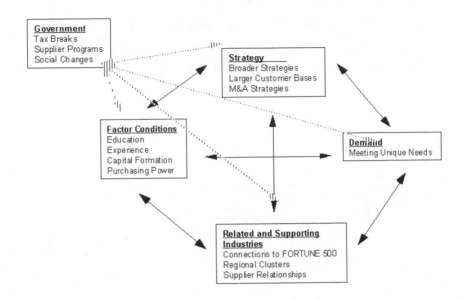

Conclusion

The character of African-American businesses has changed since 1970 and will continue to change in terms of sales growth and industry representation, away from "mom and pop stores" and toward more sophisticated internationally concerned conglomerates. Acquisitions, sell-outs, international expansion strategies, and a newfound ability to tap America's capital market will become more and more evident. The factors discussed: (1) the demands of customers, (2) factor conditions (3) firm strategy (4) and supporting industries, have illustrated the complexity of Black business growth and have offered a basis for assessing the environment which has developed over time and has allowed an increased growth of Black-owned businesses. As the growth, scope, and scale of Black-owned businesses continue to grow, knowledge of Black business history and the forces affecting it will also grow. The fact that the largest 100 Black-owned businesses have grown over 2000% during the past two-and-a-half decades is good news for the African-American entrepreneurs of tomorrow as well as for the competitiveness of America.

Section Two: Location as a Determinant of Competitive Advantage

CHAPTER THREE: CHICAGO A MODEL FOR BLACK BUSINESSES IN A METROPOLIS

At the turn of the century, in the face of racism and intense majority opposition, pure personal drive was not the only factor needed to create a business. Location also played a significant role in developing African-American businesses. Various environmental forces led some locations to develop the necessary conditions that would allow the natural entrepreneurial drive of individuals to materialize into business. Chicago, Illinois is one area where Black business roots run deep. It proved to be a positive environment for Black business growth during the late nineteenth and early twentieth century. This growth was in part sparked by massive migration from the South starting in the mid-nineteenth century, as some enslaved Africans were freed and others were looking to escape the grueling racism of the South. Many escaped enslaved Africans used the Underground Railroad to make their way from the South to Northern cities like Chicago.

Before embarking on an adventure to explore Chicago's Black business roots, it is important to note that there were scores of other locations that supported clusters of African-American businesses such as Cincinnati, Charleston, New York City, Philadelphia, Atlanta, Durham and Winston-Salem, North Carolina. Located in the various large city areas mentioned above, in the United States there were over 17,000 Black-owned businesses in 1890 and over 70,000 by 1926. This chapter will illustrate the conditions in Chicago alone, but business communities such as those in Chicago were growing throughout the country at the turn of the century.

Caselette on Chicago's founder and Businessman : Jean Baptiste Point Du Sable

Chicago's oldest connection to the African-American community comes with its foundation. Evidence stated in a 1779 British army report shows that **Jean Baptiste Point Du Sable**, a Black man, founded Chicago and was its first non-Native landed proprietor in the 1770's. Du Sable's house was the first to be built within the confines of what is now Chicago. During his stay he built various buildings such as an inn, a smokehouse and a mill. Not before long, he turned what was just an inhabited plot of land into a small village.

Born to a French father and Black mother, Du Sable was raised mostly by his father, a pirate in the West Indies, and was schooled partly in France. When he left the West Indies for America, Du Sable's first destination was Louisiana, which at the time still belonged to the French. Once he arrived there, in order to avoid the danger of being captured and sold as a slave, Du Sable sought help from a colony of Jesuit monks who gave him sanctuary and work. When he decided to move on, Du Sable built a boat and started a trip up the Mississippi River, making money by trading along the way. He stopped for a while in St. Louis, Missouri, where he lived with a Native American tribe, learned their language, and met his wife. He eventually reached the Great Lakes and stopped in Detroit, where he found employment with the governor. It was here that he came upon trouble when the British arrived in the area and questioned his settlement in a region claimed by them. Considered a French sympathizer (Britain and France were bitter rivals), Du Sable was arrested and held at Mackinac for several months. Without any charges to bring up against him, he was released. Upon his release, Du Sable moved to Illinois and settled in what is now Chicago. Du Sable's holdings in Chicago became valuable property and others became interested in acquiring it. Du Sable sold his property to Jean La Lime St. Joseph, a Frenchman, in 1800 and moved to Missouri, where his son, Jean Jr., lived.

Destiny was paving the way for what would become one of the cities with the largest number of successful Black-owned businesses. Chicago's Black community got its start in the 1840's when a group of fugitive slaves came to the city. By 1860, nearly 1,000 Blacks lived there, and a small leadership group, headed by a prosperous tailor, **John Jones**, who also was involved in antislavery activities and protested discrimination and segregation, came about. From 1870 to 1890, the Black community grew to nearly 15,000 people, and a well-delineated structure began to appear. The center of this community was located on the South Side of Chicago, with a number of Blacks also being found on the West Side. Between 1890 and 1915, the Black population of Chicago continued growing to over 250,000 people, expanding the South and West Side communities.

Most of the city's Blacks, from the mid-1800's to early 1900's, worked as domestic and personal servants. Only eight percent of the men and eleven percent of the women were involved in manufacturing of some kind. Throughout this time, however, a professional class was slowly emerging, accounting for about three percent of Chicago's Black population of the time, and an African-American elite group made up of ministers, physicians, lawyers, and business people was also emerging. One of the wealthiest businessmen of the time was a caterer by the name of **Charles J. Smiley**, whose business, like most others of the time, served exclusively the wealthy White community.

Many Black-owned businesses in Chicago, such as Smiley's catering business, started as simple ventures to serve White clientele. Examples of such catering businesses are **The French Company** and the **D. H. Weir Company**. Other fields of business were in personal care, such as the John Jones' **Cleaning and Repair Company**, the most prominent African-American Chicago business person of the late nineteenth century. As the Great Migration of Blacks from the South to the North during the late nineteenth century continued to increase the size of the African-American market, Chicago saw increasingly more businesses come to fruition, and already existing businesses grow more rapidly.

At the turn of the century, however, as new European immigrants came to the city and started taking over what had been traditionally Black industries, these immigrants and other Chicago Whites started to refuse patronage to African-American businesses. These immigrants used the American way of racial oppression to spur their beginnings, and as a reaffirmation that they were not at the bottom of the ladder. This force of non-patronage by Chicago's White community caused the eventual demise of the African-American business success in the areas of catering, barbering, tailoring, and other personal services. The forces of violence, intimidation, capital denial on the basis of race, and customer bias forced some Black entrepreneurs out of business and others to head in another direction with their ventures. New African-American-owned businesses emerged that focused on meeting the needs of the city's Blacks, which were otherwise being neglected by majority businesses. Among the most important of these new business leaders was **Theodore W. Jones**, a Canadian-born Black who owned a large South Side express company and who was a strong supporter of Booker T. Washington and the National Negro Business League. Others who were prominent in Chicago's Business League in these years were **S. Laing Williams**, an attorney, and **Sandy W. Trice**, an owner of a clothing store.

Despite the new level of discrimination in Chicago's business world, African-American businesses continued expanding with increased migration from the South. As more African-Americans migrated to the city, Chicago Blacks had a larger market to cater to, hence creating further growth in their business ventures and success. The greatest explosion in the city's Black population came during World War I and continued into the afterwar years, as Chicago became the focal point of the massive migration from the South. The city had a total of 63,355 Blacks in 1910, an amount which increased by seventy-two percent to over 109,000 in 1920. [1] During the 1920's, the population doubled. The increased population led to an increased purchasing power for Black Chicagoans, allowing the creation of increasingly more African-American-owned businesses [2]. Ninety-four percent of the population increase was the result of migration from the South. This tremendous migration and its results intensified the racism and violence that had been mounting during the prewar years, resulting in one of the bloodiest, most violent racial incidents in the country's history: the race riots of the summer of 1919. During this time, in many of the cities around the country that had become entrepreneurial havens for African-Americans, riots like these took place. Their consequences were far felt as whole Black towns, businesses, and homes were destroyed by angry mobs of racist Whites. Blacks by 1919 had developed a greater involvement in manufacturing employment in Chicago than ever before, with forty-five percent of Blacks being employed in that area by 1920. [3] Despite the growing purchasing power acquired during this time, Chicago's Black population became highly disillusioned by what had happened in their city during the riots, and many ceased to consider the city a haven of economic opportunity and racial justice.

The post-World War I migration and its effects gave rise to new civic and religious institutions which encouraged the expansion of existing institutions, as well as giving renewed impetus to the drive for Black business development. Most of this development and prosperity could be found in the area of Chicago known as "Bronzeville" (then known as the Black Belt). Bronzeville was a thriving community where African-American-owned businesses prospered and people had jobs. Around World War I it was the largest Black neighborhood in Chicago.

Before the Great Depression of 1929, Chicago's African-American community already contained a network of flourishing financial institutions: four banks, five insurance companies, and one savings and loan. The migration vastly expanded the market for Black business, but did not remove barriers such as lack of capital, inability to secure credit, and competition from better financed White companies. These forces, which had previously thwarted Black business achievement, drove Black businesses to cater to their own community's needs as opposed to a White clientele. Another force impacting the shift to serving the African-American community's needs was the sharp economic recession and massive layoffs that took place when soldiers returned home from the war.

The new businesses which focused on the Black community's unmet needs existed in such categories as:

1. **Banks and Real Estate** - such as the business run by Jesse Binga;

2. **Manufacturing** - such as Anthony Overton's cosmetic company, Overton Hygienic Manufacturing Company;

3. **Journalism** - such as Robert Abbott's *The Chicago Defender*;

4. **Insurance Companies -** such as Supreme Liberty Life and Chicago Metropolitan Insurance companies. (Four insurance companies were formed in the five years after World War I, and unlike those insurance companies that were emerging in the South, the ones in Chicago did not evolve from mutual aid and fraternal societies but rather began as corporate entities from the start);

5. **Recreational and Service Establishments** – such as the Perkin Theater owned by Robert Motts.

Many of these areas of enterprise gave rise to businesses that progressively developed into large-scale successful enterprises and gave rise to some of our current leading African-American business leaders. These leaders include John Johnson, founder of BE 100's Johnson Publishing, George Johnson, founder of BE 100's Johnson Products, and Joe Dudley, founder of BE 100's Dudley Products. These three BE 100 companies served as examples for other Chicago BE 100 companies like Ed Garner's Soft Sheen, Byron Lewis' Uniworld, Thomas Burrell's Burrell Communications, and Joy Luster's Luster Products. Finally, some members of the Black elite of Chicago were not only business leaders but were also involved in politics at the city and state level. During the early twentieth century, Black politicians were more numerous in Chicago than in any other city. Some of these businesspeople/politicians include **Oscar de Priest** and **Earl Dickerson**.

Banks and Real Estate

Real estate was a successful larger business arena, for as middle class Blacks sought to escape the slums by moving into previously White neighborhoods, real estate agents saw an opportunity to make profits. Real estate agents started buying property and obtaining leases on apartments in transitional areas on the edge of the city's Black belt found on the South Side. At least ten African-Americans were carrying on successful real estate businesses on the South Side by 1907. One example of such a businessman was **Oscar de Priest**, a real estate business owner who was also involved in politics first through a minor civil rights appointment and later by building up the Second Ward Republican organization. In addition to running his lucrative real estate business, de Priest went on to become an Alderman and then a Congressman, and was one of the founders of the National Negro Business League in Chicago.

Another example of such an African-American business leader that survived and grew despite all the hurdles in his way was **Jesse Binga.** Binga's real estate and bank business survived through repeated bombings of his home and offices, crimes for which no one ever was sent to jail.

The "Binga Block", which over time housed over 700 businesses, was at 47th and State Streets and was supposed to be the longest tenement row in Chicago. Binga used the profit from his real estate dealings to found the Binga Bank in 1908, making it the first African-American-owned financial institution in Chicago. By 1910, Binga was the Black community's leading business leader, having become a wealthy real estate broker and banker. The Binga Bank remained a private institution until 1919, when Binga took a state charter for the bank, a process which became official in 1920 making Binga Bank a state bank. The bank's boom years were between 1924 and 1930. At the peak of its prosperity it had nearly $1.5 million in deposits. Unfortunately the Binga Bank fell prey to the Great Depression and the stock market crash of 1929. The bank closed on July 31, 1930. The Great Depression hit urban Blacks in the North extremely hard, with Black unemployment hitting unprecedented levels. Even as late as 1940, thirty-six percent of Black males in Chicago were still unemployed or only had relief work.

Manufacturing

Manufacturing allowed African-American entrepreneurs to create products geared specifically toward a Black customer base. Many of these businesses created hair and cosmetic products, an arena in which majority-owned businesses had completely ignored African-Americans. Three examples of African-American businessmen that were able to break into retailing and manufacturing were **Sandy Trice**, **Anthony Overton**, and **S. B. Fuller**. Trice opened a small store of a complete line of women's, men's and children's clothing. The store prospered for a few years, but found it increasingly difficult to compete with White-owned stores in the Black Belt, and failed in 1909.

More successful was Anthony Overton, a lawyer, educated at the University of Kansas, and former municipal court judge who started manufacturing baking supplies such as baking powder, flavoring extracts as well as toiletries in Kansas in 1898. In 1911, Overton brought his company to Chicago and after a few years, a cosmetics line was added, which focused on meeting the needs of African-American women, much like **Madame C. J. Walker** had done in Indiana with her successful hair products company. By the time Overton had moved his company to Chicago "he was grossing more than $1 million a year and his "High-Brown" cosmetics had made him internationally famous". [4] Overton's cosmetics venture started with only his High-Brown Face Powder, but eventually the cosmetics line became the largest focus of his enterprise. In 1915, **Overton Hygienic Manufacturing Company** was capitalized at $268,000, with 32 employees and 62 different products. In 1920, Overton launched a magazine to advertise his products and prepared to extend his operations into banking and insurance. These other ventures emerged in the mid-1920's and included the founding of **Douglas National Bank**, the **Victory Life Insurance Company**, and the short-lived **Progressive National Life Insurance Company**. Douglas National Bank was founded in 1922 as a source of capital and credit for African-American Chicagoans, who were experiencing increasing levels of racism in this and other arenas. The bank started out with $170,000 in capital and $56,000 in bank deposits. [5] It survived the Great Depression of 1929, but unfortunately, like seventy White banks also did at the time, Douglas National Bank closed its doors in

1932. Also during his career, Overton launched *Half Century Magazine*, which eventually became the *Chicago Bee*, a South Side Chicago weekly newspaper. [6]

S. B. Fuller started his business career as a door to door insurance salesman and later as manager of **Commonwealth Burial Association Insurance Company**. In 1935, he used $25 to launch **Fuller Products**. He used the money to buy a large order of soap and began selling it door to door. As Fuller's business grew, he hired door-to-door sales representatives to sell his merchandise. Eventually, Fuller Products expanded to cover a cosmetics line. By 1939, Fuller's operations were running successfully with several salesmen, a strong customer base and a factory on Chicago's South Side. Fuller solidified his business interests by making a series of significant purchases. In 1947, he bought **Boyer International Laboratories, Inc.**, which manufactured and sold products to White customers under the name of "Jean Nadal". Fuller also purchased the Courier Newspaper Group, which included *The New York Age* and the *Pittsburgh Courier*, and owned other ventures such as Fuller-Philco Home Appliance, Fuller Department Store, Fuller Guaranty Corporation, and the Regal Theater. While building his massive business empire of real estate holdings, a department store, a newspaper and his cosmetic company, Fuller managed to mentor future business leaders such as **John H. Johnson** of Johnson Publishing, **George Johnson** of Johnson Products, and **Joe Dudley** of Dudley Products. By the 1960's, Fuller was earning $10 million annually and had sales offices in 85 branches in 38 states, a line of 300 products, staffed with over 5,000 employees. At the end of the 1960's, however, Fuller Products landed some financial and legal problems, and the company filed for bankruptcy in 1971. Fuller was able to recuperate from this time, regrouped, and by 1972, Fuller Products showed an annual profit of $300,000.

Journalism

Black newspapers were also a means of entrepreneurship for those who could provide news that was of interest to the African-American population of Chicago. Just as the needs of African-American women were not being met in cosmetics, the majority newspapers of the day were not meeting the needs of the Black community either. The *Conservator* was Chicago's first weekly Black-owned newspaper, with many others following it. Examples of these are Julius Taylor's *Broad Ax*, Sheadrick B. Turner's *Illinois Idea*, Allison Sweeny's *Chicago Leader*, William Neighbor's *Illinoise Chronicle*, B. F. Harris's *Chicago World*, and Adam Brothers' *Appeal*.

The most successful venture in journalism was the *Chicago Defender*, which was also one of America's largest Black-owned businesses of the early 20th century. It was founded by Robert Abbott in 1905, and as many of the other African-American newspapers did in the early 1900's, struggled during its first years to make profit with little advertising and a small circulation. The *Defender* turned around when Abbott hired J. Hockley in 1910, who with a flare for sensationalist and successful journalistic techniques, such as lively commentary, made the *Defender* the most successful Black newspaper in Chicago by 1915. The paper soon grew to have national circulation and became the leading Black newspaper in the country. Through its depiction of Chicago as a safe haven, free of racial prejudice and a place for economic opportunity, the *Defender* was a major factor in inducing Blacks to migrate from the South to Chicago. After a profitless beginning, the *Defender* made Abbott Chicago's first African-American millionaire.

With its readership broadened, the paper began to attract national advertisers, by the end of the migration era its columns carried not only notices for Chicago stores, but also ads for nationally distributed products. In 1920, Abbott bought a cylinder press in order to fulfill his dream of having his own printing plant. Abbott opened his new facilities in 1921, and with a plant valued at almost half a million dollars, the newspaper was by far the largest Black business in Chicago, and one of the largest in the country. Black businesses such as the *Chicago Defender*, Binga Bank, and others of the time all consciously tried to secure Black customers by emphasizing the importance of their enterprises to the cause of self-help and the buildup of the African-American community.

Insurance Companies

Chicago Black insurance companies had a different flavor than their colleagues in the South for they were built up as corporations, not as extensions of mutual aid and fraternal societies. Also, unlike their prewar counterparts in the South, Chicago insurance companies did not come about until wartime migration. During this time, Chicago was "prosperous and growing rapidly, as was the insurance market. From 1916 to 1925, the amount of life insurance in force in the United States more than tripled." [7] There were several efforts to form African-American-owned insurance companies in Chicago prior to World War I, but each of them failed. Examples of these efforts are the United Brotherhood Fraternal Insurance Company, which failed in the late 1890's when one of the founders ran off with the money, and Progressive National Life Insurance Company, which failed to materialize in 1913.

In the five years following World War I, however, Blacks founded four insurance companies in Chicago. Interestingly, the most influential entity to spur the formation of successful Black-owned insurance companies in Chicago was not African-American-owned. It was the White-owned **Royal Life Insurance Company**, founded in 1912, which was the first to hire African-American clerks and executives. It opened a district office on the South Side completely staffed by Blacks. Former employees of Royal started virtually all of the Black insurance companies started after World War I in Chicago. Among those new insurance companies were the **Public Life Insurance Company**, **Pyramid Mutual Casualty**, and **Liberty Life Insurance Company**. The Liberty Life Insurance Company (later renamed Supreme Liberty Life) became one of the most successful African-American-owned companies in the country. Like many of Chicago's leading businesspeople, Earl Dickerson, one of Supreme Liberty's leading forces, was able to not only influence the business environment of Chicago, but also became involved politically. Dickerson started out by winning the seat of Alderman of the Second Ward in 1939, and later in his career became involved in President Roosevelt's Committee of Fair Employment Practices. Dickerson was instrumental in bringing about the mass conversion of Chicago's African-American community to the Democratic Party during the 1930's and 1940's.

The Great Depression (which was preceded by the return of soldiers from the war) took with it many of these companies, mostly because of the high level of unemployment and recession that it caused. As Blacks lost their jobs, and as income levels fell, Black Chicagoans could no longer afford to keep their insurance premiums. The effect of these years on Black insurance companies was not only felt in Chicago, but nationwide as well, with some of the largest Black-owned companies going out of business.

During the 1940's and 1950's, as the United States became involved in World War II, Black employment and wages began to increase rapidly, leading mortality rates to drop sharply for Blacks, finally coming closer to the national average. This again made the insurance arena a more profitable one for Chicago's business leaders. An example of a firm that survived all the ups and downs experienced by Chicago's Black community is **Chicago Metropolitan Mutual Assurance Company.** Founded in 1927, it was an outgrowth of a consortium of Black funeral companies, which in 1925 had united in order to provide death benefits for poor African-Americans in Chicago. **Robert A. Cole**, once the manager of a gambling establishment in the city, started the company in the 1920's. In the 1950's, after Cole's death and an agent strike at the firm, the growth of the company was slowed for a while, until it came under the control of **George S. Harris** in 1961. After this, Chicago Metropolitan began to expand. In 1965, Harris explored the possibility of a merger with Supreme Liberty Life Insurance, but the plans never went through, mostly because of resistance from the personnel of both companies. In 1971, Harris was replaced by **Anderson M. Schweich**, who led the company successfully into the 1990's. Schweich took Chicago Metropolitan into the group insurance market, getting some of the group insurance business of General Foods Corporation, Jewel Companies, Inc., and Commonwealth Edison. By 1992, Chicago Mutual had over $2.8 billion of insurance in force, compared to the just $1 billion for the other prominent Chicago insurance firm, Supreme Liberty Life (see next chapter for case study).

Recreational and Service Establishments

Blacks were completely excluded from White-owned commercial establishments such as skating rinks, dance halls, and amusement parks. To meet these demands, some entrepreneurs ventured into recreation, such as **Robert T. Motts** who owned the Perkin Theater, the only Black-owned theater of its time. Other prominent Black-owned recreational establishments during this time were saloons and other businesses of marginal reputation such as pool halls and gambling establishments.

Black baseball teams and various other recreational establishments were also organized during this time. **Robert L. Jackson** and **Beauregard F. Moseley** promoted the first successful baseball team on the South Side: The Leland Giants. The Leland Giants Baseball and Amusement Association raised funds for an "all-Black-owned" baseball park, operated a dance hall and roller skating rink, and attempted to establish an amusement park and summer hotel for African-Americans. The first attempt in creating a baseball league came in 1910, when Moseley called together a group of Black baseball officials throughout the Midwest and South to organize the **National Negro Baseball League**. Chicago fielded two baseball teams in 1911, one more than it could support. This first attempt at a Black baseball league failed to materialize and the only team in Chicago played in a White-owned park. The dream of a Black baseball league was not realized until after World War I.

Service establishments such as barber shops, restaurants, hotels, wood and coal companies, and development companies also predominated during the early twentieth century. One reason for their existence is that Blacks already had experience in these service trades, more than they did in retailing and manufacturing. Also, these industries usually required only a small amount of capital to start off, less than it would to establish a factory. Few Black businessmen had either the ready cash or credit necessary to stock goods for a store or invest in expensive equipment, not to forget the denial of capital Blacks experienced from majority banks during this time. Finally, an African-American who opened a clothing or hardware store would face fierce competition from well-established, well-financed White merchants. A Black barber, saloonkeeper, or restaurant owner, on the other hand, found relatively little competition, as Chicago's White business people were hesitant to provide these types of services to African-Americans.

Cooperative business enterprises were another type of business that developed during this time, which like Black service institutions, resulted from White discrimination. They were also the outgrowth of the ideology of self-help and racial solidarity that drove many of Chicago's other Black-owned businesses. Their leaders were motivated by a desire to provide services and facilities that were otherwise unavailable to African-Americans. Struggling African-American retailers sought, through cooperation, to bolster their difficult position. A number of African-American shopkeepers organized the **Colored Commercial Club of Chicago** designed to promote the common interests of its members through joint business and legal advice. Despite these efforts, however, majority store owners maintained their control over most retail businesses on the South Side and held a virtual monopoly of grocery, clothing, furniture, hardware, and department stores.

Of the various cooperative business ventures, cemetery associations were most able to achieve a relative measure of success. Encountering discriminatory prices and even exclusion in White cemeteries, African-Americans opened two cemeteries of their own in the Chicago area: Mount Glenwood Cemetery and Lincoln Cemetery. Several other cooperative businesses had shorter lives, especially in prewar Chicago. They encountered the same problems faced by individual Black businesses. They failed as a result of strict discrimination, inexperience, inadequate capital, and the difficulty in securing credit from financial institutions.

CHAPTER FOUR: CASE: SUPREME LIBERTY LIFE INSURANCE COMPANY

Supreme Liberty Life has been chosen as a case study of a business created in the city of Chicago during the early twentieth century. By understanding the issues that faced this insurance company as it was created and grew, the forces that were present in Chicago at the time will become apparent. These forces created a fertile environment for the creation of successful businesses, many of them insurance companies and other businesses geared towards meeting the needs of the African-American community. The result was the creation of a thriving Black elite made up of professionals, business people and politicians in the city.

Profile

- Supreme Liberty Life Insurance Company is still the oldest Black-owned insurance company in Chicago and was once the largest Black-owned business in the North.

- In 1992, Supreme Liberty Life was the tenth-largest African-American-owned insurance company in the country. It currently remains a profitable entity.

- Supreme Liberty Life is currently part of John H. Johnson's Chicago business empire, which includes the renowned Johnson Publishing, publishers of *Ebony* and *Jet* magazines.

- From its start in the early twentieth century, Supreme Liberty Life has played a vital and active role in the development of Chicago's African-American community.

Summary

Supreme Liberty Life Insurance Company was founded in 1919 (then under the name of Liberty Life Insurance Company) by a Black migrant from the South named Frank L. Gillespie. The company received its Illinois state charter that year, a year after Gillespie had started to plan the creation of the company, together with a couple of other prominent Black business leaders. The insurance company was able to acquire the necessary $100,000 in deposits to open, and started business by the summer of 1921. At this time, Gillespie's two most significant partners were Earl B. Dickerson, who served as the company's legal counsel for three decades, and W. Ellis Stewart, the company's secretary.

One thing which differentiated Liberty Life from other insurance companies of the time was the fact that they focused more on the ordinary life insurance market, rather than on the more widely used industrial insurance. Since ordinary life insurance policies were more expensive, the company focused on the city's expanding Black middle class.

The first few years of business were difficult, with few profits and high expenses. Despite these problems, sales managed to rise every year through 1925. That year, Gillespie passed away and the presidency of the company was taken over by Dr. M. O. Bousfield. Under his leadership, the company achieved its first profit. Bousfield led the company until 1929. In 1929, a major change came about in the company with the merger to Supreme Life and Casualty Company and Northeastern Life Insurance Company. This merger changed the company's name to Supreme Liberty Life Insurance Company, and brought about a number of advantages to the firm. The merger brought with it two very talented executives: Harry H. Pace, who served as the new company's president, and Truman K. Gibson, who served as Chairman of the Board. This new extra strength came just in time to help the company survive the Great Depression of the same year. Many companies were not able to survive this economic crisis; Supreme Liberty Life was one of the few that, as a result of excellent leadership, did.

Another crisis hit the company in 1933, when an examination by the Illinois Department of Insurance resulted in a devaluation of the company of nearly fifty-percent. This devaluation would have caused the bankruptcy of Supreme Liberty Life were it not for the drastic maneuvers taken on by Dickerson, the firm's legal counsel. Dickerson was able to increase the company's value and the firm was saved. Supreme Liberty Life entered the next decade strong, reaching an insurance in force of over $53 million by 1942. In 1943, Gibson took over the presidency of the company and led it successfully until 1955, when the presidency was taken over by Earl B. Dickerson.

The early 1950's brought new problems to the company. Its profits were low and its growth was decreased, thus decreasing its ranking among other insurance companies. Fortunately, by 1955, and with the change of power into Dickerson's hands, Supreme was on its way back to recovery. By 1961, Supreme Liberty Life was listed as the largest Black-owned business in the North and the third-largest in the country, and held over $200 million of insurance in force. In part, due to the Civil Rights movement going on in the whole country, the 1960's proved to be one of the company's most successful decades ever. By 1970, unfortunately, the firm started having financial troubles again. The company lost a significant amount of money and started to quickly slip in the rankings.

In 1971, Dickerson retired and the presidency was taken over by John H. Johnson, who still currently runs the company. Johnson, who got his start with Supreme Liberty Life, and now runs a powerful business empire, was a major stockholder at the time he took over the management of Supreme Liberty Life. Under his command, the firm grew strongly over the 1970's and 1980's, reaching a record $2.3 billion of insurance in force in 1988. The early 1990's were less fortunate for the firm, however, but not deadly. With 1991 came a significant decrease in the company's assets as well as a decreased staff to fit the new smaller size of the firm. Although not listed on **BLACK ENTERPRISE**'s Top 10 insurance companies since 1992, the firm has been able to continue being a profitable and successful midsize insurance company under Johnson's rule, and has found a comfortable niche in the market for the future.

History

Supreme Liberty Life Insurance Company was started under the name of Liberty Life Insurance Company, receiving a charter from the state of Illinois on June 3, 1919. [1] The company was founded by one of the many Black migrants that made their way to Chicago from the South during the World War I years. His name was **Frank L. Gillespie**.

Gillespie was born on November 8, 1876 in Osceola, Arkansas. When he was a young boy, his family relocated to Memphis, where he received his formal education in public schools. As a teenager, Gillespie lived in St. Louis, Missouri, where he attended Sumner High School. He did not get to graduate from Sumner, for after three years he was sent to the Boston Conservatory to study music. It was there that he received his high school degree. After finishing his studies in Boston, Gillespie pursued a law degree at Harvard Law School. [2] Unfortunately, his family started experiencing some financial difficulties and he was not able to finish his law degree. Instead, he moved to Chicago, where he got a job working as a private secretary for J. C. Yeager, an important White business leader in the city.

When Yeager died, Gillespie again had to find a means to support himself. He found a position with the Automatic Telephone Company, becoming the first African-American employee to ever be hired by that firm. Gillespie did not stay at the telephone company for very long because he left to join Oscar De Priest, a powerful Black businessman, congressman and politician, in the real estate business. Two years later, in 1916, Gillespie joined the agency in force of the Royal Insurance Company of Chicago, the first White firm to hire Blacks in the city and the first firm to begin pursuing business in predominantly African-American areas. Gillespie was initially hired to head what was known as the "department for colored people", but only in a matter of months, in August of 1916, was promoted to superintendent of the company. With this appointment, Gillespie became the first African-American superintendent of a northern, White-owned, old-line insurance firm.

During World War I, despite the mounting racial tensions due to increased Black migration, Royal Insurance made impressive efforts to hire and promote a number of Blacks like Gillespie. Gillespie, however, grew eventually frustrated by his work at Royal Insurance, finding it difficult to advance any further in the company, so just over a year after starting his position as superintendent, he gave up his job. In turn, he became organizer and officer of the Public Life Insurance Company of Illinois, a company organized by a group of former African-American Royal Insurance employees. Gillespie ran that firm successfully as an officer for about two years, after which he moved on to his next venture. In early 1918, Gillespie had started meeting with a group of prominent Black business leaders in the city who wanted to create a new insurance company. The timing was perfect for such a venture, for Black migration from the South was at its peak, thus increasing the market for such services.

As soon as Gillespie and his partners received the necessary state charter, they started creating Liberty Life. By late 1920, the 10,000 initial shares issued were being held by more than 800 persons, the founders holding over 3,500 of those shares. However, they were not able to start business until the summer of 1921, this slow start mostly due to Gillespie and his partners' overestimation of the capacity of the city's African-American community. It took the new company a few years to be able to acquire the required $100,000 in deposits necessary to start an insurance business. The necessary $100,000 was "finally raised by enlisting the aid of [the] president of the Lincoln State Bank." [3] Once open for business, Frank Gillespie served as the company's first president. Two significant players in running the firm with Gillespie were **W. Ellis Stewart**, who acted as secretary, and **Earl B. Dickerson**, who served as legal counsel.

One of the things that differentiated Liberty Life from Black insurance firms in the South was the fact that they offered ordinary life insurance, instead of concentrating on the more common industrial insurance. Industrial insurance was more prevalent during this time, where premiums of just a nickel or a dime a week were collected to supply only a basic burial insurance. Liberty Life collected higher premiums, only once or twice a year, while providing their patrons with an insurance of greater substance than that of a simple industrial insurance. There were fewer potential policyholders, but, because of the higher expense of it, Liberty's insurance policies were designed to be sold to the expanding, higher-income African-American middle class, which over the early twentieth century had become an expanding and lucrative market. There was no real competition for Liberty Life at the time, for White-owned companies refused to sell any type of insurance to African-Americans, mostly on the pretext that Black mortality rates were higher than those of Whites.

Liberty Life started doing business during a time of crisis, which had come about as a result of the tensions that had been growing in Chicago since the late 1910's.

Following the summer riots of 1919, Blacks in the city had become greatly disillusioned in the potential of Chicago as a place free of racial prejudice. The return of soldiers to the city at the end of World War I had brought about major layoffs and thus a massive economic recession to the Black community. These conditions forced Gillespie and his staff to have to try hard to convince the disillusioned community that it was worth investing in their insurance plan. To do this, Gillespie hired and trained an army of well-educated, young African-Americans. This was a financial strain on the company, however, for given the hard times, they had little money with which to pay the salaries of these professionals. As a result, Liberty Life was forced to eventually rely on part-time ministers and postal workers to do some of the agents' work.

In 1922, Liberty Life had to sell additional shares in order to come up with enough money to survive. The move proved successful, and by 1923, their sales income was enough to cover operating expenses, although their policy reserves still had to be covered with surplus funds. Investments throughout the 1920's were primarily in real estate, and in 1924 a home office building was erected. During the early 1920's, Liberty Life also bought a number of mortgages on Black residential property, providing an economic benefit to themselves as well as a social service to Chicago's African-American community, which was routinely refused mortgage financing from White institutions.

Despite these hard times of high sales expenses and lapsed policies, sales still managed to rise every year through 1925. By the end of 1925, Liberty Life had over $8 million of insurance in force and $495,000 in admitted assets. [4] 1925, unfortunately, also brought bad news to the company, when in May, Gillespie, the company's co-founder and driving force, passed away. Gillespie was a powerful driving force and tremendous leader not only of Liberty Life, but was also one of the founders of the National Insurance Association, a trade association of Black-owned insurance companies. With the presidency turned over to **Dr. Midian O. Bousfield**, Gillespie's death caused a temporary setback for the firm.

Bousfield was born in Missouri and was a graduate of the University of Kansas and Northwestern Medical School. After his education, Bousfield served various internships and traveled to various countries, eventually landing in Chicago in the late 1910's, where he began working for the Railway Man's International Benevolent Association. While an employee there, he met Frank Gillespie, who asked him to help organize Liberty Life. Bousfield took him up on the offer, and became vice president and medical director of the company until Gillespie's death. Bousfield was president of Liberty Life successfully until 1929, leading the company in achieving a significant reduction in expenses and its first real profit of $12,000 in 1928.

In 1929, Liberty Life's leadership decided it was time to reenergize the company through merging with other insurance companies. That same year, it accomplished this goal by merging with **Supreme Life and Casualty Company** of Columbus, Ohio and **Northeastern Life Insurance Company** of Newark, New Jersey. This merger changed the company's name to **Supreme Liberty Life Insurance Company** and brought about a number of advantages to the company. Supreme Life had large holdings of industrial insurance, with salesmen trained in those operations and Northeastern had an astounding investment portfolio and highly experienced management, all things that Liberty Life could use to make its firm stronger. Also, neither company, unlike Liberty, had been profitable in 1928, so the merger was beneficial for all parties involved.

Financial Effect of Merger

Company	Assets	Ordinary Insurance in Force	Industrial Insurance in Force
Liberty Life	$832,000	$10,401,000	$1,964,000
Supreme Life	$470,000	$4,519,000	$5,429,000
Northeastern Life	$157,000	$1,709,000	None
Combined	$1,458,000	$16,629,000	$7,393,000
Supreme Liberty (12/1929)	$1,621,000	$16,644,000	$8,953,000

Source: "Supreme Liberty Life: The History of a Negro Life Insurance Company, 1919-1962." Business History Review, Spring 1969.

The merger brought with it not only financial gain and trained sales personnel, but also very talented chief executives. **Harry H. Pace**, who had been the president of Northeastern, became the president of the new and improved Supreme Liberty Life, and **Truman K. Gibson**, who had been the president of Supreme Life, became the Chairman of the Board. Gibson was also responsible for working out the complicated merger, and for this work was awarded the Harmon Medal for distinguished achievement. The merger proved to be a success, and was, at the time, the biggest financial deal ever negotiated by an African-American-owned business. With its new leadership and combined business in force of $27 million, Supreme Liberty Life was able to survive the Great Depression. [5] During this time, Bousfield, who had given up the presidency to Pace, became again medical director and vice president, his previous position, while also serving as director of medical services for the Julius Rosenwald Fund.

Pace and Gibson, Supreme Liberty's new leaders, had various things in common. They were both Georgia natives and both attended Atlanta University, graduating in 1903 and 1905 respectively. Both men were also officers of important Black-owned Atlanta insurance companies (Herman Perry's Standard Life Insurance and Alonzo Herndon's Atlanta Mutual Life Insurance, respectively). It was after his work with Standard Life Insurance and a stint as president of Motown-forerunner Black Swan Records (the first major Black-owned recording company) that Pace, with the financial support of a number of wealthy Blacks, went on to form Northeastern Insurance Company. [6] After becoming president of Supreme Liberty, Pace decided to further his education and enrolled in University of Chicago Law School, where he received his law degree in 1933. During the late 1930's, while continuing as president of Supreme Liberty, Pace also practiced law as a member of the law firm Bibb, Tyree and Pace. Pace remained involved in these endeavors until he passed away in 1943.

Gibson's road to Supreme Liberty was comparable to that of Pace. After receiving his bachelor's degree from Atlanta University in 1905, Gibson attended Harvard University, where he received another Bachelor's degree, this one in Business Administration in 1908. After his education, Gibson moved to Virginia, where he taught for two years. In 1910, a fellow teacher and friend convinced him to enter the insurance field. That year he started working at Atlanta Mutual, where he stayed until 1919. During the nine years at Atlanta Mutual, Gibson advanced from the agency side to manager, increasing his annual earnings over time from $600 to over $2,000. In 1919, wanting to escape the racism of the South, and wanting to be an entrepreneur and own his own business, Gibson and a few partners organized the Supreme Life and Casualty Company of Ohio. Gibson served as the company's only president for ten years, until the merger with Liberty Life and Northeastern Insurance. Gibson served as Chairman of the Board of the new consortium until Pace's death in 1943, after which he took over as president. His tenure as president lasted until 1955, when he again became Chairman of the Board and then Chairman Emeritus until his death in 1972.

The merger of 1929 came just in time to give all three companies involved extra strength needed. Just after the merger, the devastating Great Depression struck the country, leaving many companies in complete turmoil. The Great Depression was especially hurtful to Black insurance companies for it made more pronounced the already large amount of unemployment in the African-American community. (More than ten years after the Great Depression, in 1940, still thirty-six percent of African-American Chicago males were unemployed.) [7] This unemployment trend had been taking place since the return of soldiers at the end of World War I, and was allowing progressively fewer of the city's Blacks to afford their insurance premiums. Without having had time to fully coordinate its procedures, the new company, under Pace and Gibson's leadership, was faced with trying to survive in an economic recession of unprecedented proportions. As a result, Supreme Liberty Life's first few years of existence were ones of mere survival. The situation was especially difficult for Supreme Liberty Life because its income relied more heavily on the more expensive ordinary life market as opposed to the industrial insurance market most other insurance companies dealt in. Another source of strain at the time was the company's heavy investment in the real estate market, which, with the rapid devaluation of real estate, especially in Black areas, had caused a sharp decline in the value of the company's assets. Not only could the increasing numbers of unemployed

Blacks no longer afford their insurance premiums, they could also no longer meet their mortgage payments. Despite all these downhill battles, however, and unlike many other companies, Supreme Liberty Life was able to survive.

Some of Pace and Gibson's strategy during these difficult times involved, among other tactics, the reducing of the company's operating expenses. They also focused the company more on the less expensive and more widespread industrial insurance market. Under Pace and Gibson's leadership, and with the move to industrial insurance, the company was able to survive hard times, but did experience financial hardship. The company was left standing with a significant loss of $250,000 dollars over four years, from $1.83 million in 1930 to $1.58 million in 1934, and had virtually no investment income by the mid 1930's. [8]

Besides the Great Depression, Supreme Liberty Life was faced by another crisis in 1933, when the Illinois Department of Insurance began an examination of all insurance firms in the state. As part of their investigation, the department reduced the book value of most of the real estate items in Supreme Liberty Life's insurance portfolio from $743,000 to $360,000. This sharp decline put the company, which, at the time had only a small surplus of $76,544 and was experiencing no profits on current operations, at the brink of bankruptcy. [9] A drastic move became necessary to save the company. **Earl Dickerson**, the company's counsel came up with the perfect, and later to become illegal, plan to increase the company's assets. Dickerson was forced to take his plan to the Illinois Supreme Court, which, after a five-to-two vote, was allowed to be implemented. [10] The plan was to convince the company's policyholders to sign a lien by which they acknowledged an indebtedness to the company of either fifty percent or the whole amount of their policies' reserves. Dickerson's move added some $300,000 in policyholders' liens to the company's assets, thus saving Supreme Liberty Life. With the liens retired in 1937, the company became increasingly profitable, making the late 1930's a turning point for Supreme Liberty Life. Surplus funds grew from $100,000 in 1935 to $280,000 in 1941, a recovery due, for the most part, to the switch to industrial life insurance. Also, a new strategy had been put in place by **James G. Ish**, the agency director, that mass-produced these policies. With Ish's strategy, an impressive $460,000 worth of industrial insurance policies were sold between 1935 and 1942, bringing Supreme Liberty Life's insurance in force up from less than $9 million in 1929 to over $53 million by 1942.

In the early 1940's, with America's entrance into World War II, conditions for Chicago Black insurance companies again improved. The increase in employment and income experienced in the African-American community, as well as a decrease in Black mortality which came about during this time, gave rise to conditions which gave Supreme Liberty Life a renewed opportunity to sell the more profitable ordinary life insurance. These new conditions, in turn, increased their profits further. On the other hand, the improved conditions in the African-American community made the Black market more attractive to large White-owned firms, thus increasing the level of competition experienced by Supreme Liberty Life. Truman K. Gibson successfully served as president of the company during this time, and especially during his first seven years (1943-1950) the company experienced significant growth. Despite high operating expenses, by the end of the war, Supreme Liberty Life was experiencing financial success. Both surplus and dividends had increased over the years, the company was able to raise its stock value to its original $10 price, and the company's surplus had reached an unprecedented one million dollars by 1948. [11] Feeling comfortable with the company's financial stability, toward the end of his tenure as president, in order to allow a further diversification of the company, Gibson pushed for more aggressive moves. Examples of these moves are the 1949 absorption of Carver Mutual Insurance Company of Detroit and the 1952 take over of Twentieth Century Life Insurance Company, also of Detroit.

After 1950, problems again arose for Supreme Liberty Life. Despite a greater volume of business, profits never rose above $180,000 after 1951, a number well below the company's average of the previous eight years. Supreme Liberty Life's growth also significantly decreased, now ranking below other Black insurance companies, unlike its growth in the 1940's, which had exceeded other companies' growth. Industrial insurance in force fell by about $10 million between 1950 and 1955, and its holdings of ordinary life insurance grew by only thirty-three percent, seventeen percent below the growth experienced by other Black insurance companies. [12]

Supreme's leadership realized that the core of the problem was Gibson's management of the company. When Gibson had taken helm, Supreme was a much smaller firm, but as it had grown, he had not been able to deal with the increasing business, growing size of employees and more complex problems that arise in a larger company. Changes had to be made to save the company. A number of changes in the administrative structure and flow of communications were made starting in 1953, ending with the 1956 replacement of Gibson by **Earl B. Dickerson**, the person responsible for saving Supreme Liberty Life in the 1930's. Gibson remained involved in the company's operations as Chairman of the Board until 1971 and honorary Chairman Emeritus until his death, at age ninety, in 1972. During his lifetime, Gibson also served as chairman of the Joint Negro Appeal Drive, was a sponsor of the United Negro College Fund, and was a member of the National Negro Insurance Association, the Urban League, and the NAACP.

Earl Dickerson was born in Mississippi on June 23, 1891 and was educated in his hometown until 1907, when at the age of sixteen, he moved to Chicago to attend the Evanston Academy, then the preparatory division of Northwestern University. Dickerson graduated from Evanston in 1909, after which he enrolled in the University of Illinois at Urbana, where he graduated from in 1914. After teaching at the Tuskegee Institute in Alabama and at a high school in Indiana, Dickerson entered law school at the University of Chicago. Before he could finish his law degree, however, the United States entered World War I, and Dickerson was drafted to serve in France, where he served as first lieutenant in the 365th Infantry. After finishing his service, Dickerson returned to Chicago and his law studies, graduating from University of Chicago in 1920. In 1921, Dickerson was admitted to the Illinois Bar Association, and in the same year was asked by Frank Gillespie to draw up the articles of incorporation for Liberty Life Insurance. Dickerson accepted, and after the creation of the company became general counsel of the firm. Dickerson remained legal counsel for the company for thirty years while also having a successful career as a lawyer, politician, and civil rights leader in the city.

When the company started exhibiting problems in the 1950's, Dickerson started taking on a more active role in Supreme Liberty Life's management. During this decade he was instrumental in bringing about the necessary changes for the company's survival of a difficult time. In 1954 he became executive Vice President and a year later became General Manager before succeeding Gibson as President and Chief Executive Officer in 1956. When Dickerson took over Gibson's job in April 1956, the company was under financial strain so his main objective was to increase the company's rate of growth. Under his leadership, the most significant move taken by the company to serve this purpose was the shift from industrial insurance back to ordinary life insurance. In order to do so, he replaced the current agency director, the 'king' of mass industrial insurance, James Ish, with **J. F. Morning**. Morning proved to be a perfect pick, successfully reducing the company's expenses. Morning also made great improvements in the selection, training, and compensation of the company's agents, making possible the shift from industrial to the higher quality, more lucrative ordinary life insurance market.

With Dickerson's appointment came better times for Supreme Liberty. Dickerson's initial steps included a centralization of the control of the company and a reduction of agency expenses. Already one year prior to his taking over as president, Supreme was well on its way to recovery. In 1955 the company reported an insurance in force of $124 million and had more than 1,000 employees with offices in twelve states and assets of more than $15 million invested in buildings and equipment. By 1956 it was rated as the North's largest African-American-owned business "with 38 branch offices in 28 cities…over 300,000 policyholders in 12 states and the District of Columbia." [13] Supreme's insurance in force during this time was reported to be in excess of $125 million and had more than $17 million in assets with 600 employees nationwide. [14]

Another endeavor taken on by Dickerson during his tenure as President was the 1956 renovation of the company's corporate headquarters building. Between 1956 and 1961 Dickerson also absorbed Friendship Mutual Life Insurance Company, the Beneficial Life Insurance Company of Detroit, the Dunbar Life Insurance Company of

Cleveland, and the Federal Life Insurance Company of Washington, D.C. By 1961, Supreme Liberty Life was listed as the largest Black-owned business in the North, and the third largest in the country. The company had over $200 million of insurance in force, and had some $31.5 million in assets, thirty-eight branch offices in twelve states with 600 employees, and more than 350,000 policyholders nationwide.

Also in 1961, Dickerson bought over Domestic Life Insurance Company of Louisville, Kentucky, adding one-third as many policyholders to their holdings as well as bringing the Supreme Liberty Life into Kentucky, Ohio, Indiana, and Tennessee. All these acquisitions usually took place through stock purchases or reinsurance and were made possible by the increased administrative capacity created under Dickerson and Morning's leadership. Over a six-year period these moves added almost $58 million to Supreme Liberty Life's insurance holdings and brought the company an unprecedented profit of $500,000. [15] Unlike its growth rate in the early 1950's, its growth rate from 1957 to 1962 was much higher than the average of other Black insurance companies. By 1965 it was reported to have assets of over $33 million and $208 million of insurance in force, sixty percent more insurance than it had ten years prior. [16] By 1970, however, the company started experiencing some financial strain again, losing more than half a million dollars that year alone, and had reported assets of $37 million, an insurance in force of $222 million, and an annual premium income of $7.3 million. By 1970, Supreme Liberty Life stood at number 517 among all insurance companies in the country and was also quickly slipping in ranking among Black insurance companies.

Dickerson remained Chief Executive Officer until 1971, when he retired and took on the position of Chairman of the Board until 1973. From 1973, until his death in 1986, Dickerson served as honorary Chairman Emeritus. Outside of his leadership of the company, Dickerson led a successful career as a leader in Chicago politics and civil rights. His interest in politics was first sparked while a student at the University of Illinois, and first put into practice when in 1923 he was named head of the Negro Division of Democratic Mayor William Dever's campaign. With Dever's election, Dickerson was named assistant corporation counsel for the city, a significant move for him since at that time virtually all of Chicago's African-Americans were supporters of the Republican Party. Throughout the 1920's, Dickerson continued to work for Democratic national, state, and citywide candidates, but never ran for office himself during that time. His first run for office was in 1929, when he ran as an independent for the position of alderman of the Second Ward. Dickerson lost the race and in 1931 returned to the Democratic Party. Also throughout the 1920's, Dickerson became involved in the National and Chicago Urban Leagues, as well as the NAACP, and he was a vocal protest leader on behalf of public housing.

During the 1930's, as one of the first African-American Democrats in Chicago, Dickerson was in a unique position, instrumental in implementing Franklin Roosevelt's New Deal policies, which were key in converting the mass of Chicago Blacks to the Democratic Party. During these years he protested police brutality both in person to Chicago Mayor Cermak and through leading public protests. In 1939, Dickerson again ran for the position of Alderman of the Second Ward, this time victorious and on the Democratic ticket. He reached an agreement with William Dawson, his predecessor, to join forces after the election, and through the agreement Dawson, a Black Republican, converted to the Democratic Party. Dickerson grew to be a powerful person in the new African-American Democratic elite group that was growing in the city. Dickerson's tactics in achieving his many social and civil rights goals were often not well-liked by his political colleagues. As a result, in 1941, in part 'to get him out of their hair', the powerful Black Democratic elite of Chicago convinced President Roosevelt to appoint him to the Committee of Fair Employment Practices. This committee had good intentions of investigating claims of discrimination in the workplace, but had no enforcement powers and was only able to make suggestions to the government. Throughout the late 1940's, and through the 1950's, 1960's, and 1970's, Dickerson's multifaceted career made him an important figure in the civil rights struggle in Chicago. During this time he served as director of both the NAACP and the National Urban League, and served as president of the Chicago Urban League. He spent most of his life fighting discrimination and pushing for integration, and at his death in 1986 was considered one of the most important and powerful figures of Chicago's African-American community.

At the time of Dickerson's retirement, Johnson Publishing's **John Johnson**, then majority stockholder of Supreme Liberty Life, took over the management of the company. (Johnson's history is featured in Chapter Five, the Case Study on Johnson Publishing). During his first two years as head of Supreme Liberty Life, Johnson applied the successful leadership qualities which had made him a success in his other business ventures, and through these was able to turn around the insurance firm for the better. Only two years after Johnson took on the helm of the company its insurance in force had climbed to over $1 billion, its assets stood at $41 million, and its premium income had increased over forty percent to $10.2 million. In only three years its ranking among all insurance companies had risen 153 spots up to number 364 and its rank among Black insurance firms was also on the rise. In the fall of 1973, Johnson decided to keep his role as Chief Executive Officer but dropped his role as president and took on the role of Chairman of the Board of the company. The role of President was given to **Ray Irby**, the company's former vice president and agency director and Johnson's right-hand man during Johnson's takeover of Supreme Liberty Life's management. Under Irby and Johnson's leadership the company continued to grow, setting a record in 1975, when it reached over $1.5 billion of insurance in force and ranked 244th among all insurance firms of the nation.

Supreme Liberty Life's performance remained strong during the 1970's and 1980's, reaching new crossroads in the early 1990's. In 1988 it had a reported $2.3 billion of insurance in force, a premium income of $21 million, and assets of over $55 million. With 1991 came a decrease in the company's assets with a set of significant sales of assets arranged by Johnson. During that year he sold off $39 million in assets to the United Insurance Company of America, a sale which cut the company's total in assets from $53 million to a mere $14 million. The sale also wrote off nearly $4 million in real estate loans between 1985 and 1990, further decreasing the worth of the company. By 1992, Supreme Liberty Life was still alive and kicking, with all its claims paid off and a decreased staff to fit the decreased size of the company. At this size, Supreme Liberty Life was no longer a contender for being the North's largest Black-owned business nor was it close to being ranked among the top Black insurance companies anymore, yet it managed to hold its own comfortably, still making profit in its market niche. Throughout the years, Supreme Liberty Life continued sliding down **BLACK ENTERPRISE**'s listing of top insurance companies, being listed for the last time, as number ten, in 1992. Today, the company is still under John Johnson's control and continues to be a medium-scale profitable insurance company.

Section Three: Cases in the History of Black Business

CHAPTER FIVE: JOHNSON PUBLISHING COMPANY, INC.

Profile

- Publishers of *Ebony, Jet & Ebony Man* (EM) Magazines; book publishers; radio broadcasting; television production; and the manufacture of cosmetics.

- Owned by John H. Johnson and wife Eunice; current operations run by daughter, Linda Johnson Rice.

- Sales of $274 million in 1993; located in Chicago, Illinois; founded in 1942.

- Pioneer in advertising and publications geared at the African-American consumer; number two in **BLACK ENTERPRISE** Top 100 companies of 1993; pioneering efforts in publishing, media, broadcasting, and radio with diversification efforts in fashion and beauty products as symbiotic businesses.

- Enhanced relationship with Supreme Life Insurance Company – once largest and first Black-owned life insurance company in Chicago. Large installed base with African-American consumers and corporations.

- Talented writer pool and unmatched library of African-American history.

Summary

There has been a history of Black publishing since the early nineteenth century; Johnson Publishing continues that history. In 1942 John H. Johnson founded what is now the world's largest Black-owned publishing company. This came about after Johnson graduated from high school, had taken courses at the University of Chicago and Northwestern University, and had begun working at the Black-owned Supreme Liberty Life Insurance Company.

Realizing that there was no single source of articles of interest to Black Americans, Johnson came up with the idea of a *Reader's Digest*-style magazine for Blacks. Unable to raise money from either Blacks or Whites, Johnson borrowed $500 using his mother's furniture as collateral. Supreme Life gave Johnson access to its 20,000 policyholders and Johnson used the $500 he had borrowed to send a description of his idea to each of them.

3,000 people (15%) responded by October 1942 and sent in $2 subscriptions to *Negro Digest, a Magazine for Negro Comment.* By mid 1943, Johnson was selling more than 50,000 copies a month. *Ebony Magazine* followed shortly thereafter. Six years later *JET* was born and added to Johnson's portfolio, and *Ebony Man* then finally followed in 1985.

History

John Harold Johnson was born in Arkansas City, Arkansas on January 19, 1918, the only child of Leroy and Gertrude Johnson, a saw mill laborer and a domestic worker. After his father's death in 1924, Johnson was raised by his mother and stepfather, James Williams. At age fifteen Johnson moved with his family to Chicago, where he was an honors student at Du Sable High School. He developed an intense interest in journalism which was tempered by positions such as managing editor of the school newspaper and yearbook. As a senior, Johnson was chosen by the Chicago Urban League to be honored for his academic excellence. His speech, delivered at the League's banquet in his honor, impressed Harry Pace, then President of the Black-owned Supreme Liberty Life Insurance Company, enough to offer him a job as an office clerk. Upon graduation from high school in 1936, Johnson sought this employment opportunity with Supreme Life Insurance Company, while attending the University of Chicago part-time, and later, the School of Commerce at Northwestern University. At Supreme Life, one of his tasks was to summarize magazine and newspaper articles about the Black community for a company newsletter. From this task, Johnson conceived the idea of a *Reader's Digest*-style magazine for and by Blacks. He sought support and capital for the purpose of bringing his concept to reality, but found none. Those he approached did not think that the Black community would be interested in such a magazine. Undaunted by the criticism, Johnson was determined to make and sell his creation. In 1942 he secured a $500 loan using his mother's furniture as collateral. He used this money to send out a description of *Negro Digest, A Magazine of Negro Comment* and a subscription form to all 20,000 of Supreme Life's policyholders. The response was more than positive. Of the 20,000 policyholders, 3,000 sent in two-dollar subscriptions. With this $6000 Johnson produced the first issue of a soon-to-be historic journal of Black achievements. The *Negro Digest* was a monthly compilation of articles about and for the African-American community. With the conception of *Negro Digest* came the conception of a soon-to-be even bigger entity, Johnson Publishing. Johnson, it seemed, had discovered and given the greater society privy to an untapped market. The *Digest* was a raging success: within one year, three thousand subscriptions of the monthly magazine turned into fifty thousand.

Johnson did not stop there. He surmised that *Life* magazine was the second most popular magazine among African-Americans (the first, of course, being *Negro Digest*) and, inspired by this statistic, created a magazine for Blacks that was comparable to *Life*. Thus, in 1945, *Ebony,* the brain-child of a Black man with a vision for his people, was born. Johnson brought *Ebony* into being as a showcase for the accomplishments of African-Americans: *Ebony* would show by example. He wanted it to focus on the positive, to inspire and to motivate its readers, to instill in them a sense of pride both in who they were and who they could become. In order to do this, *Ebony* employed engaging photographs and interesting articles about, for, and by Blacks. It was an immediate and smashing success. Within hours, twenty-five thousand copies had been sold and another twenty-five thousand printed to meet the demand. *Ebony* instantly became the premier Black magazine in the United States, easily outdoing its forerunner and sister publication, *Negro Digest*. Johnson's biggest obstacle with *Ebony* was persuading national advertisers to tap the Black market. These advertisers were skeptical about any gains to be made off of the newly "discovered" Black consumer market, but this obstacle was finally overcome in 1947, when Johnson secured three advertising contracts from major corporations. His goal, "to make *Ebony* and the Negro consumer market integral parts of the marketing and advertising agendas of corporate America" [1], was well on its way to realization.

After the 1950 creation of a third, but relatively minor women's magazine, *Tan Confessions* (which was later renamed *Black Stars,*) Johnson reluctantly put *Negro Digest* to rest in November of 1951. In that same month, Johnson launched a new magazine,

Jet, which was another instant and smashing success. *Jet* is best described as a Black news and entertainment weekly. (Incidentally, *Hue,* a weekly feature magazine was also launched by Johnson Publishing in 1951. It was only marginally successful, and thus, short-lived.)

By the sixties and seventies, *Ebony* and *Jet,* the diamonds in the crown of Johnson Publishing Company, were enjoying tremendous success. By 1973, *Ebony* had achieved the highest monthly paid subscription of any African-American magazine. In 1975, Johnson Publishing hit the $37 million revenue mark. *Negro Digest* was revived and flourished for a short time, once again under a new name, *Black World*, only to be put out of commission for a second time in 1975.

During the early 1960's, Johnson Publishing prepared itself to break into a new and promising dimension: book publishing. The book division of Johnson Publishing, started in 1962, is now said to be one of the nation's leading producers of books on Black history and culture. [2] The sixties also saw the beginning of the diversification of Johnson Publishing Company. In 1964, John H. Johnson became president of Supreme Liberty Life Insurance Company. Becoming president and chief stockholder of the very company for who he was once but an office boy—Johnson had seemingly come full-circle!

Not surprisingly, there was more to come. Since the sixties Johnson has founded two cosmetics companies and a hair care products company, Fashion Fair Cosmetics, Ebony, and Supreme Beauty Products respectively. All three have proved themselves extremely profitable. Within ten years of its conception, Fashion Fair Cosmetics had sales exceeding thirty million dollars. Fashion Fair Cosmetics currently accounts for approximately thirty-five percent of Johnson Publishing's sales. [3] Johnson Publishing also currently owns three radio stations and a travel agency, produces a nationally syndicated television show (Ebony/Jet Showcase), and stages its own traveling fashion show. In 1985, JPC launched *EM (Ebony Man)* a magazine geared towards the Black man and Johnson Publishing's answer to *GQ (Gentleman's Quarterly.)* In 1991, JPC sold controlling interest in Supreme Liberty Life Insurance Company and announced a new venture: a mail order catalog selling women's apparel together with Spiegel.

Johnson Publishing Company Incorporated is currently America's second largest African-American-owned and operated business. In 1992 Johnson Publishing posted revenues of $274.2 million. [4] It is the nation's leading publisher of magazines geared towards Blacks. *Ebony*, as it is well-known, has double the circulation of its closest competitor, *Essence* magazine, in which Johnson owns a twenty percent interest. [5] It is estimated that collectively *Ebony* and *Jet* reach over fifty percent of African-Americans. Johnson Publishing is undoubtedly a financial success and a formidable competitor, and is, perhaps more importantly, a major contributor to African-American entrepreneurship, consumerism, and political and social participation. [6]

John Harold Johnson, age eighty, still plays an extremely active role in the running of his empire. While he has relinquished the Presidency and Chief Operating Officer position to his daughter, Linda Johnson Rice, he retains the offices of Chief Executive Officer and Chairperson of the Board.

CHAPTER SIX: TLC BEATRICE INTERNATIONAL

Profile

- Diversified food company, created and led by Reginald Lewis until his death in 1993. Currently being led successfully by Lewis' widow, Loida Nicolas Lewis.
- Major acquisitions are McCall Pattern in 1984 (later sold in 1987) and Beatrice International in 1987.
- TLC Group, an investment group, was launched by Lewis in 1983.
- In 1970, a law firm, specializing in business matters affecting New York City's African-American community, was Lewis' first venture.

Summary

Lewis was born in Baltimore on December 7, 1942. His mother and father raised him until he was five years old, at which point he moved in with his mother and grandparents. When he was nine years old, Lewis' mother remarried and Lewis moved in with his mother and new stepfather. He graduated from Dunbar High School in 1961, after which he attended Virginia State University. The summer before his 1965 graduation, Lewis attended a summer school program sponsored by Harvard University meant to introduce undergraduates to the study of law. Despite a strict code that the program was not to serve as a venue for the summer school students to apply to Harvard Law School, Lewis accomplished his life long goal: to be accepted to Harvard Law School. He spoke with the necessary people and stated his case convincingly until he got his way. He started law school in the fall of 1965 and graduated in 1968, after which he worked at a prestigious Wall Street firm. In 1970, he started his own law firm, which specialized in raising venture capital for small and medium-sized minority firms. By 1983, he had launched his own investment group, TLC Group. TLC bought McCall's Pattern Company in 1984 with $1 million of Lewis' own money and $24 million in debt. Three years later he sold McCall for $63 million with the purchaser assuming the outstanding debt.

Lewis set his sights on Beatrice International with an acquaintance, Michael Milken, who proved to be a powerful ally. Lewis acquired Beatrice International Companies, more than doubling the company's sales in one year. Lewis successfully led TLC Beatrice International Holdings until his sudden death of brain cancer in 1993. Since 1994, Lewis' widow, Loida, has been heading the company successfully. She was able to take it out of a slump, which it had been in since the European recession of 1992, and is currently working on taking the company public.

History

Reginald Lewis was born on December 7, 1942 and was reared in a middle-class Baltimore family. His parents are Clinton and Carolyn Cooper Lewis, but Lewis only lived with his father for the first five years of his life. At age five, Lewis and his mother moved in with his maternal grandparents. 'Grandpop Cooper' was a strong influence on Lewis' life, teaching him many of the values that would later be instrumental in his success. Lewis' mother, although away much of the time because of a heavy work schedule, was also an influential person in Lewis' life, and always made sure she had time with her son. Life changed again for Lewis when in 1951, when he was nine years old, his mother Carolyn married Jean Fugett. The new family moved from East Baltimore to the more middle class West Baltimore. Lewis did not stay an only child for very long. His first sibling to come was Jean Jr., who later on worked with him at TLC Beatrice. After Jean Jr. came Anthony, Joseph, Rosalyn, and Sharon.

When Lewis was ten years old he got his first job. He took on a paper route for Baltimore's African-American paper. He impressed everyone when he was able to increase his route from ten customers to more than 100 in a short period of time. After having increased his route by ten fold, Lewis decided to take on a new paper route. He began to deliver the *Baltimore News American* and sold his other route to a friend for profit. Surely an early sign of things to come!

When Lewis was fourteen, he left the parochial school system he had been in all his life and enrolled at Dunbar High School, a public high school in East Baltimore. Lewis showed incredible focus and discipline, becoming involved in football, baseball, and basketball. Lewis became starting quarterback for his school, and fell in love with the sport. He also excelled in his schoolwork, and took on after school jobs to earn extra money. During his junior and senior years Lewis worked in a drugstore every night after practice, after which he would go home and study. At age sixteen, Lewis took a summer full-time job at The Suburban Club, a Baltimore country club. He worked at the same country club every summer until he was eighteen years old, making $50 a week, plus any tips he got from selected club members. Once he entered college, Lewis continued to work occasional weekends at the club until his sophomore year. Lewis had promised himself that he would not be a financial burden on his family, and used the money from his jobs to pay for his clothing and other expenses. With money he had saved from his jobs, Lewis was able to afford his own car, and while still in high school he bought a Hillman, an English convertible.

Lewis graduated from Dunbar High School in 1961, and got a scholarship to attend Virginia State College in Petersburg, Virginia, the oldest publicly-funded Black university in the country. He played college football and hoped for a shot at the pros, but fortunately for the business world, his hopes were dashed after a shoulder injury brought his playing to a premature end. That is not to say that Lewis' only dreams were in professional sports, quite to the contrary. By the time he entered college, Lewis had dreams of becoming a successful lawyer. When Lewis quit football and lost his scholarship he restructured his college life, taking on a job to be able to support himself through school. He also got very serious about his studies, focusing 100 percent on his dream of attending law school. Among the jobs which Lewis held during this time was one as night manager of a bowling alley and another as a salesperson for a photography studio.

During Lewis' senior year at Virginia State, a life-altering opportunity came up. Lewis found out that Harvard Law School had started a program where selected few African-American college students would be introduced to legal study through allowing them to attend summer school at Harvard. Lewis saw in this program a perfect opportunity to attend the country's best law school, and wrote the university for more information on the program. After he read through the information, he applied to be accepted to the program. The selection process was to be done by Virginia State, and only five students of the college would be selected to apply to the program. Lewis made the first cut by Virginia State and sent off his application to Harvard. Soon thereafter Lewis got a letter from Harvard saying he had been accepted to the summer program. This one opportunity proved to be a life-altering one for Lewis. He left for Cambridge in the summer of 1965, not yet aware of what lay ahead of him.

The Harvard program was designed to make students familiar with law school life as well as give them an edge in the law school application process. It was strictly outlined, however, that it would not serve as an alternative admissions route to Harvard Law School. This would not hold Reginald Lewis back from accomplishing his dreams. All the while at the summer program, his underlying goal was to be admitted to the law school. He did his best to grasp the attention of the professors and made himself known to important people at the law school. One of the people initially impressed with Lewis was a professor, Frank Sander, who mentioned him to the Harvard Law School Dean of Admissions. Towards the end of the summer program, the Dean of Admissions, Louis Toepfler, contacted Lewis and asked him to come to his office. Toepfler went on to say that he had heard many professors were very impressed with him, and that many believed Lewis could excel in the study of law. Toepfler promised to contact several law schools on Lewis' behalf and give them his vote of confidence on Lewis. Lewis really wanted to attend Harvard Law School, and not any other law school, but he kept his hopes up. At the end of the summer program, he left back to Baltimore, hoping he would be able to return to Cambridge and fulfill his dream. A couple of days later, on Toepfler's request, Lewis called his office. Toepfler was not in, but he spoke to his secretary, who informed him that she was in the process of writing him a letter offering him a place in Harvard Law School's fall class! To make the offer even better, Harvard was offering Lewis a one-year grant from the Rockefeller Foundation as well as financial aid. For the first time in his life, Lewis would be able to focus exclusively on his studies without having to work his way through school.

Lewis' first task when he arrived in Cambridge in the fall of 1965 was to fill out an application to the law school. Reginald Lewis is the only person in the near 150-year history of Harvard Law School who has ever been admitted to the school without submitting an application. By the time Lewis arrived at Harvard, Toepfler had already filed the necessary paperwork for his educational loans and a check had already been drawn out in his name. Lewis was set. Much later on in his life, in 1992, Lewis repaid Harvard for its generosity by donating a $3 million gift, the largest gift ever given by someone at the time. In response to the generous gift, Harvard Law School named its international law building The Reginald F. Lewis International Law Center. This building remains, until now, the only building of Harvard University's campuses to be named after an African-American.

During the summer after his second year of law school, Lewis took a job with the Baltimore law firm of Piper & Marbury. The firm would have liked for him to return at the end of law school for a permanent job, but Lewis decided he wanted to try his luck in New York City. When he started interviewing with law firms during the fall of his third and last year in law school, Lewis aimed at large New York City firms. Lewis graduated from Harvard Law School in 1968, and accepted an offer for $10,000 per year with a renowned Wall Street law firm, Paul, Wiess, Rifkind, Wharton, & Garrison, and was assigned to the corporate law division. It was here that Lewis started acquiring the necessary skills that would become necessary in his future business endeavors. Among other things, Lewis learned how to set up corporations, prepared joint venture agreements, worked on small venture capital deals and set up initial public offerings (IPOs).

It was during his first couple of months at Paul, Weiss that Reginald Lewis met Loida Nicolas, whom he proposed to in May of 1969. She became his wife on August 16, 1969. Nicolas, who after Lewis' death took over leadership of TLC Beatrice, had grown up in a wealthy Phillipino family and had come to the United States as an adult. Their first daughter, Leslie, was born in 1973, and their second daughter, Christina, was born in 1980. Loida Nicolas Lewis was a support for Lewis through all his ventures, trials and tribulations that led to his business success.

In 1970, Lewis' destiny took him away from Paul, Weiss when a fellow Harvard Law School graduate, Fred Wallace, contacted him. Wallace was recruiting lawyers to form a law firm that would deal with issues regarding housing for people of low economic means. Wallace and Lewis met and discussed the firm's goals in servicing the New York Urban Coalition's programs designed to create more and better housing for the city's disadvantaged. Lewis considered the offer to join Wallace, and eventually decided to go for it. The idea of starting his own practice became increasingly appealing and he left the prestigious Paul, Weiss, Rifkind, Wharton, & Garrison after only two years with them.

Lewis joined Wallace and a couple of other lawyers and formed a Black-owned law firm. The new Wallace, Murphy, Thorpe and Lewis was one of the first Black-run law firms on Wall Street. There were many small businesses in the city trying to raise money and there was a rising market in development work in New York's African-American community. The time could not have been more perfect to create a law firm such as Lewis', and as a result, the firm did well. There was, however, some quick turnaround in the partnership of the company. Two of the initial partners, Rita Murphy and Josephine Thorpe, left after only two years with the firm. At this time, Lewis bought Murphy's and Thorpe's partnerships out for about $30,000 and assumed all of the law firm's liabilities, in turn giving him more power in the firm. Lewis hired Charles Clarkson, who remained with him until his death, first with the firm and later as part of TLC Beatrice. In 1978 the firm was eventually renamed Lewis and Clarkson. Some of Lewis' clients from those first couple of years on his own include General Foods, Equitable Life, Norton Simon, and Aetna Life. The firm's expertise grew to include not only housing matters but also small business investment companies. Lewis and Clarkson raised capital and other resources for budding minority-owned businesses with a perceived high amount of potential. They focused progressively more on the emerging market of MESBICs (Minority Enterprise Small Business Investment

Companies), venture capital firms formed by corporations which operate under the supervision of the U.S. Small Business Administration. With time, Lewis became the top MESBIC transaction lawyer in the country.

Aside from a comfortable life style, Lewis' success as a MESBIC lawyer was bringing him something more important: knowledge on how to acquire companies. During his time leading Lewis and Clarkson, Lewis was chosen to be general counsel for the American Association of MESBICs, a position that further allowed him to gain vital information and contacts on corporate acquisitions. As early as 1973, Lewis was dealing with tremendous clients such as his work on the large MESBIC Equitable Capital Corp. Between 1970 and 1984 Lewis and his firm became progressively more well-known and worked on a significant amount of MESBIC deals. The more Lewis became involved in corporate acquisitions, the more he decided it was something he wanted to do himself. As early as the mid 1970's Lewis began looking for possible companies he could acquire.

Lewis' first chance at acquiring a company came in 1975 with the Black-owned Parks Sausage based in his hometown of Baltimore. Lewis traveled to Baltimore to meet with Henry Parks several times and offered around $3 million for the company. He came up with the necessary financing, but much to his chagrin was not able to close the deal. Another buyer, offering roughly the same Lewis was offering, was given the deal. Lewis was immensely disappointed, and for a couple of years thereafter, went back to focusing on his law firm completely. The next acquisition attempt came in 1977 with the company Almet. A meeting was arranged between Lewis and Almet's president, after which Lewis spent one and a half years of his time "courting" Almet's executives. During this time, Lewis created Republic Furniture and Leisure, Inc. (RFL, Inc.) to serve as the company through which he would acquire Almet. He was able to get $5 of the $7 million necessary in financing from Chemical Bank, and got some of his MESBIC clients to put up the rest of the money. Up to this point, everything seemed to be going smoothly. Money was wired to California, where the closing would take place and Clarkson flew to California to deal with the closing legal matters. However, yet again the deal did not go through. On the day of the closing, Almet's president decided not to go through with the closing. Lewis was so angry and disappointed, he sued Almet's president for breach of contract. Lewis was compensated for all of his expenses and was paid a break-up fee as a result of the suit. Only a short time later, Almet was sold to another company for $11 million, $4 million more than Lewis had offered.

With two deals gone awry, Lewis was not about to give up on his desire to buy a company. He continued studying successful takeovers and began to come up with a plan for his next attempt. In 1979, he moved the offices of Lewis and Clarkson from their original 30 Broad Street address to a bigger and better 99 Wall Street location, where he rented the entire 16th floor of the building. The 1980's brought some new faces to Lewis and Clarkson. In 1981, Lewis hired two new associates for his firm: Kevin Wright, a Black Harvard Law School graduate, and Laurie Nelson, a graduate of Brooklyn Law School. Wright stayed with Lewis until his death, becoming his "trusted right-hand man" at TLC Beatrice. Finally, by 1984, the year he would acquire McCall Pattern Company, Lewis' brother Jean Fugett, Jr. was hired as an associate and as a law librarian. Fugett had graduated *cum laude* from Amherst, after which he had played professional football first with the Dallas Cowboys, and then with the Washington Redskins. While with the Redskins, Fugett attended George Washington University where he obtained his law degree.

Lewis' next acquisition attempt came in 1982 with two U.S. Virgin Islands radio stations, WCRN-FM in St. Thomas, and WSTX-AM in St. Croix. Lewis' first step was to try to obtain financing for the deal. He first tried to obtain the necessary capital through a Washington MESBIC, Broadcast Capital, Inc., which specialized in broadcasting loans for minorities. Lewis went to Washington with a business plan and met with the head of Broadcast Capital, Inc. Broadcast Capital was not too thrilled with the prospect of financing Lewis' venture, most of its reservations being due to the fact that Lewis would not be the hands-on operator of the radio stations. Also a concern was the fact that Fugett, who would be in charge of the radio stations, had no background in radio management. Lewis felt these reservations and took it upon himself to personally lobby his case with each of Broadcast Capital's board members. Lewis also made sure he was present at the meeting where Broadcast Capital's president would go before the board. The meeting turned out to be yet another let down for Lewis, with the board rejecting his offer to get the loan necessary for the purchase of the two radio stations. The next company he went to for financing was CVC Capital, another MESBIC that specialized in lending money to minorities buying broadcast properties. This time, at last, the request was successful. CVC made Lewis a loan of $150,000, and Lewis obtained an additional $275,000 from Banco Popular, a Puerto Rican bank. With all the financing taken care of, Lewis was finally able to make his first acquisition. He bought the station in St. Thomas in July of 1982, and passed up on the purchase of the St. Croix AM radio station.

Unfortunately for Lewis, his first acquisition did not turn out to be a profitable one. Business with the radio station never really took off, and the station ended up spending more time off air than it did on air. The disc jockeys that had been hired quickly proved not to be up to the work that had to be done, and before Lewis knew it, his station's revenues never covered expenses and came to represent only financial trouble for Lewis. Finally realizing that his dream for a Caribbean Basin Broadcasting Network would never be successful, Lewis sold the radio station in July 1986.

More important things had been taking place during Lewis' tumultuous years of owning his radio station, however. In August 1983, he was given a tip on a company, which could be a potential acquisition. The company's name was McCall Pattern Company, an old company that specialized in the making of home sewing patterns. Lewis decided to go after McCall right away. The first step toward his plan was the creation of a company with which he would acquire McCall: TLC Pattern, Inc. (TLC being an acronym for The Lewis Company). He also created a holding company, based in Delaware, called TLC Group, Inc. For a couple of weeks, Lewis educated himself to the greatest extent possible on McCall, its financials, its competition, and any other information which was important to determine its worth and how much Lewis would offer. Lewis decided the company was worth at least $18 million, and went forth to write a letter of intent where he outlined his offer to buy McCall. The letter of offering was made in the name of TLC Group, not Lewis individually, and the Group (which, in order to ensure that race would not play a negative role in the acquisition, Lewis claimed was a group of investors, not just himself) offered to pay $22.5 million.

Lewis' meeting with McCall ended with a deadline being set for Lewis to come up with a commitment letter from a financial institution pledging to come up with the offered $22.5 million. Lewis first decided he needed to meet McCall's leadership and get their trust such that they wanted him to be the one to buy the firm. He set up a meeting with McCall's CEO, Earle Angstadt and discussed with him his plans for an acquisition. Lewis had made a good move by trying to woo McCall people and it paid off. Angstadt was impressed by Lewis and decided to lobby in favor of Lewis. He was now free to go and try to find the necessary financing. Lewis was able to secure a $19 million loan from Bankers Trust, but Lewis still had a few things to address. He needed to come up with an additional $1 million in investor equity, and he still needed to negotiate the terms and conditions of the deal. In order to come up with the necessary $1 million, Lewis went to one of his MESBIC contacts, Equico Capital, who gave him a $500,000 loan, and then asked the Morgan Bank, his personal bank, for a personal loan of the other $500,000 needed. Lewis was successful at obtaining loans from both investors and was finally ready for the deal with McCall Pattern. When the final terms of the agreement were finally reached, Lewis was set to pay $20 million in cash, as well as a note worth $2.5 million and a warrant for 7.5 percent of the new company. The closing finally took place on January 29, 1984, almost one year after Lewis had started working on the deal. After many years of trying for such a major acquisition, Lewis had managed to buy a company for $22.5 million without having to risk any of his own capital in the transaction. Lewis took over as chairman of McCall Pattern Company in February 1984.

After the transaction, because of the highly leveraged nature of the deal, Lewis' first priority was to increase the amount of cash being generated by the company. One of the ideas Lewis came up with during this time was to use some presses not being used to make sewing patterns to make greeting cards. This was a smart move by Lewis, greeting cards becoming an important area of profit for the new McCall. Also to increase cash flow, Lewis restructured McCall's pension plan by instituting a 401k program, a move which made an additional $648,000 in cash available to pay off the company's debt.

By the summer of 1986, McCall Pattern was financially strong, and Lewis decided it was time to do something new. Initially, Lewis had hoped that McCall would serve as a venue through which he would acquire other companies. So by 1986 he decided that he was going to try to take McCall public in order to come up with significant amounts of money, which he could in turn use to acquire other companies. He went through Bear, Stearns, & Co. to handle the IPO (initial public offering), which decided to put 2.2 million shares of the firm on the American Stock Exchange. Unfortunately, in part due to a negative article that came out in the *Wall Street Journal* during the time of the IPO, the Lewis' public offering did not go through.

Before finally selling McCall Pattern in 1987, Lewis tried one more plan to create increased capital for the firm and its shareholders, namely a plan where Bankers Trust would put a large sum of money into the company, in turn making the bank a forty percent partner in the firm. This plan did not go as smoothly as he would have wished, and Lewis backed out of the deal before it completely went through. It was becoming clearer and clearer to Lewis that what he really needed to do in order to get a significant return on his investment was to sell McCall Pattern. Since Lewis' acquisition of McCall, the TLC Group had taken steps that had more than doubled the sales of McCall and had given the company two of the most profitable years in its one hundred and fifteen year history. Under Lewis' leadership, McCall's income doubled between 1985 and 1986, and Lewis significantly increased his income during this time as well. Lewis and Clarkson continued practicing law, but as the years passed after the McCall deal, their law practice became less and less of a priority for the partners. By December 1986, the amount of cash on McCall's balance sheet had gone up to $23 million, up $20 million from what it had been when Lewis acquired the firm. In January of 1987, Lewis met with McCall's executives and prepared an offering document that would be presented at the auctioning off of the firm. First Boston was set to handle the auction, and offering documents were sent to about eighty possible buyers. The final closing of the sale took place on June 30, 1987, where Lewis sold McCall to a publicly-held British company by the name of the John Crowther Group for $63 million dollars, an additional $2 million for expenses, and $32 million of buyer-assumed debt.

Two weeks before the McCall deal closed, an associate from Bear, Stearns & Co. contacted Lewis and the two met for lunch. Lewis was told that KKR (Kohlberg, Kravis, and Roberts) was selling a company by the name of Beatrice International through an auction, and was asked if he would have any interest in such a purchase. Lewis was not interested at first for he was still tired from the dealings with the McCall sale, and was still tying up loose ends, but nonetheless he asked for the purchaser's brochure to be sent to him. Lewis got up early the next morning to read the write-up on Beatrice International and within two hours, after weighing out all the pros and cons, Lewis decided that TLC would go for it. He would bid on and win the Beatrice deal.

Lewis was up against other much larger bidders such as Citibank, and it was important for him to decide, first and foremost, what price he was going to offer for Beatrice. Lewis and his right hand man of the time, Cleveland Christophe, studied Beatrice intensely, and came up with a price of $950 million. On June 24, 1987, the vice president of Solomon Brothers, who was in charge of handling the sale for KKR, got in touch with Lewis to discuss his plans. Solomon Bros. wanted to be put up to date about Lewis and his company, which up to this time were still relatively unknown. Lewis was prepared for this meeting and presented Solomon with all the necessary information, making sure that his acquisition and sale of McCall Pattern was stressed. After Lewis talked with Solomon Bros., the time to make his bid was drawing nearer and nearer. He needed to get an investor who would make the $1 billion dollars available to him, and at the same time give him credibility as a relatively unknown player. In the back of his mind, he intended to be able to rely on his acquaintance Michael Milken, but he first went to other sources. He first tried to speak with Bankers Trust Company, but when he found out that they were already working with another bidder, Lewis gave them up. Next, he went to Equitable, but that did not convince him either, so he went to Milken at last. Lewis had already laid the groundwork for a possible deal with Milken by calling him when the sale of McCall Pattern had gone through and Lewis had decided to go for Beatrice International. Milken had been impressed with Lewis' return on his investment in McCall, and expressed to Lewis that he needed to go for something larger the next time. Lewis had remained in contact with various people at Drexel, the investment bank Milken worked with, so when time came to get the financing needed for the deal, Lewis was not only getting the credibility needed through his association with Milken, he was also dealing with investors which already had a history of dealing with him. Drexel pledged $1 billion, and Lewis' official deal was made on July of 1987 for $950 million.

The leveraged buyout of Beatrice International Companies spelled opportunity for businesspersons with a taste for acquisitions. Reginald Lewis and TLC Group happened to be very hungry. Beatrice's International Foods division was a powerhouse with sixty-four food and consumer products companies in thirty-one countries. Its combined sales by 1987 amounted to 2.5 billion dollars. [1] It was a smart buy for a smart person with a lot of capital. Lewis wanted that person to be him. Lewis' plan was to bid on the entire company, but before the closing of the deal, he would already sell of portions of the company, such as to use those profits to reduce some of the debt accrued through the purchase. If his plan worked, it would enable him to reduce the $1 billion deal to one half that size. The portions of Beatrice he was most interested in selling were its Canadian operations for $200 million, Australian operations for $75 million, and Latin American operations for another $100 million.

One thing Lewis needed to take care of in order to be able to buy Beatrice and put all these plans into action, however, was to build a tax structure that would fit the kind of acquisition that was taking place. Because a majority of Beatrice's earnings came from overseas, a total of sixty-four companies located in thirty-one foreign countries, those earnings were being earned in foreign currencies. Lewis' major challenge would be to devise a way through which to get that income into the United States, have it converted into U.S. Dollars, while still keeping the cost of these transactions at a manageable level. Furthermore, these expenses needed to be made tax-deductible in some way such that the financial strain of bringing in money from overseas did not become a financial burden for the new company in paying off its debt. Lewis had to devise this tax structure all on his own for he had no precedents to study, no one had ever pulled off such a large off-shore leveraged buyout (LBO) in the history of business. Lewis and Christophe worked on the tax structure and created a financial model, all in preparation of their meeting with Drexel.

Christophe arranged for Lewis and himself to fly to Los Angeles to meet with the Drexel people on July 30, 1987. Drexel was not as enthusiastic as it had been initially, but Lewis was prepared to convince them that it was worth for them to invest in this deal. By the end of the meeting, Lewis had succeeded at restoring Drexel's confidence in him and the viability of the acquisition of Beatrice. After some tough bargaining, Lewis agreed to sell twenty-six percent of what would be TLC Beatrice International to Drexel for a token amount of money. This was a move that Lewis ended up very much regretting, and spent much of the last days before the deal trying to take Drexel and others out of the deal completely. Throughout all this courting of Drexel, Michael Milken remained firmly in support of Lewis, which eventually convinced Lewis that it was best to leave Drexel in the deal. Initially, Lewis bid $950 million, with the plan in mind to sell off some of Beatrice's businesses for a total price of $400 million, and keep a "core group" of businesses that could bring in significant income.

Only two days before the deal was going to be finalized, Lewis got word that there was another major bidder taking action. Not to take any risks of losing Beatrice, Lewis decided to top his bid to $985 million. This bid was soon accepted and the deal was closed on August 6, 1987. Lewis always believed that KKR was going to give him the deal all along, but had just created the idea in his mind that there was a strong competitor in the works so that Lewis would increase the bid amount. This acquisition turned TLC into TLC Beatrice International Holdings, turned Lewis into chairman, principal stockholder, and chief executive officer, and turned the company's sales from $63 million to $1.5 billion in one year. Lewis then went forth with his plan to further sell off numerous holdings to reduce the company's acquisition debt and streamlined TLC Beatrice International into a primarily European food firm. As planned, he sold off operations in Australia and Latin America and most of its Canadian interests to Toronto-based Onex Corporation. He sold the company's stake in Winner Food Products, Ltd. to a Japanese group including Nissin Food and C. Itoh & Co. "In 1990 he sold Boizet, a specialty meats holding in France, and its French hypermarkets. The next year the company sold its holdings in Beatrice Canada and in French Tropicana orange juice distributor Maxime Delrue." [2]

A dairy company for half a century, Beatrice had begun to expand into other food areas after World War II. Decades of dizzying acquisitions finally came to an end when the company was taken public through Lewis' leveraged buyout in August of 1987. Under new leadership, Lewis trimmed the company radically, selling $7.3 billion worth of assets in two years. Beatrice today consists primarily of Beatrice/Hunt-Wesson, a packaged foods producer; Swift-Eckrich, a producer of prepared meats; and Beatrice Cheese. [3]

A 1993 company overview published in Hoover's Handbook of American Business read as follows:

TLC Beatrice International Holdings is a privately owned food company created by the 1987 spin-off of Beatrice's foreign operations. The company is engaged in 2 primary business segments: wholesale and retail food distribution, and the manufacturing and marketing of grocery products. Although the company is based in New York and is the nation's largest Black-owned enterprise, it is focused on Western Europe. Food distribution includes Baud, distributor of products to nearly 500 independent grocers operating in the Paris area under the name Franprix. In addition, TLC Beatrice owns and operates 38 Franprix and 16 Leader Price stores (featuring limited selection, lower prices, and private label goods) in France through the majority-owned Minimarche Group. The grocery products segment makes ice cream, dairy, and dessert products under names including La Menorquina (Spain), Interglas (Canary Islands), Sanson (Italy), Artic (Belgium and France), and Premier Is (Denmark). The Tayto subsidiary is the leader in the Irish potato chip market, and TLC Beatrice bottles soft drinks under several names. The grocery products division is expanding geographically and is the company's growth segment. [4]

Through TLC Beatrice, Lewis reportedly amassed a $400 million fortune, becoming the richest African-American man in the country. He donated $1 million to Howard University, a historically Black university in Washington, D.C. He also donated $3 million to his alma mater, Harvard Law School, to build the first building at that university named after an African-American. Even before TLC Beatrice, Lewis used his power and money to help those he felt were worthy of it. In 1984, when Jesse Jackson made his first attempt at the presidency, Lewis held a fund-raising dinner for him in New York City. Lewis also supported other African-American politicians during his life time by holding fundraisers for people such as former New York City Mayor David N. Dinkins, Virginia Governor Douglas Wilder, Los Angeles Mayor Tom Bradley, former Manhattan Borough President Percy Sutton, and Jackson's 1988 presidential campaign.

At the height of TLC Beatrice's success and at age fifty, Reginald F. Lewis died of brain cancer. His sudden and tragic 1993 death left his company scrambling for leadership. Without Lewis having thought much about his succession, Beatrice director and Reginald's half brother Jean S. Fugett, Jr. took over as Chairman and CEO, while roughly fifty-five percent of the company's stock remained in the control of Loida Lewis and their two daughters. Loida Lewis took that year off to mourn her loss, deal with the estate that had been left to her, and finish work on Lewis' autobiography. Fugett spent 1993 leading TLC Beatrice through a European recession and currency fluctuations which pulled down the revenues of the food processing and distribution company by nearly one-and-a-half percent, to $1.2 billion. [5] He also led the company through restructuring and cost-cutting, and made talk about Beatrice buying the Baltimore Orioles, all of which made him quite unpopular with analysts and shareholders. Realizing Fugett was not the man cut out for the job, in January 1994, Loida replaced Fugett as Chairperson and Fugett agreed to relinquish the position of CEO to a more qualified candidate. By July of that same year Loida Nicolas Lewis herself took on the position of CEO.

Despite the fact that Loida, an immigration lawyer, had little experience in business management, she took on the challenge of leading her late-husband's company successfully. She was able to get Beatrice out of the slump it had been in since the year prior to Lewis' death, when operating profits had decreased fifty-two percent to $47 million and the company had reported a loss of $17 million. Loida managed to restore TLC Beatrice's credibility and turned the company around and out of the red. The same year that Loida took over, the company reported its first profit since 1991. By 1995, sales for Beatrice were up by 17% from $1.8 billion to $2.1 billion. Some of her strategies involved that of consolidating power and downsizing her late-husband's company. After her takeover, she sold off the corporate jets and limousines, as well as other luxuries and moved the company's offices into a less lavish location. Also as part of her strategy, Loida sold various Beatrice businesses including ice cream companies in Denmark, Germany, Belgium, and Italy, and a beverage company in France, and cut about 500 jobs from the TLC Beatrice payroll. Finally, she shutdown TLC Capital, a division whose purpose had been to pursue possible takeover targets.

Beatrice continues to be America's largest minority-owned business, and holds sales of $2.1 billion from twelve companies in twenty different countries. TLC Beatrice is not very well-known in the United States, but Loida hopes to change this through some future domestic ventures. Beatrice is currently the leading seller of potato chips in Ireland, is the leading seller of ice cream in Spain, and until very recently held the largest supermarket chains in France, Franprix and Leader Price.

In September 1997, Groupe Casino, a French food retailer, agreed to acquire the French food distribution businesses of TLC Beatrice International Holdings Inc. The deal was made for 2.8 billion French Francs ($459 million), plus the assumption of debt, which adds up to a deal worth some $573 million. This will allow Groupe Casino to take control of the 250-store Leader Price discount supermarket chain and Franprix, a Paris-area operator of about 400 stores. Casino paid $459 million in cash and reimbursed TLC for an intercompany loan of an additional $115 million. [6] The sale came a month after TLC announced a 33% increase in net earnings, from $41 million for the first half of 1996 to $55 million for the same period in 1997. [7] Beatrice has said that it will use proceeds from the deal to repay debt and for general corporate purposes. The deal left TLC Beatrice with core food-manufacturing operations producing 1996 sales of $358 million and an operating income of $30 million.

The only negative factor hanging over Loida and her leadership of TLC Beatrice until very recently was a lawsuit by the very investors who made the LBO of Beatrice possible in 1987. Investors linked to Drexel and Michael Milken, who with the deal had acquired some twenty-six percent of the company's stock, sued TLC in 1994, claiming that Lewis took undeserved money from Beatrice to cover his personal expenses. TLC's lawyers, as well as Loida Lewis, saw this suit as merely a desperate action taken on by a group of investors who no longer wished to have their money tied up in the company. The company always held faith that the suit would be able to be resolved favorably for the company, and in 1997 it was. On May 30 Chancellor Allen of the Delaware Court of Chancery approved a $14.9 million settlement negotiated by the Special Litigation Committee of TLC Beatrice Holdings International, Inc. On July 24 of that same year, Carlton Investments, a partnership composed of former Drexel Burnham Lambert, Inc. executives, finally agreed as part of the overall settlement, to withdraw their lawsuit. Although it had initially appealed the May settlement, Carlton withdrew its appeal at this time and agreed to end all pending litigation against the company.

Despite these distractions and new developments, Loida always continues with business as usual. With a growth in the company, and another year "in the black", Loida hopes to continually unlock greater value for Beatrice. The initial steps in that direction have already been taken with the sale of its food division for $576 million and its European beverage group for $44 million. As chairperson, owner of fifty-one percent of Beatrice with her two daughters (Leslie and Christine), Loida expects the future of TLC to be a bright one.

CHAPTER SEVEN: JOHNSON PRODUCTS

Profile

- Leading developer/manufacturer of personal grooming products for African-Americans (Ultra-Sheen, Afro-Sheen). 1992 sales grew to $42M.
- Owned by the Joan B. Johnson family since its 1954 founding, it is one of the largest African-American controlled corporations in the U.S. Sold in September 1993 for $70M to majority-owned IVAX Corp.
- Manufacturing facility and product development center located in South Side Chicago. European distribution facility located in the United Kingdom.
- Its seven thousand square foot development center is the largest of its kind devoted to African-American consumers.
- Targets urban areas with substantial African-American populations with branded African-American products for large national chains.
- Distributes through large retail chains as well as small salons and barbershops.

Summary

George Johnson was born in Richton, Mississippi but was raised in Chicago from an early age. His career in cosmetic products began at age sixteen, when he quit high school to become a door-to-door salesman for African-American-owned Fullerton Products. During his time at Fullerton, Johnson also worked as a laboratory assistant and later as head production chemist. It was during this time that Johnson and Orville Nelson, a Black barber, developed a hair-straightening product. They soon formed a partnership and in 1954 leased out a space on the South Side of Chicago to do their work. Johnson began selling their product at Nelson's barbershop for about four months, after which the two parted and began marketing separate formulas. Johnson named his product 'Ultra Wave Hair Culture' and with a $250 loan began what is now Johnson Products. In a short period of time Ultra Wave became a household name all over the country. By the end of the 1960's Johnson Products had surpassed the one million-dollar revenue mark, occupied a three-story building, and had added additional products to its hair care line. During the 1970's, Johnson Products faced increased competition from both new Black-owned firms as well as majority-owned companies trying to get a share of the Black consumer base. Johnson continued running Johnson Products until 1989, when, as part of his divorce settlement from his wife Joan, he was forced to resign as Chairman and CEO. One of his sons, Eric, was promoted from COO to CEO and Joan took over as Chairperson. Under the leadership of Eric Johnson, Johnson Products' sales rose significantly, marking a much more prosperous period for the company than the 1980's. After an unsuccessful attempt to take the company public, Eric stepped down and Joan was left with complete power as majority stockholder, CEO and Chairperson. Sales continued a slow and steady rise until 1993, when the company was sold to majority-owned IVAX Corporation for $70 million.

History

In 1954, George Johnson, equipped only with an innovation and determination, founded a company that was to become a pioneer in the field of Black hair care. Born in Richton, Mississippi and raised in Chicago from the age of two, Johnson was no stranger to work. At kindergarten age he collected milk bottles for money; as he grew older he worked as a shoeshine boy, paperboy, sweeper, and waiter. After quitting high school in his junior year, he joined his brother as a door-to-door salesman for Fuller Products, a African-American-owned cosmetics company. After one year as a salesman, Johnson became a laboratory assistant and soon afterwards, the head production chemist. In 1953, George Johnson met Orville Nelson on an elevator at Fuller Products: Nelson was a well-known African-American barber of the day that was trying to develop a new and better hair-straightening product for his customers. The two men developed a relationship and Johnson went to his drawing board in order to come up with a new product. They formed a partnership in 1954 and leased out a space on the South Side of Chicago where they could do their work.

Along with a friend and colleague, Herbert Martini, Johnson created a lye and petroleum hair-straightener that he allowed Nelson to try on his customers. Realizing that the finished product was effective, Johnson and Nelson began selling it at Nelson's barber shop; but only after four months the two parted and began marketing separate straightening formulas. Johnson was able to market his product, which he named Ultra Wave Hair Culture, with a two hundred-and-fifty dollar loan. Before long, Ultra Wave was a household name in Black homes all over the country. The nation was impressed by a product made and marketed by a Black man, for the Black man. Johnson, it seemed, had the right idea, in the right place, at the right time. [1]

Things moved quickly: in 1958, Johnson Products occupied the second floor of a Windy City warehouse; in 1960, it occupied an entire three-story building. By the end of the decade, Johnson Products had reached and surpassed the one million dollar revenue mark, added its popular Afro Sheen hair care line and a no-base creme relaxer, and survived an electrical fire which burned down the company plant and most of its inventory. [2]

With the seventies came the good, the bad, and the ugly. "In 1970, sales were at $12 million. In 1971, the company became the first Black-owned company to trade on the American Stock Exchange." [3] Thirty percent of its stock was held by the public, two percent by Johnson Products employees and the remaining sixty-eight percent was owned by Johnson. But with this good fortune came some bad. National, majority-owned companies had finally caught on to the Black consumer base (and all the money to be made there) and began to rear their well-known heads in what was formerly Johnson territory. Even worse for Johnson Products, another Black-owned hair care company came into being (Soft Sheen) and offered some stiff competition. Also, the Federal Trade Commission's 1975 order to place explicit warnings of lye content on hair relaxers caused a major setback in sales. "George Johnson said the incident almost killed the hair relaxer end of his business, which then accounted for more than fifty percent of sales. "It was an absolute assassination of the brand name Ultra Sheen.'"[4] These factors, along with a failed effort to manufacture in Nigeria and a negative tendency to lag behind market trends, including the development of a no-lye relaxer, contributed to a dip in sales that sent Johnson Products into a tail-spin.

The late 1970's and 1980's were an unstable period for the company, its sales going back and forth between lows of $29 million and highs of $45 million during this time. [5] Additionally, the Johnson family began experiencing internal conflicts that had significant impacts on the company. One Johnson son, John Johnson, was dismissed from his position within the firm by his father, and another, George Johnson, Jr. left to pursue musical interests. In 1989, George Sr. was forced to resign as Chairman and Chief Executive Officer and to give up control of Johnson Products as part of a divorce settlement with his wife, Joan B. Johnson. At this juncture, Joan Johnson, who had filled the office of the treasurer under her then-husband's guidance, gained the majority of the voting stock and was elected Chairperson. The only remaining Johnson son, Eric, was promoted from Chief Operating Officer to Chief Executive Officer (CEO).

As President and CEO, Eric Johnson showed the world the resiliency and tenacity of Johnson Products Company. He is largely credited with bringing the proverbial head of a company in danger of floundering well above water. He took a number of proactive steps in order to accomplish this task, including the development of a new marketing strategy, expense controls, a stronger focus on research and development, and the addition of Johnson's first new products in three years. In 1990, "he paid M&M Products $2.5 million for two of its hair care product lines. These actions produced fast results. Sales, which had dipped from $46 million in 1983 to $29 million in 1989, grew to $34 million in 1990 and $44 million by the end of 1991. Net income, which was negative for most of the 1980's, blossomed to $3.2 million ($1.3 million due to tax loss carry-forward credit) in fiscal year 1991. And [the company's] share price, which had been as low as $1.63 at the end of 1989, ran up to $23.75." [6]

However, JPC's internal problems returned in 1991 when Eric made a move to take the company public in a $20.6 million leveraged buyout attempt. This plan, which would have gradually reduced the power and influence of Joan Johnson, placing it in Eric's willing hands, folded with stern opposition from some of the shareholders, including, not surprisingly, Joan. [7] This caused a great deal of tension within the upper echelons of the company, tension which was reportedly exacerbated by still more family squabbling. There is much speculation that Joanie, the only Johnson daughter, felt slighted by her older brother as a result of his positioning of her as the director of market research, a position that she felt well beneath her abilities. Her mother apparently sided with her in the latest family feud and ousted her son after he refused to share power with his sister. [8] An official press release stated that "Eric Johnson had left to 'pursue personal business interests'" and quoted Chairwoman Joan B. Johnson as rather stoically saying, "Eric Johnson has made a significant contribution at Johnson Products...I understand his decision and wish him well in his future endeavors...Internally, it's back to business as usual at the company." [9 & 10]

Eric Johnson's departure left Joan B. Johnson majority stockholder, Chairperson, and Chief Executive Officer. It also caused a relative panic. The company's shares took a nose dive, but eventually rebounded. Once again, Johnson Products came out of potential disaster a little wounded, but not a casualty. A four-person office of the president, which included Joanie Johnson, was formed to compensate the loss of the last Johnson son. Johnson Products experienced a slow, but steady increase in sales and production. According to Thomas Polke, Vice President and Chief Financial Officer, Johnson Products accounted for about ten percent of the Black hair-care market and was approximately half the size of its main competitor, Soft Sheen Products, Incorporated. [11] One analyst said, "It's remarkable how well they've done in a tough economic environment", and the Turnaround Management Association listed the company as one of ten "Turnaround of the Year" companies for 1992. [12]

One year after Eric's buyout attempt, Joan Johnson announced her decision to merge Johnson Products into a wholly owned subsidiary of Ivax Corporation, a White-owned, Florida-based producer of specialty chemicals, pharmaceuticals, and medical diagnostics. Under the agreement, Johnson stockholders received one IVAX common share for each share of Johnson stock. The sixty-seven-million-dollar sale removed Johnson Products from thirty-nine years of Black family ownership. Opponents of the acquisition saw it as a major loss for Black and minority communities alike; Johnson Products was "selling out." John Johnson was quoted in the Chicago Tribune as saying,

"It's like the worst nightmare I could have ever had. Never in my wildest dreams when I was building this company did I believe it would wind up out of the Black community." [13]

Some had mixed reactions. William Cunningham, president of Creative Investment Research, said, "On one hand, it's a sign of progress because it shows that a non-minority firm recognizes the value of a Black company. On the other hand, I don't see any remaining Black manufacturers with the historical prominence of Johnson Products." [14]

Proponents of the merger felt it was a pragmatic move and a great opportunity for the company. The merger would potentially expand distribution and create jobs. Joan Johnson, reportedly stood to gain over thirty-seven million dollars in IVAX stock as well as the retention of the title of President for at least one year with a minimum salary of three hundred thousand dollars, plus stock options. To this Joan said, "I believe that this transaction will benefit our stockholders, employees and community. Strategically, this transaction has the potential to expand Johnson Products' current distribution and increase the utilization of our Chicago facility. All of us in Johnson Products' management look forward to working with IVAX." [15]   IVAX executives saw Johnson Products as a compatible match for IVAX units Flori Roberts (acquired by IVAX in 1992 for twenty million dollars) and Baker Cummins Dermatologicals.

Divorced in 1989, George and Joan Johnson came together in 1995 at the Ritz Carlton in Chicago. By then, Joan had gotten more than $33 million from the sale of Johnson Products to IVAX and had retired. George was, and still is, the Chairman of Indecorp, the largest U.S. Black-owned bank [16]. He remains heavily involved in supporting various organizations such as Rev. Jesse Jackson's Operation PUSH, the Chicago Urban League, the Boy Scouts of America, Junior Achievement, the YMCA, Chicago Youth Centers, and Provident Hospitals, and it has recently been reported that he and Joan have reconciled.

CHAPTER EIGHT: BLACK ENTERTAINMENT TELEVISION (BET) HOLDINGS, INC.

Profile

* Incorporated in 1991, BET Holdings, Inc. is a Washington, D.C.-based entertainment media holding company with cable, publishing, and production operations.
* Its original company, Black Entertainment Television Network (BET Network), was founded in 1979 by Robert L. Johnson.
* Its subsidiaries are in television entertainment (**BET Network, BET Action Pay-per-View, BET International and BET Jazz**), publications (**Paige Publications, Inc.** and 70% of **Emerge Communications, Inc.**) radio (**BET Radio**), and marketing of specialty merchandise (**BET Direct**).
* In 1996 was listed as # 10 on **BLACK ENTERPRISE**'s Top 100 list of Service Companies, with total sales of $115 million for the 1995-1996 fiscal year.
* Produced two movies: "Once Upon A Time...When We Were Colored" and "Out of Sync".
* Publishes *Emerge* magazine and until late 1996 published *YSB* (Young Sisters and Brothers).
* Its first public offering made in 1991, BET became the first Black company to be listed on the New York Stock Exchange.
* BET offices and other facilities can be found in Washington D.C., Burbank, New York City, Chicago, Rosslyn, VA, San Francisco, and Detroit.

Summary

A holding company for firms created since 1979 by Robert L. Johnson, BET Holdings, Inc. is a Washington, D.C.-based entertainment media holding company with cable, publishing, and production operations. BET Holdings, Inc. was incorporated in Delaware in July 1991. As a result of a series of related transactions completed in September 1991, Black Entertainment Television, Inc. (BET), a District of Columbia corporation formed in 1979, became the wholly-owned subsidiary of BET Holdings. Black Entertainment Television Network currently cablecasts 24 hours a day to over 32 million subscribers. BET was the first advertiser-supported basic cable network to target the viewing interests of African-Americans and the first Black company to be listed on the New York Stock Exchange (NYSE).

BET, a company of approximately 350 employees, transmits via satellite from its $15 million headquarters in the industrial corridor of Washington, D.C.   BET Holdings is a diversified media holding company with two primary operating groups that conduct operations through a variety of subsidiaries. The Entertainment Group includes the BET Network and BET Action-Pay-Per-View, and since the beginning of fiscal 1994, BET International, BET on Jazz and BET Radio (the only non-television unit of this group).   The Publishing Group reaches Black Americans through its publications *Emerge* and, until 1996, *YSB* (Young Sisters & Brothers), published by Emerge Communications, Inc. (of which BET holds seventy percent control) and BET's own Paige Publications, Inc. respectively. Ninety-four percent of BET Holding's consolidated revenues come from its Entertainment Group (including all revenues obtained through television advertising).

The BET Cable Network provides a broad mix of Black-oriented programming. Programs are produced in-house or are acquired from a variety of sources. The BET Cable Network's in-house productions (BET has production facilities in Washington, D.C. and Burbank, California), most of which are live, include hosted music video programs, talk shows, sports, news and public affairs, game shows, children's programs and variety shows. Acquired programs include situation comedies, gospel music programs and sports and entertainment specials. Through a series of partnerships with respected names, such as actor/producer Tim Reid, and gold-star companies such as Blockbuster Entertainment Corporation, BET finances, produces, and distributes new film and video products and recycles classics. A joint venture with Baruch Entertainment has produced three hour-long specials: " A Tribute to Black Music Legends", "YSB Bookin' it Back to School", and " BET Yearbook 1994".

Eighty-seven percent of BET's $100 million in revenues is generated by the BET Cable Network through the sale of advertising time and the collection of subscriber fees from cable system affiliates. The BET Cable Network currently generates approximately forty-five percent of its revenues from subscriber fees paid by cable system affiliates. Under affiliation agreements, BET contracts to receive a monthly fee per subscriber from each affiliated cable system operator that carries the BET Cable Network.

History

Robert L. Johnson, founder of Black Entertainment Television (BET), was born in Hickory, Mississippi on April 8, 1946 and was the ninth of the family's ten children. When he was a young boy his family moved North to Freeport, Illinois, an industrial farming town of about 30,000 people, where both his parents worked in a factory to be able to make ends meet. Johnson attended a predominantly White high school, and was not particularly interested in going to college until a teacher encouraged him to go speak with his guidance counselor. During that visit, Johnson found out that the University of Illinois offered a good teaching program, with low-percentage tuition loans and decided to enroll. He graduated from high school with honors in history and was able to secure himself an academic scholarship to attend the University of Illinois. He graduated from that university in 1968 with a teaching baccalaureate in history degree. Only a year later, in 1969, Johnson was accepted to Princeton University's Woodrow Wilson School of Public and International Affairs, where he went on the pursue a Master's degree in public administration. He graduated from Princeton sixth in his class in 1972.

With a Master's degree in Public Affairs from Princeton University, Robert L. Johnson was able to get himself a job at the Corporation for Public Broadcasting as a press secretary, which was then followed by a job at the Washington Urban League. Following the Washington Urban League, Johnson continued his public servant career as a press secretary for D.C. city councilman Sterling Tucker, and Walter Fauntroy, a non-voting member of Congress from Washington, D.C. Finally, from 1976 to 1979, Johnson worked as Vice President of government relations for the National Cable Television Association. It was during his last year at this job that thirty-two year-old Johnson began his effort to start a cable channel aimed at Black viewers. With only $15,000 to invest himself, the first step was finding other investors with more significant funds. Getting investors for his project, however, proved difficult at first, for most potential investors did not believe he had enough experience to be able to make the project work. One person, however, did see a future in Johnson's idea: John C. Malone, the head of the Denver-based Telecommunications, Inc. (TCI), the nation's largest cable operator. Malone was so intrigued by Johnson's idea that TCI (who currently owns seventeen percent of BET) backed Johnson and provided him with $500,000 to help him launch Black Entertainment Television Network. BET Network was formed in 1979 and began operations in 1980, with Johnson serving as President, Chief Executive Officer, and director since its creation. Between 1982 and 1984, one of the companies that joined the list of BET investors was American Broadcasting and Home Box Office (HBO). Since 1991 Johnson has also held the position of Chairman of the Board of Directors. He currently holds all these positions as well as the positions of Chairman of the Board of District Cablevision, Inc., a Washington, D.C. cable system operating company which he founded in 1980, and the position of director of Liberty Media Corporation.

Headquartered in the Georgetown section of Washington, D.C., and cablecasting a variety of programs including music videos, news, and infomercials to Black audiences, BET quickly took off and became successful, surviving recessions that devastated other media companies. The BET Cable Network began operations in 1980 by providing two hours of programming per week to approximately 3.8 million cable subscribers. Within four years, by 1984, it had jumped from two hours to twenty-four. Media Research estimated that, as of September 30, 1993, the BET Cable Network reached approximately 37.3 million subscribers, representing approximately sixty percent of all cable households in the United States. By 1995, BET reached 41.3 million cable households.

On April 11, 1989, BET acquired a forty-nine percent equity interest in Haricom Advertising, Inc., an advertising agency that attracts advertisers seeking to place a portion of their advertising dollar with minority companies. In 1990, United Image Entertainment (UIE), a joint venture with actor and producer Tim Reid and his production company, was formed to facilitate the production of "Black-oriented" films, mini-series, and situation comedies for cable television, pay television and the broadcast networks. In December of 1990, as part of the joint venture terms, BET committed to invest up to $1 million over a two-year period in UIE. By 1990, advertising revenues had multiplied four times to $29.9 million. The joint venture agreement was amended in February 1993 to add Butch Lewis Productions, Inc. as a joint venture partner.

1991 brought many new developments to BET. BET ventured into previously unchartered territory: publishing. In August 1991, Johnson launched *YSB* (Young Sisters and Brothers), the only national lifestyle magazine targeted at Black American teenagers and young adults, through its wholly-owned subsidiary Paige Publications, Inc. By 1993, its circulation had already reached 80,000 and it was a finalist in two categories of that year's National Magazine Awards. The magazine was published until late 1996. Four months after the launching of *YSB*, in December, BET acquired a seventy percent controlling interest in Emerge Communications, Inc., the publisher of *Emerge* magazine, an issue-oriented publication primarily targeted toward an upscale Black audience, providing news, commentary and analysis from the Black American perspective. BET's Publishing Group represents only a modest portion of its revenues, only six percent of BET's total operating revenues came from their magazines in 1993, which is not to say, however, that it is not a successful venture.

The event that most marked 1991 for BET, however, came in October, when BET successfully completed an initial public offering, breaking new ground for Blacks in the capital market. Twenty-one percent (or $4.2 million in shares) of the eleven year-old firm was sold on October 30, netting $72.3 million for Johnson and his investors. BET itself sold 1.5 million shares, raising $25 million before expenses, approximately half of which was used to reduce debt, and the rest was used to improve operations. Finally, Cincinnati-based Great American Broadcasting Co. sold its entire stake in the company for $40.9 million and Johnson sold 375,000 of his own shares for $6.4 million. In November 1991, the company completed the stock offering and became the first Black majority-controlled company listed (under the symbol BTV) on the New York Stock Exchange. Parts of the company stock that were not sold were the 18.1 percent owned by New York-based Tele-Communications Inc. and the fifteen percent owned by Time Warner Inc. Johnson owns an additional 4.5 million publicly traded shares worth an estimated $104.5 million, as well as 4.8 million shares that he does not trade but allow him 56 percent of the voting control of his firm. Johnson currently owns well over $200 million worth in BET stock.

1993 proved to be a monumentous year for BET. By that year, the BET Cable Network transmitted programming to approximately 2,422 local affiliate systems in forty-six states, the District of Columbia, certain United States territories and possessions, and portions of the Caribbean. BET has also been granted the right to distribute its programming in Canada, to Canadian operators who are currently permitted to distribute the programming when packaged with a Canadian pay service. Currently, BET holds cable affiliation agreements with two Canadian operators. During 1993, BET expanded into several related media and other business ventures. In June 1993, BET launched BET Direct, a subsidiary that distributes merchandise to BET viewers. BET Direct's first two products were 'BET on Music' and the 'Color Code Skin Care' line. In July, it acquired eighty-one percent of the common stock of Avalon Pictures, Inc., owner of a Santa Monica, California based pay-per-view service, Action Pay-Per-View. [1] Since the acquisition, BET has operated the service as BET Action-Pay-Per-View, and has approximately six million subscribers. In August 1993, the company entered into a joint venture with Straford Research Partners to establish the BET Radio Network. Also, BET International was formed, a distributor of programming initially to the United Kingdom through a joint venture with Identity Cable, England's first television service to target some 500,000 Afro-Caribbean viewers who live within London's franchise area. BET International eventually expanded to Africa and other foreign markets. Finally, in December, BET formed two joined ventures. One venture involved the joining of Liberty Media Corp's Encore movie channel division and LIVE Entertainment Inc. with BET Film Productions. The second was a joint venture between Blockbuster Entertainment Corporation and BET Pictures. Both ventures were geared toward Black-oriented projects. BET reported a net profit of $3.3 million for the second quarter of 1993, increasing 14.2% from 1992's figure mostly due to significant gains in advertising and subscriber revenues. By the end of

1993, BET reached a record thirty-five million subscribers. [2]

In April of 1995, Johnson opened a 50,000-square-foot film and video production facility, one of the largest on the East Coast, which allowed BET to produce large-scale events, concerts and music videos. BET's market value in 1995 was estimated to be one of $500 million. Current projects include the building of the first Black-controlled studio, a project meant to "break the color barrier" in Hollywood. Johnson believes that in order for African-Americans to gain some control in Hollywood, the key is having ownership of copyrights of film and television show libraries, music, and images. Johnson is currently trying to enlist support from top Black stars, an effort that has yet to come to full fruition. The idea is for talent to appear in two to three low-budget movies for which they would get cut-rate pay as well as a piece of ownership of the movie's rights. The biggest stars would have bigger budget movies, the money to make the movies coming not only from BET's profits but also from other Black and White investors. So far, two low-budget movies have been put on a limited amount of screens: "Once Upon a Time...When We Were Colored" and "Out of Sync".

In October 1995, BET finalized arrangements for the January 1996 launching of its new 24-hour cable channel, BET on Jazz, a cable television jazz network featuring jazz concerts and interviews with jazz artists. Its sister channel, Jazz Central, will become the flagship program and will feature various jazz music shows. [3] Less than a year later, In September 1996, Encore Media Corp and BET formed a joint venture to create a Black-film pay cable channel, BET Movies/Starz!3. The new channel debuted in February 1997, and targets the minority and urban market, offering movies from Encore's film library in addition to original entertainment and movies. [4] With all these new projects and ventures, the company has continued its steady growth, listed as number 10 on **BLACK ENTERPRISE**'s 1996 list of Top 100 service companies, and showing an increase in revenues of $41 million between 1992 and 1996. In 1996, BET Holdings posted profits of $22 million on revenues of $133 million, and since its 1991 IPO, its stock has more than doubled.

Sales Revenues from 1992-1997:

1992	$61.6 million
1993	$74.2 million
1994	$97.5 million
1995	$115.2 million
1996	$133.3 million
1997	$154.2 million

Other current projects include a joint venture with Microsoft to produce interactive programming on the Internet. [5] The new site, MSBET, will replace BET's current website, BET Networks, and will target primarily African-Americans on the World Wide Web. Also in early 1997, BET opened a posh theme restaurant in the greater Washington, D.C. area. The $65 million, 12,000 square foot, 365-seat restaurant, BET SoundStage, was inaugurated on January 17, 1997, with others planned to be opened in cities like Charlotte, Atlanta, Dallas, Denver, and Indianapolis, and one opening as a joint venture with Disney Co. at Pleasure Island in Orlando, Florida. [6]   Also, in early 1997, BET and Hilton, Corp. announced a possible partnership in developing a Las Vegas hotel and casino. [7] The partners are in the initial stages of the development of their deal, a Hotel-Casino that would be called BET SoundStage Casino. The venture would target the more than two million African-Americans that visit Las Vegas every year. Hilton Corp. will bring with it to the partnership its management of gaming activities and general hotel and recreational facilities management expertise (they own two hotel-casinos in Las Vegas), while BET will provide the entertainment and bring with it its marketing expertise. Undoubtedly, Robert Johnson and his multi-million dollar company are on the right track into the next century of business. Finally, on March 31, 1997, BET announced that it was teaming up with Chevy Chase Bank to sell financial services nationwide to African-Americans. [8] The venture, to be called BET Financial Services, plans to offer Visa credit cards to African-American consumers and hopes to "offer a range of financial products, which could include mortgage and brokerage services, mutual funds and home equity loans". [9] BET and Chevy Chase will share in the profits. BET, what started as just a modest cable television venture, has now become a diverse, multi-faceted enterprise.

CHAPTER NINE: HARPO, INC.

Profile

- Produces "The Oprah Winfrey Show" as well as a variety of television After School Specials.
- Owned and run by Oprah Winfrey; started in 1986.
- Made up of Harpo Studios and Harpo Productions. Harpo Studios is the best television production facility in the Midwest.
- Winfrey is the first African-American to own a major studio facility.
- Grossed $130 million in sales in 1995.
- Produced films such as *The Women of Brewster Place*, and *Aint no Children Here*, and recently completed shooting Toni Morrison's *Beloved*.

Summary

Oprah Winfrey was born in Mississippi in 1954, and until she was six was raiscd by her grandmother. Later, she moved to Milwaukee, Wisconsin, to live with her mother. When Winfrey's mother found it difficult to give Winfrey the attention she needed, she was sent to live with her father in Nashville. It was in Nashville that, as a 17-year old high school senior, Winfrey started her broadcasting career. [1] Winfrey started out as a news broadcaster at a local radio station, a job which lasted until the end of her freshman year at Tennessee State University (TSU). In 1973, Winfrey had her first job offer for television as a news anchor. Winfrey quit college, and took on the $15,000 per year job, and stayed with WTVF-TV of Nashville for three years. [2] Winfrey's next big move came in 1976, when ABC-affiliate WJZ-TV of Baltimore offered her a news anchor position. [3] Winfrey worked in Baltimore from 1976 to 1983. She started as anchor but her style did not go over well with the station nor with her co-anchor, so she was fired from the anchor position. Upon her losing the anchor position she was asked to co-host a morning talk show called "People Are Talking". In 1984, Winfrey moved from Baltimore to Chicago, where she had received an offer to host another talk show: "A.M. Chicago". Winfrey's popularity rose quickly, as it had in Nashville, beating the very popular Phil Donahue in ratings, as she had in Nashville. In order to be able to combine work on her talkshow with work in the movies, Winfrey decided to gain better control of her show by forming her own studios and production company: Harpo, Inc. Only one year after having started to air on "A.M. Chicago", the show had become nationally syndicated, had been renamed "The Oprah Winfrey Show", and Winfrey had taken over complete production of her show.

History

Oprah Gail Winfrey was born January 29, 1954 in Kosciusko, Mississippi. Oprah's parents, Vernon Winfrey, a soldier, and Vernita Lee were never married and Oprah grew up being shuffled between her grandmother and her two parents. Vernon was living 250 miles away in Fort Rucker at the time of Oprah's birth, and first learned of Vernita's pregnancy and Oprah's birth at that time through a written birth announcement sent to him by Vernita Lee. Vernita's sister suggested that Vernita's baby girl be named after the Bible's Orpah from the book of Ruth in the Old Testament. Somehow the letters of Orpah were transposed and the name Oprah ended up on the birth certificate instead. In search of a better life, away from the deep racial prejudice of the South, Vernita moved to Milwaukee soon after Winfrey's birth, leaving Oprah to spend her early years on the Kosciusko pig farm of her maternal grandmother, Hattie Mae, and her husband Earless. Hattie Mae was well aware of the need for an education, and pushed Winfrey from an early age to learn. Winfrey could read, do arithmetic, and write by the time that she was three years old. This, as well as her involvement in their local church, made her appreciated by adults from an early age, but by the same token gave her a difficult time being accepted by her peers.

In 1960, when Winfrey was six years old, Vernita decided she wanted to have her daughter back, so Winfrey was sent to live with her mother in Milwaukee. Life in Milwaukee was cramped compared to life at the farm, where Vernita, Winfrey, and Patricia (Winfrey's new half sister) lived in a single room in a rooming house of the downtown ghettoes of the city. As she had in Mississippi, Winfrey excelled in school and developed a deep love for books. In 1962, Winfrey's father Vernon and his new wife Zelma decided to take Oprah in to give her a better life. So Winfrey moved to Nashville, Tennessee and moved in with her father and stepmother. Like Hattie Mae, Zelma valued an education very much and was strict with Winfrey, making her read one book and write a report on it every week. Winfrey's stay with her father only lasted one year, however, for after a summer visit in Milwaukee, Vernita decided not to let her go back to Nashville, and moved Winfrey back in with her. They now lived in a crowded two-bedroom apartment with Vernita's new boyfriend, Oprah's half sister Patricia, and a new half-sibling, Jeffrey.

During her early teenage years in Milwaukee, Winfrey excelled in school and remained involved in church activities. It was in 1964 that Oprah first fell in love with television and the entertainment industry. Watching 'The Supremes' on the Ed Sullivan Show inspired her with the possibility of being on television. The dream was still almost a decade from coming to fruition. [4] In 1968, Gene Abrams, one of Winfrey's teachers at Lincoln School, recommended her for an Upward Bound scholarship. That year, Winfrey received a full scholarship to and enrolled in Nicolet High School, an all-White school in suburban Milwaukee. Being the only Black student in a large affluent all-White school was difficult for Winfrey, and she struggled to feel accepted, causing her to rebel against her parents and her home. She started running away from home and hanging out with the wrong crowds. This rebellious behavior led Vernita to feel she could no longer handle raising her daughter. In order to 'straighten her out', after an unsuccessful attempt at committing Winfrey to a home for troubled teens, Vernita called Vernon and arranged for Oprah to go back to Nashville to live with him and Zelma. Winfrey's stay in Nashville lasted until 1976, from ages fourteen to twenty-two. Like it had been during Winfrey's brief stay in 1962, life with Vernon and Zelma was one of academics and strict discipline. Vernon made Winfrey give up her bad attitude and rebellious ways and encouraged her to do well in school.

From the time Oprah had been a little girl living with her grandmother, she had been a great speaker and student and had always enjoyed performing in church groups. Living with her father, Winfrey again became very involved in church and school activities while attending East Nashville High, and became active in drama classes and in student politics. In 1970, Winfrey was invited to travel to Los Angeles to give one of her recitations to a church congregation. She also landed her first job working in her father's small grocery store. In 1971, she was invited to the White House Youth Conference and represented Nashville in a national speaking competition. That same year she was also the first Black woman to win the Miss Fire Prevention contest and won the Elks Club beauty contest, which awarded her with a four-year scholarship to Tennessee State University. Finally, to top off her senior year in High School, what started as a sponsorship by a local radio station in a walkathon, led to an opportunity to be on the radio. A disc jockey, John Heidelberg, talked her into doing a demo tape, and had the station manager hear it. His manager was impressed, and Winfrey was hired to do news reports on weekends and after school. Winfrey worked at the radio station through the end of her senior year in high school. In the fall of 1971, she entered TSU as a drama and speech major, and continued her work at the radio station until the end of her freshman year.

Then, in 1973 came an offer Winfrey could not resist, and the first step towards that dream which had first sparked in a little girl's heart nine years prior while watching the Ed Sullivan show. CBS affiliate WTVF-TV of Nashville offered Winfrey a $15,000 a year job starting as the weekend news anchor. Taking the job meant quitting TSU at age nineteen. She accepted the offer, became the first woman and first Black newscaster in Nashville's television history, and was quickly moved to the weeknight news co-anchor position.

In 1976, Winfrey moved to ABC affiliate WJZ-TV in Baltimore, which offered her a job as co-anchor of their evening news show. Winfrey and WJZ-TV were not a good match from the start, however. Problems arose as a result of Winfrey's style of reporting, a style which was considered by her superiors as being too compassionate, not like the unemotional traditional style that was expected of anchors at the station. Winfrey's untraditional style of reporting was not only too emotional for the taste of the station, she would also ad-lib what she read on the Tele Prompter, further creating a problematic relationship between herself and the station. Her style had worked well in Nashville, but did not work well with her co-anchor Jerry Turner. She was quickly disliked by her station management, her co-anchor, and was considered too nice for television.

By April 1977, nine months after she first went on the air in Baltimore, Oprah was pulled off the news anchor desk. She had signed a seven-year contract with Baltimore, however, so the station had to find something for her to do. WJZ-TV assigned her to co-host a local morning talk-interview show - "People are Talking" - geared at a Baltimore audience. She was slotted to air opposite Phil Donahue on a competing station. Winfrey and her co-host, Richard Sher, clicked instantly, and although Donahue offered stiff competition, the show was a hit, and they beat Donahue in Baltimore ratings. Winfrey spent the full seven years of her contract in Baltimore, of which she hosted "People are Talking" for six. It was here in Baltimore that Winfrey met who would become her long time producer, Debra DiMaio.

DiMaio produced her show in Baltimore, until 1983, when she took a job in Chicago to produce the show "A.M. Chicago". Knowing that Winfrey's contract in Baltimore was up at the end of 1983, and seeing that she was beating Donahue in Baltimore ratings, DiMaio arranged for Oprah to fly to Chicago during Labor Day weekend, 1983 in the hope of getting her to do the same in Chicago. Oprah was subsequently hired to host "A.M. Chicago" and started January 1984, accepting a $200,000 per year, four-year deal with WLS-TV. [5] She would now be up against Donahue in his own hometown, and she rose to the challenge. Within twelve weeks she beat Donahue in the local ratings, giving "A.M. Chicago" its highest ratings ever. [6] Seven months from her debut in Chicago, the show was expanded to one hour. By the time the show had been on for one year, Winfrey was making all decisions concerning guests and topics.

1985 brought Winfrey her first chance at national exposure. First came her appearance on the "Tonight" show with Johnny Carson in January of 1985. Winfrey's appearance on that show attracted the attention of Quincy Jones, who subsequently offered her the role of Sofia in the highly-acclaimed film, *The Color Purple*. The offer to star in *The Color Purple* presented scheduling problems for Oprah's show, and Winfrey had to reach a compromise with WLS-TV so they would allow her to take the time off that was required by the film. Although she was able to reach a compromise relatively easily, Winfrey realized that she wanted to gain control of her show from a business perspective in order to avoid a similar problem from coming up again in the future. Once she had control, she would be able to rent her own program out to WLS-TV and any other station that wanted to broadcast it. What she needed to do was make a deal so that WLS-TV would become part of the syndication deal. It was during this time that King World syndicators first came into play.

Syndication is a multi-million-dollar business that rents programs to television stations to show on the air. Like an agent, the syndicator is paid a percentage of the income brought in by the shows. Dennis Swanson, the man who had hired Winfrey in Chicago, had made a deal in 1984 with King World to bring in a new popular syndicated game show, "Wheel of Fortune". King World was making enough money from "Wheel of Fortune" and their other hit "Jeopardy", allowing them to cast about for more shows to syndicate. This all came just in time for Winfrey to be able to strike a deal and gain more control of her show. In September 1985 a deal was worked out to syndicate Winfrey, setting her compensation at twenty-four percent of the gross income from syndication. [7] In December of 1985, *The Color Purple* was released, helping Winfrey gain national publicity. After only twelve months on the air with Winfrey as a host, the show had been sold to television stations across the nation, had had its name changed to "The Oprah Winfrey Show", and by September 8, 1986 was being broadcast nationally on 138 stations. [8]

This success, as well as Winfrey's ongoing desire to be in control of as much of her show as she could, led to the creation of Harpo Incorporated. In 1986, with the guidance of her longtime lawyer and business manager, Jeffrey Jacobs, Winfrey formed her own studios and production company. The studio was created with the idea in mind that it would give her more freedom to do more movies, and would give her control over the production of "The Oprah Winfrey Show" as well as other special projects. Since the law dictates that the television networks are not allowed to syndicate shows they own, King World continued syndication of the show as had been arranged in the 1985 deal. By the end of 1986, "The Oprah Winfrey Show" had grossed $125 million and Winfrey's share came out to $30 million for that one year. [9] Her new company, Harpo Inc. grossed $2.2 million on its first year of existence.

Coverage of the show grew quickly from 138 to 198 stations and a daily audience of ten million. By 1993, the show was King World's main money maker, accounting for forty percent of its 1993 income of $474.3 million. Today, King World grosses $20 million a week on the show, with a production cost of only $200,000 a week, making it a lucrative deal for both Winfrey and King World. Her first year producing her own show, Winfrey had arranged a twenty-five percent share of the program's gross for herself from King World, bringing her $7.5 million. In 1987, King World increased the fees paid by stations by four-fold, and by the end of that year the show was reaching nine million homes and was among the top five in syndication. Winfrey's income rose significantly, bringing her $25 million by 1988. Winfrey used some of her share of the income to buy interests in various television stations: WIVB-TV of Buffalo, NY, WEEK-TV of Peoria, IL, and KBJR-TV of Duluth, MN.

Also in 1988, Oprah invested $10 million, an investment that involved money from King World as part of a deal struck to ensure the happiness of their main investment, to remodel a newly acquired studio facility located in the West Loop of Chicago. [10] The facility was called Harpo Studios and became the best film and television production facility in the Midwest. This venture made Winfrey the first African-American to own a major studio facility. Oprah created commotion in the broadcasting industry by hiring mostly nonunion crews on the talk show. Most unions are predominantly White and male and Winfrey wanted to provide jobs for Blacks, women, and other minorities. Unions were hesitant, however, to confront someone as powerful as Winfrey had become, and Winfrey was able to continue hiring crews at her discretion. Winfrey took over production of her own show and moved its shooting from WLS-TV to Harpo Studios. She had two additional studios built, which opened in January 1990, meant for other attracted productions. *The Women of Brewster Place* became the first television series produced by Harpo Productions, a project which was initially a difficult sell to the older White men who ran the networks, but eventually was sold to ABC and aired in March, 1989 with huge ratings. That same year brought "The Oprah Winfrey Show" a gross income of $55.6 million, a substantial part of her wealth being in shares of stock of King World.

The October 1, 1990 issue of *Forbes* magazine listed Madonna as the highest grossing female entertainer of the year, but Winfrey probably took more money home that year for, unlike many other artists, Winfrey did not have an expensive entourage to pay for. The only person working for her was her long time lawyer and business manager, Jeffrey Jacobs. 1990 also saw Winfrey syndicated to twenty million viewers internationally, these earnings giving her a net worth of $250 million. Winfrey's contract with King World was set to end in 1991, but in an effort to come up with a deal with King World and Cap Cities/ABC, Winfrey agreed to do the show through August of 1993. Jacobs, her manager and guiding force in the creation of Harpo Incorporated, however, wanted a better deal than that, and in 1991 was able to obtain ownership of the show for Harpo Productions. As part of the deal, Oprah would keep the same level of control and was given a guarantee that stations owned and operated by ABC would carry it for five years. Under this new deal, King World still agreed to continue distribution of the show until August of 1993, and later extended the contract to September of 1995.

1992 marked the sixth season King World had syndicated Oprah, giving Winfrey a yearly income of $30 million and King World a six-year gross income of $750 million. Winfrey's net worth continued to grow and Harpo Studios began to attract an increasing amount of business, meaning more money for Harpo Inc. By the 1993 National Association of Television Programming Executives (NATPE) convention, Winfrey was by a wide margin the top talk show in the country. In September of that year, Winfrey made the cover of *Forbes* magazine as the wealthiest entertainer in the world. By this time she was being seen in 99 percent of United States television markets, in 64 countries, and was generating over $170 million in revenue.

1994 was another successful year, "The Oprah Winfrey Show" was still the number one show in America, going up by twelve percent in its ratings, and Winfrey struck up a lucrative new deal with King World. Since Winfrey's contract with King

World was set to expire in September of 1995, 1994 was a year of negotiations for Oprah. Given that Oprah was still a major source of income for King World, there was great interest on King World's part to keep syndication of "The Oprah Winfrey Show". A deal was struck in March of 1994, extending Winfrey's contract with King World, giving them the exclusive right to distribute the show until the year 2000. [11] As part of this deal, Winfrey received the option on one and a half million shares of King World stock to add to the one million shares she already had. To top the deal off, King World also gave Winfrey the option to buy another 500,000 shares at the time of the new contract signing plus the option to buy another 250,000 shares per year each year she renews her show with King World between 1997 and 2000. In exchange, Oprah agreed to a five-year 'anti-competition' clause, ensuring King World she would not go to another syndicator if she left them before the end of their contract. However, if King World is sold or merged with another company, the anti-competition clause is automatically canceled. Finally, under the new contract, the percent profit taken by King World would drop from forty-three percent to thirty-five percent and ultimately twenty-five percent. To pay for this new expensive contract, King World increased the prices stations were to pay for broadcasting "The Oprah Winfrey Show" by ten to twenty-five percent. The future of Winfrey's show will significantly affect King World's financial future, given that "The Oprah Winfrey Show" accounts for 40% of King World's revenues (twice of what any other show brings the syndicator). [12]

With the signing of this new contract, 1994 turned out to be a very lucrative year for Winfrey, making her worth about one-third of a billion dollars. And she keeps on making lucrative deals. 1995 was marked with numerous movie deals. In April of that year Harpo Films, Winfrey's production division, optioned the rights to Dorothy West's book "The Wedding". [13] In the summer of 1995, Harpo Films optioned the rights to another movie, "The Keepers of the House". [14] This film is an addition to the other six films Harpo Films had already agreed to produce in a May 1995 three-year-deal with Capital Cities/ABC-TV. [15] Two weeks after her deal with ABC, Winfrey signed a five year, exclusive deal, this one with The Walt Disney Motion Pictures Group. [16] Under this pact, Harpo will produce feature films, some of which Winfrey is expected to star in.

A recent project developed for this deal was the big screen version of award-winning Toni Morrison's novel "Beloved", which was released in the fall of 1998, starring Winfrey and Danny Glover. In September of 1996 Winfrey was featured as *Forbes* magazine's wealthiest entertainer with a two-year income of $171 million. According to *Forbes* Winfrey's net worth was $340 million in 1995, $415 in million in 1996, and $550 million in 1997. As her five percent stake in King World and the other business ventures continue to grow, Winfrey's estimated net worth will reach $1 billion by the year 2000.

CHAPTER TEN: MOTOWN

Profile

- From 1959 to 1988 owned and run by Berry Gordy, first as Motown Record Corporation, and then as Motown Industries, a corporation made up of record label companies, a production company, a distribution company, and an artist management group.
- Motown held the number one slot on the BE 100s between 1973 to 1984, at its highest point in 1986 having sales of $152.4 million.
- Among the successful films produced by Motown are *Lady Sings the Blues*, *Mahogany*, *The Wiz*, and *Last Dragon*.
- Produced stars, among many others, like Diana Ross and the Supremes, Smokey Robinson and the Miracles, the Contours, the Commodores, the Jackson 5 and Michael Jackson, the Four Tops, Martha and the Vandellas, Gladys Knight and the Pips, Stevie Wonder, Marvin Gaye, Lionel Richie, and the Temptations.
- In 1988, Motown was sold to MCA, Inc. for $61 million.

Summary

Berry Gordy III was born in Detroit in 1929, and grew up in a supportive, hard working family with seven other brothers and sisters. His father owned his own plastering contracting company, as well as a grocery shop, and his mother was an insurance agent. Gordy's two first loves as he was growing up were boxing and music. As a child he dreamed of becoming a boxer like his hero Joe Louis, and when he was fifteen started training at the Brewster Recreation Center. Gordy quit school in 1948 to pursue a professional career in boxing, but discovering there was not much money to be made and having kept his love for music, he quit fighting two years later and dedicated himself full-time to songwriting. In 1951 he was drafted by the Army, and spent two years on duty, a time during which he earned his GED and was sent to Korea to fight in the war. When he returned home, using his army severance pay and a $700 loan, he opened a record store in 1953. When this project did not work out, he took a series of different jobs: one as a salesperson for a cooking utensils company, and jobs at two different auto manufacturing plants. Gordy, however, still continued to compose music and dream of going into the music business. In 1957, he quit his job at a Lincoln-Mercury plant and dedicated himself to being a full-time songwriter, and in 1958, began working as an independent record producer. He recorded songs by singers such as the Miracles and Marv Johnson and wrote songs for people such as Jackie Wilson. Gordy did not like having to deal with other companies to distribute and nationally produce his work, and disliked how little money he was being paid by the big companies. So by the end of 1959, when Gordy was thirty years old, he established his own record company: Motown. Motown began as a small company with only six employees, out of a small building on 2648 West Grand Boulevard, which Gordy named "Hitsville USA", and grew to be the largest independent record company in the world. By launching singers such as the Supremes, Stevie Wonder, and the Jackson 5, Gordy and Motown made history in the world of entertainment.

Throughout the 1960's, Motown produced one Number One hit after the other, and Gordy proved himself not only to be a talented songwriter, but also a gifted spotter of talent and "hit material". Gordy's next step came in the movie business with films such as *Mahogany* and *Lady Sings the Blues*. To accommodate his increasing work in movies and movie soundtracks, in 1968 Gordy moved Motown's corporate headquarters from Detroit to Los Angeles. In 1973, Gordy established Motown Industries, an umbrella company to head all his ventures: Jobete Music Company Inc. (a record label and publishing company named after his first three children), IMTI (an artist management company), Motown Records, and MPI (his movie production company). In 1983, Motown celebrated its 25th anniversary with a special "Motown 25 - Yesterday, Today, and Forever", the most watched variety show in the history of television, and a nine-time Emmy Award nominee. Unfortunately, over the next couple of years, Motown came to find itself in deeper and deeper financial trouble, and after various attempts at saving the company, in 1988 Gordy finally sold Motown to MCA, Inc. for $61 million. He continues to run Gordy Company, which includes the film, television, and record publishing divisions of Motown Industries. He is the proud father of eight children (Hazel Joy, Berry IV, Terry, Kerry, Rhonda, Sherry, Kennedy, and Stefan). He is very close to his family, and many members have held key executive positions in his company. Motown's success was built on Berry Gordy's extraordinary ability to spot and develop talent in the African-American community. In those days, there were no music companies that would open doors to Black artists or gamble on the 'Black' sound. His business acumen allowed Gordy to develop this new sound which would become known around the world as the 'Motown' sound. Gordy's Motown shaped and influenced the history of entertainment not only of the United States but also of the world.

History

Berry Gordy was born in Detroit on November 28, 1929 to Berry Gordy and Bertha Ida Fuller. Gordy grew up during the Depression in a family of eight children. The family was on welfare for a while, until Gordy's father took over a small, failing grocery store and turned it around into a profit-making venture. Gordy's country-born father turned himself into a successful businessman, owning his own grocery store and later his own plastering contracting business. Gordy describes himself growing up as "mischievous, terrible in school, [and] always in trouble" [1]. He did, early on, find his true love, music, while learning to play the piano. As a teenager, Gordy worked with his father at his contracting business, and tried out various different ventures such as a homemade shoeshine stand, which was not very successful, and selling Detroit's top colored weekly newspaper, *The Michigan Chronicle*.

When Gordy was about fifteen years old, when he was not working for his father, Gordy started going to the Brewster Center after school, a recreation facility for inner-city kids that offered training in boxing. Ever since Gordy had seen Joe Louis box, he had dreamed of boxing. He started training with Eddie Futch, the man who had trained Joe Frazier, among others, and soon Gordy decided he wanted to make boxing his career. He quit school to turn professional and in November of 1948 had his first professional fight, on the same card with his hero and boxing inspiration: Joe Louis. During his boxing time, Gordy also became attracted to Jazz and became an avid fan of many of the time's greats. These two loves had always been in conflict, and in 1950 music won. In August 1950, Gordy decided to give up boxing and dedicate himself to music. Gordy spent the next year of his life writing songs. One of his earliest accomplishments came during this time with a radio commercial he wrote and sang in for his brother Fuller's printshop. Gordy got a local disc jockey to record it in his basement and to play it at the radio station where he worked.

1951 brought a radical change in Gordy's life as he got drafted to fight in the Korean War. He was first sent to training in Arkansas for three months, during which time he picked up his high school diploma through the GED test. While in Korea, he learned the Korean language perfectly, and he prided himself on being able to communicate with locals. Gordy returned home in 1953, and went back to the music business. He opened a Jazz record store: 3D Record Mart - House of Jazz using money from his severance pay, a loan from his father and an investment from his brother George (who became his partner in this venture). Initially, business was scarce for popular demand was for Blues music, and Gordy only carried Jazz artists. When Gordy finally realized he had to diversify his products, the store was almost broke. Gordy started carrying Blues and business picked up, but this attempt to save the store came too late. Gordy was too far in debt to turn things around, and he lost the store less than a year after he had opened it. With this venture having left him in financial trouble, Gordy took a 'regular' job selling cooking utensils for "Guardian Service Cookware". Realizing that he was a good, successful salesman, Gordy decided he wanted to go back to what his real dream was, music, so he quit his salesman job and devoted himself full-time to songwriting. Unfortunately, he was not able to make enough money doing this to support his wife and three children, so he had to go back to a steady job. With the help of his mother-in-law he found a job at Lincoln-Mercury working at the conveyor belt, making $86.40 a week. While at work, Gordy would sing and write songs, having devised a simple numbers code to help him memorize the melodies he composed. After about two years at the factory, Gordy again decided to fully pursue his dreams, and quit his job at the auto plant. During the day he would write songs, and at night he would frequent Jazz clubs in order to meet people who worked in the music business. His favorite place was the Flame Show Bar. Here he met Al Green, who owned the club, managed a few singers and owned Pearl Music Company, a music publishing company. Gordy started writing for, among others, Al Green's artists. This would prove itself to be the beginning of Gordy's illustrious and successful career in the music business.

At Pearl Music Company, Gordy met Roquel Billy Davis, and together they became a successful songwriting team, as well as long time friends. Between 1957 and 1959, Gordy and Davis began to be sought out by more and more artists, and found their first big hit in Jackie Wilson's "Reet Petite". It was during this time that Gordy's sister Gwen joined the ranks and that he met William "Smokey" Robinson, who went on to become a songwriting partner and his closest friend to date. Those first few years of songwriting, however, brought little money, and the bit of money that came in had to be split in three between Gordy, Davis, and Gwen. Also, record companies were not using their songs on the 'B' sides, which meant less money for Gordy and his team. Gordy's attempt to convince Pearl Music to give them the 'B' sides was unsuccessful, and as a result, Davis and Gordy parted ways with Jackie Wilson and Pearl Music Company. Gwen Gordy and Davis started their own record company, and Gordy decided to stay on his own promising to keep writing and producing for his sister and partner. Because of his acquired notoriety in the Detroit music scene, artists were being referred to him to audition, making Gordy's new found solo career go in the direction of artist manager. The first group he managed was the group led by his friend Smokey, The Miracles.

Based on his bad experiences with not getting royalties from his songs, Gordy started a company for songwriters where they could publish and get paid for songs they wrote. He called this company Jobete Music Company, Inc. after his first three children: Hazel Joy, Terry, and Berry IV. That business was not as fruitful as he thought it would be, producers' royalties were low, so Berry started trying to come up with enough money to produce his own records and start his own record label. Finding investors proved to be difficult, so he resorted to using the family savings, pledging his future royalties as security to his family. So in 1959, when Gordy was barely thirty years old, the future Motown Industries was created out of a house in Detroit on 2648 West Grand Boulevard, a house which he named "Hitsville USA". He named his record label 'Tamla' and signed a long-term deal with United Artists to produce and distribute records for them. Not long after starting Tamla, after only a few hits, Gordy started his second record label. He named the label 'Motown' in honor of his hometown, Detroit, also known as the Motor City. These two labels, as well as Gwen Gordy's label 'Anna Records', increased his ability to distribute his music, but Gordy realized that he needed to do more. He needed to get his songs released nationally and needed to directly distribute his records in order to make some more substantial money. With this in mind he decided to go at it alone, without United Artists.

Gordy's first national hit came in 1960 with a song by The Miracles, and to make it happen he advertised the song in a magazine and promoted it at various radio stations. He started off promoting his music at Black radio stations and then worked himself into getting airplay on White radio stations. The 1960's were successful years for Gordy as he finally was able to create the kind of company he had always envisioned: "I wanted [that] concept for my company...I wanted a place where a kid off the street could walk in one door an unknown and come out another a recording artist - a star" [2]. Among many of the stars signed by Gordy during this decade were Marvin Gaye, Diana Ross and the Supremes, the Temptations, the Marvelettes, the Contours, Martha and the Vandellas, Stevie Wonder, the Four Tops and the Jackson 5. Between 1960 and 1961 alone, Motown released over twenty records and produced hit after hit. As the company began to grow, Gordy acquired two more companies: Golden World (a publishing company) and Ric-Tic Records. Gordy created the "Motortown Revue", a tour all across the country of his most popular artists. In 1962, Gordy bought the Greystone Ballroom in Detroit, where his stars could perform all of their latest hits. As other independent record labels were failing, Tamla-Motown was thriving. By the Fall of 1963, Motown artists had become visible also in Europe, so Gordy signed an international foreign distribution deal with EMI and set up his own publishing operation throughout Europe. Motown soon saw wide international success. That same year, a West Coast office was opened for the A & R publishing activities and West Coast recruiting. Motown had become the largest independent record company in the world and the third largest recording company, RCA Victor and Columbia being numbers one and two.

In 1965, as the Supremes were becoming increasingly popular and Motown was in the midst of its most successful times, Gordy started a second publishing company. This venture was meant for the publishing of 'standard-type' songs that Gordy wanted the public to believe had been around for years, and which did not match the Motown sound. He called this company Stein and Van Stock, two names he had picked out of the telephone book. That same year, after selling 200,000 albums, Motown opened a New York office and began selling to the pre-recorded market. Two years later, Motown moved in yet another different direction when the Supremes were asked to guest star on the popular "Tarzan" television series. The Supremes episode brought the highest ratings of any "Tarzan" episode and gave Gordy his first taste for the television and movie business.

In 1968, Gordy's largest problem yet, since the inception of the company in 1959, arose with the strike and threat to leave of Gordy's most prolific writing and hit-producing team. The team, known as HDH, was made up of Eddie Holland, Lamont Dozier, and Brian Holland, who aside from being important songwriters also happened to hold powerful positions in the company. Knowing that the departure of HDH could mean disaster for Motown, Gordy sued them for breach of contract. After the suit, HDH never came back to work. At this point, the company was in disarray, a significant part of its creative genius had been lost and the departments headed by Holland, Dozier, and Holland were in chaos. Gordy realized he needed to take charge to save his company. He let his legal team take care of the pending lawsuit, appointed new people to head divisions that had previously been headed by Holland, Dozier, and Holland, and hired a new team of songwriters to produce a new hit for his hot commodity, the Supremes. HDH countersued, accusing Gordy of, among many other things, cheating its artists, and dragged the situation on for close to four years, when it was finally settled. Gordy always felt that these kind of accusations and rumors of cheating his artists, as well as those about Motown's connections to the Mafia, were attempts at finding crooked reasons for Motown's incredible success: "How could one of the most successful independent record companies in the world be owned and operated by a Black man without being crooked?" [3]

Despite all the turmoil created by the departure of HDH, 1968 ended up being a good year for Motown. Motown received its first Grammy award that year and by the end of the year Motown had five records out of the Top 10 on *Billboard*'s Hot 100. Motown songs captured and held the number one to number three spots on the Top 10 for one whole month. By the fall of 1968, Gordy was spending most of his time working out of Motown's Los Angeles office and was involved with various Motown television projects. Given Motown's increased involvement with television and its increased success, Gordy decided to move his whole operation to the West Coast. Under the leadership of Vice President Suzanne de Passe, Motown began its diversification into stage, screen, and television. Between 1968 and 1974 Motown produced six television specials including the weekly cartoon classic about the Jackson 5.

Shortly before the move to Los Angeles, a group of five brothers from Indiana had auditioned for Gordy and he had been very impressed with their talent, but was hesitant at first about signing and having to be responsible for minors. In 1969, he finally decided to sign them and moved the Jackson 5 to Los Angeles. This group would prove itself to be one of Motown's most famous musical groups ever, and would create one of the most successful entertainers in the world: Michael Jackson. Gordy used Diana Ross to help promote them by calling their first album "Diana Ross presents the Jackson 5" and by allowing them to open for Diana Ross and the Supremes. The Jackson 5 went on to become a smash hit on the Ed Sullivan Show, quickly their first song "I Want You Back" rose to number one on the charts, and by January of 1970, the Jackson 5 made Top 100 history by becoming the first group ever to have their first four singles go to number one, all within an eleven month period. The growth of the Jackson 5 was accompanied by the break up of Diana Ross and the Supremes, the beginning of Diana Ross' solo career, and a new era of business for Motown.

In the summer of 1971, Gordy's dream of being in the motion picture business finally came true with a deal with Paramount Pictures. Gordy was presented with the opportunity of doing a film about the life of singer Billie Holiday; it would be made by Paramount and would be produced by Motown. To top the deal off, Diana Ross would star in the role of Billie Holiday, and Gordy was named executive producer. Gordy went on to hire an up and coming African-American entertainer, Richard Pryor, a comedian he had discovered in the mid 1960's. The movie opened in October 1972 with rave reviews as the opening credits read: *Berry Gordy Presents Diana Ross as Billie Holiday in Lady Sings the Blues*. That next spring, the film received five Academy Award Nominations, one of them being for Diana Ross as Best Actress. Although Ross did not win the Oscar, she was honored for her part in the film by receiving a Golden Globe Award for Best Actress in January of 1973. By 1974, the movie had grossed over $8.5 million.

Motown's second film opportunity came soon thereafter, this one proving itself to be even more successful than *Lady Sings the Blues*. *Mahogany* was not only produced by Motown, but Gordy also ended up directing it after things with the original director did not work out. Motown only had to put half of the budgeted money down, instead of the full amount it had had to put down on *Lady Sings the Blues*. Starring Diana Ross and Billy Dee Williams, *Mahogany* was a great hit, breaking records with its release in 1975. With this new facet of Motown's business came a restructuring of Motown Record Corporation. In 1973, Gordy formed and became Chairman of Motown Industries, an umbrella company meant to oversee all other companies: Motown Records, Jobete Music, MPI (a movie production company), and ITMI (an artist management company).

Unfortunately, by the late 1970's, financial trouble started arising for the company. Although popularity and overhead were growing, revenues and the roster of stars had been progressively shrinking. During these years, not only had Motown lost the Jackson 5 to CBS, it had also lost other valuable stars such as Martha and the Vandellas, Ashford and Simpson, and Gladys Knight and the Pips. Major record companies, who in the past had not wanted to sign Black artists, were now aggressively going after Black talent. These large companies were not only going after Motown artists, but also were developing their own Black artists, and going after Motown writers and producers. The value placed on artists had jumped into the multimillions and artists under contract were being taken away by simply offering them more money. What had seemed as a move towards growth, the move of Motown to Los Angeles had rather proved itself to be one that harmed the company, by placing it in the midst of competition with many other larger and more powerful record companies. Motown found itself having financial worries, problems in middle-management, and low productivity. And to make matters worse, Stevie Wonder, someone who had been with him since age eleven and one of Motown's major stars, was considering leaving Motown. After a tough negotiation, Gordy managed to keep Wonder and a new album by Wonder was released, making Gordy feel he could perhaps revive his company. Another act that came along just in time was the Commodores, bringing Motown various hits in the late 1970's. However, because the company had become so dependent on only a handful of stars, whenever no new music was being produced, without developing successful new acts, the company could find itself in great trouble very quickly. By November of 1979, Gordy was informed by his financial advisors that he was bankrupt - his liabilities were higher than his assets.

Motown and other companies like it had been dealing with a decline in independent distributors over the years, thus forcing them to switch distribution over to the larger, more powerful record companies, which served only to make those companies even more powerful. In an attempt to set up his own distributorship that would be strong enough to defend itself from the major players, Gordy had joined forces in 1974 with A & M records, another independent company like Motown. Together they set up their own distributorship called 'Together'. This alliance, unfortunately did not last its five year deal, and six months before its end, A & M announced it was making a deal with RCA for national distribution. With this came a continuation of Motown's previous financial problems. Gordy knew the company was overstaffed, so he was suggested to get rid of half of his employees. Gordy found this difficult to do, given he felt close to most of his employees, as if they were family, so instead he took other measures to help alleviate his financial woes. Gordy put through a fifteen percent cut for all executive salaries and outside consultants and went and got himself a business loan from the bank. Luckily for Gordy, Smokey Robinson and Diana Ross came through with big hits just in time, helping him survive this crisis. After one year, Gordy was able to pay off his bank loan and Motown was able to survive this episode of his financial rollercoaster. With the hiring of a new president for the record company came a new period of growth for Motown. Old hits were re-released in "best-of" compilations and new acts such as Lionel Richie, De Barge, and Rick James were broken.

The 1980's, unfortunately, brought with them more financial trouble. It all started with the loss of Diana Ross to RCA in 1981. This not only left Gordy personally devastated, for Diana and he were very close, it also left Motown without one of its greatest money-producing artists. One of the only highlights of the decade came on March 25, 1983, with the 25th anniversary celebration in honor of Motown and Berry Gordy. *Motown 25 - Yesterday, Today, and Forever* became the most watched variety show in the history of television and was nominated for nine Emmy Awards. By May 1983, Motown was in financial trouble again and given the previous dissolution of the deal with A & M, the decision was made to go with MCA for national distribution. With this deal, MCA would get a major foothold in the Black record business and in return, Motown would have one reliable distributor as opposed to many different distributors. Everything seemed to be going well again at Motown, for a while at least. In 1985, a new person was hired to head Jobete and previously untapped worldwide opportunities for Motown songs were taken advantage of, causing Jobete's revenues to rise. Hits by Stevie Wonder, Lionel Richie, and Debarge, along with Jobete making soundtracks for movies like *The Big Chill*, were moving Motown up to $137 million in sales. Motown Industries as a whole, however, did not recover as well. Marketing costs were skyrocketing, the company was losing money and to make matters worse, Gordy was losing the motivation to keep going. Making the decision to sell had come across his mind but had been a difficult one to come to grips with for not only did he feel like everybody involved was like family, he also had actual family members in important executive positions. He had also hoped to be able to keep the company in the family, eventually passing it on to his children.

Gordy knew what would come next as a result of having signed the distribution deal with MCA, as he expressed matter-of-factly in his 1994 autobiography:

"It was a natural conflict when a major record company takes over your smaller record label for distribution. They really want to sell *their* records, not *your* records. And the only way to make *your* records *their* records is for them to buy you out". [4]

Gordy struggled with making the decision to sell, evaluating all the other possible scenarios first. He could decide to go public, merge with other companies, sell off personal assets, or auction off rights to some of his master recordings to come up with enough money to save his company. Gordy decided to go with none of these, and decided that the only way to keep the company intact and still protect its legacy would be to sell. On November of 1986 MCA made its first offer. By this point the foundation of the deal had already been worked out, and a meeting was set only for working out details that would dictate the degree of Gordy's involvement in the MCA family. Before the deal could be closed, however, Gordy needed to speak to Stevie Wonder, who years ago in the negotiating of his contract had had a clause included that stated that Motown could not be sold unless he approved of the buyer. Wonder and Gordy met on Christmas Eve, a week before the deal's deadline, and Wonder gave Gordy the necessary approval.

Gordy, however, was still not convinced with the MCA deal. He did not feel the deal reflected Motown's real worth, but rather its current financial statements. Also, Gordy wanted to make sure that other stipulations were taken care of such as an assurance that a specific portion of the company would be held for minority ownership and that he would be allowed to continue in and still use his name in the business. MCA's original deal had various elements that Gordy at the time was not willing to settle for and after various back-and-forth shuffles of the contract between MCA and Motown for revisions, Gordy decided not to sell. On December 30, 1986, only 24 hours before the deadline, Gordy called the whole thing off. Once more, Gordy decided to try and save his company. He knew he would need a quick string of hit records and that quick decisions would have to be made to put a plan into action that could save Motown. Gordy decided to cut costs through various measures such as scaling back further on personnel and cutting salaries. None of these measures, however, proved themselves to be able to pull it off, and by early 1988, Gordy decided the only real way to save the company was to sell it. MCA was still interested, as were other companies, something that helped Gordy's bargaining position. Tough negotiations began, and this time MCA met most of Gordy's demands, including an offering price more than fifty percent higher than the price that had been offered in 1986.

The deal was set. Gordy would sell the Motown name and record catalogue, the masters and the artists' recording contracts, and MCA had to agree to keep intact Motown's body of music as well as establish a set percentage of minority ownership of the company. He did not sell Jobete Music Company, Inc. (which owned the publishing rights to most of the Motown songs) or his film and television company. On June 29, 1988 the sale was official: MCA (through a deal with Boston Ventures) had bought Motown for $61 million. In 1990, MCA parted with Motown, selling it to Netherlands-based Polygram Records for some $325 million. [5]

Motown Sales over the years (in $ millions):

Year	Sales in MM	Year	Sales in MM
1973	46	1980	64.8
1974	45	1981	91.7
1975	43.5	1982	104.3
1976	50	1983	108.2
1977	51.4	1984	137
1978	58	1985	149
1979	64.8	1986	152.4
		1987	100

In the months following the sale, Gordy occupied his time by finalizing details such as a bonus and severance pay structure for all Motown employees, and the transferring of all the property and documentation to MCA. Also, a new company, Gordy Company was set up to oversee the divisions Gordy had not sold, Jobete and Motown Productions (which was renamed Gordy-de Passe Productions after the sale). Gordy remained chairperson of the company and put his son Berry IV, an employee of Motown for several years already, in charge of Gordy Company. Today, Gordy continues to run Gordy Company with his son and in 1994 released his autobiography titled "To Be Loved - The Music, the Magic, the Memories of Motown". In July of 1997, Gordy sold half of his stake in two of his music publishing companies: Jobete Music Publishing and its sister company Stone Diamond Music. In the deal, EMI paid $132 million for the 50% stake and took over Jobete's management (significantly more than the $61 million he had been able to sell Motown Records for in 1988), while Gordy kept his position as chairman. "Gordy says the deal will free him to spend more time on other Motown ventures, such as a Broadway musical collaboration with Motown CEO Andre Harrell and producer Dick Clark to be directed by George Wolfe." [6] Other projects Gordy is currently involved with include a TV miniseries on the Motown era, which he is working on with long-time associate Suzanne de Passe.

Throughout the decades with stars like Martha and the Vandellas, Diana Ross and the Supremes, the Commodores, Smokey Robinson, Stevey Wonder, and Michael Jackson Motown brought African-American music into the fabric of mainstream American music and culture. Through its music and movies, Motown Records and Berry Gordy have left a legacy that will never fade.

CHAPTER ELEVEN: NORTH CAROLINA MUTUAL INSURANCE COMPANY

Profile

- Listed #1 on the June 1996 BLACK ENTERPRISE Top 100 list of Insurance Companies with 475 employees, over $9.5 billion in insurance in force and $215.814 million in assets. Has been number one for the last 25 years.
- Formed in 1898 by John Merrick and Dr. Aaron McDuffie Moore with the purpose of making insurance more available to the poor of Durham, NC.
- Most influential forces on the company over the years have been Merrick, Moore, Charles Clinton Spaulding, his cousin Asa T. Spaulding, William Jesse Kennedy, Jr., and William Jesse Kennedy III. Current leader is Bert Collins.
- Part of its philosophy involved extensive philanthropic work to benefit Durham's African-American community.
- One of few minority-owned insurance companies to have survived the Great Depression and other recessions.
- Company leaders instrumental in involving Durham's Blacks in politics through organizations such as the Urban League and the Durham Committee of Negro Affairs (DCNA).
- Has been instrumental in creating a strong African-American business community in Durham as well as a solid Black middle class.

Summary

North Carolina Mutual Insurance Company was created by John Merrick and Dr. Aaron McDuffie Moore in 1898 to primarily serve the insurance needs of Durham's low-income African-American population. North Carolina Mutual's first president was Charles Clinton Spaulding, who ran the company from 1900 until 1952. C. C. Spaulding was hired by Merrick and Moore just in time to save the young company from faltering. Under his leadership, the company grew steadily and consistently, and in the process got Durham's Black business community off the ground. Spaulding expanded the company's business over time, first in North Carolina, later into other states. He proved to be successful at getting the company through various rough periods, the worse of them being the Great Depression of the late 1920's and early 1930's.

The deaths of Merrick and Moore, in 1919 and 1923 respectively, brought new leadership to North Carolina Mutual. For the three decades following their deaths, C. C. Spaulding led the company with his second cousin Asa T. Spaulding and William Jesse Kennedy, Jr. By the time of C. C.'s death in 1952, North Carolina Mutual had reached assets of $38 million and had an insurance in force of over $179 million.

William J. Kennedy, Jr. succeeded C. C. Spaulding as President, a position he served until 1959, leading the company through continued growth. In his seven-year tenure, North Carolina Mutual's assets increased to over $67 million and its insurance in force increased to $337 million. Asa T. Spaulding took over as President of the company in 1959. Spaulding, who in 1932 had become the country's first Black actuary, led the company successfully during the Civil Rights era, increasing its assets and insurance in force consistently. Spaulding retired from his position in 1967 and even after his retirement remained involved in the growth of Durham's African-American community through his involvement in politics and various community organizations.

Spaulding was succeeded by John Goodloe, who served as President for five years, until 1972. Goodloe was in turn succeeded by William Jesse Kennedy III, the son of William J. Kennedy, Jr. Under his leadership, North Carolina Mutual hired increased numbers of White insurance salespeople to service the increase in White clientele, including large corporations that had been serviced since the 1960's. The company continued growing consistently under his rule. Kennedy was the President of North Carolina Mutual for almost two decades, until 1990, when Bert Collins took over the position. Today, North Carolina Mutual is listed as number one on **BLACK ENTERPRISE**'s top 100 list of insurance companies with total assets of over $200 million and a staff of 475.

History

Various men have been instrumental in the building and success of North Carolina Mutual. One of them is Charles Clinton Spaulding, who ran North Carolina

Mutual from 1900 until his death in 1952, and in the process got Durham's Black business community off the ground. Over his career, C. C. Spaulding became not only an important businessman but also an important political leader.

Spaulding was born on August 1, 1874, near Wilmington, North Carolina. Spaulding's father was a successful farmer, blacksmith, cabinetmaker, and community leader. As a child, Spaulding received only a limited amount of formal education for he spent most of his time working for his father. Barely literate, at age twenty, in 1894, Spaulding moved to Durham to live with Dr. Aaron McDuffie Moore, his uncle and one of the organizers of the North Carolina Mutual. While under Moore's wing, he enrolled in the Whitted School, a private school, and worked at a variety of jobs, such as waiter and dishwasher, in order to support himself. When he found it difficult to keep up with his schoolwork, Spaulding spent two years working as a cook for a wealthy White family. It was finally at age 24, in 1898, that Spaulding obtained his high school diploma. After graduation, Spaulding embarked onto his first, albeit unsuccessful, business venture. Spaulding became the manager of a local cooperative grocery store in which twenty-five of Durham's leading Blacks had invested. It did not take long before the store started to experience financial trouble, leading most investors to withdraw their investments. Within two years Spaulding was left with a bare grocery store and $300 in debt.

Dr. Moore and a man by the name of John Merrick brought Spaulding luck at this time of despair. Merrick, the son of a slave, and Moore, the son of free landowners and owner of Durham's first African-American-owned pharmacy, had formed North Carolina Mutual Insurance Company in 1898 but had had trouble keeping it above ground. [1] By 1900 the company was almost on the brink of collapse. As Moore and Merrick were trying to reorganize and save their company, they bought out their partners and started looking for someone to devote himself to the management of their company. Moore had witnessed the collapse of Spaulding's grocery store, but had also observed an impressive entrepreneurial ability in his nephew during those two years. This, as well a the fact that he was family, led Moore and Merrick to offer then twenty-six-year-old Spaulding the position of general manager of the company.

During those early years, Spaulding's responsibilities included recruiting agents, and selling policies on street corners and door to door. Spaulding proved successful, and as he signed more and more policyholders, the company's premium rose consistently, allowing Spaulding to begin recruiting a sales force. Within six months of beginning to hire a sales force, Spaulding had agents in twenty-eight towns in North Carolina. The increase in premiums was beneficial to the company but also doubled expenses, so for Spaulding this was a difficult time financially, for there was very little money to spare after all expenses were paid (Moore and Merrick had other business interests to provide them with income). North Carolina Mutual's most critical times took place during these years, especially during 1901 and 1902. Given that 1901 was a year of many sick and death claims, and Spaulding's office and travel expenses were steep, in the fall of that year, Moore and Merrick had to loan the company $300 to save it. Early 1902 did not fare any better, losses continued to exceed the company's profits, and, in February, again Moore and Merrick had to advance money to save the company. Spaulding continued his hard work, however, helping to bring the company past the crisis. By 1903, the company was still fighting a slight deficit, but was finally finding itself with premiums exceeding claims for the first time in two years.

1903 was also a significant year for Spaulding because it was then that he became the first of the three to receive a set salary. The company was financially stable; Moore, Merrick, and Spaulding were finally receiving a steady income, so it was decided that in order for North Carolina Mutual to continue its upward movement, it was time for an aggressive expansion. Spaulding realized that the only way to do this would be by advertising their services to the greater population. That same year the company started what would become a very successful advertising approach. Spaulding decided to publish *North Carolina Mutual*, a company newspaper that could serve a dual purpose, as a community newspaper for the Black community of Durham, as well as a powerful advertising tool. The monthly magazine, as well as other advertising tools such as pencils, matches, fans, thermometers, and blotters, proved to be successful.

Given the success of his twenty-eight offices in North Carolina, Spaulding next set out to expand the company's range outside of North Carolina, mostly into

South Carolina, as well as expand its insurance services. Previously, the company had sold affordable combination life, sickness, and accident policies to the poor on an "industrial basis", which meant that payments were made in small weekly premiums (which the insurance agents had to make house calls to collect). This system was more expensive for the policyholder and costly for North Carolina Mutual to administrate, so in 1903 Spaulding began to offer the option of "straight life" policies without the sickness and accident benefits. In 1904, he introduced North Carolina Mutual's first ordinary whole life plans as well as their first twenty-year endowment plans. Spaulding was on his way to turning North Carolina Mutual into a full-line life insurance company.

With all the expansion of services taking place, Moore, Merrick and Spaulding decided it was time to expand their headquarters, so they decided to build a new office building on the edge of White-dominated downtown. Between 1904 and 1906, the company bought additional lots to this building and added to it, forming a large Black business complex which housed not only their offices but also the offices of two Black lawyers, medical offices, clothing stores, offices of the Black newspaper, and others. North Carolina Mutual's offices stayed in this building the next two decades, until 1921, when they moved their offices into a marble-trimmed, modern, six-story complex Spaulding had decided to build a year prior.

Spaulding's first decade with North Carolina Mutual proved itself a successful one. The company experienced impressive growth during this time, reaching 1911 with a premium income of $250,000, assets of nearly $120,000, insurance of over $2 million, and almost 500 employees. By 1913, Spaulding had also used the company for philanthropic work, helping the Black community of Durham by supporting its churches, helping it found a hospital, North Carolina Central College, three newspapers and setting up a library. [2] Finally, Spaulding hired increasing numbers of Black college graduates, which in turn served to help create a thriving Black intellectual community in Durham.

The company experienced its first major change in the 1920's with the death of John Merrick in 1919 followed with the death of Dr. Moore in 1923. Fortunately, the deaths of Merrick and Moore did not affect the company's profits, and it continued to grow steadily, becoming increasingly profitable during the first half of the 1920's. North Carolina Mutual transitioned from being led by John Merrick, Dr. A.M. Moore, and Spaulding, to after 1925 being under the leadership of C.C. Spaulding, William J. Kennedy, Jr., and Asa T. Spaulding (Spaulding's second cousin). In 1921, to less success, Spaulding created the Negro Insurance Association, and during this decade served as vice president of Bankers Fire Insurance of Durham, and was a member of the National Negro Bankers Association. The second half of the 1920's proved a little less fruitful, in part due to the Great Depression of the late 1920's. Problems in southern agriculture forced cutbacks after 1926, and by 1929 North Carolina Mutual's insurance in force had fallen from $46 million in 1926 to $39 million. Although these times were testing ones for the company, under C. C. Spaulding's leadership it survived without any major setbacks. By 1939, the company's premium income had been restored and insurance in force had recovered from its 1929 fall, managing to surpass their previous record set in 1925.

In 1938, in yet another of his philanthropic gestures, Spaulding rescued the faltering National Negro Business League, of which he had been a life-long member and served as its President for several years. The Great Depression also marked Spaulding's increased involvement in politics, where he became a strong supporter of Franklin Roosevelt's New Deal. He became a vital figure in leading North Carolina Blacks from the Republican to the Democratic party and before long became known as the most influential Black democrat in North Carolina. Spaulding advocated African-American involvement in politics and became increasingly more influential both at the state and the national level. The governor of North Carolina appointed Spaulding to the state Council on Unemployment and Relief, and he became national chairman of the Urban League's Emergency Advisory Council. Spaulding's most significant political and community contribution was his leadership of the Durham Committee of Negro Affairs (DCNA), which organized in 1935, had as its primary goal to encourage and make voting accessible to Blacks, thus bringing about political and social reforms. Through his work in this organization, Spaulding was instrumental in bringing about Black political, economic, and civil rights victories.

During World War II and the years following it, the company continued its growth under C. C. Spaulding's leadership, reaching assets of almost $38 million and an insurance in force of over $179 million by 1952. North Carolina Mutual was now the largest Black business in the United States, a position it maintained for several years. Spaulding passed away in 1952, and given the enormous success of North Carolina Mutual, most people thought he had died a millionaire. In fact, he was worth much less than the general population was made to believe. Spaulding owned no stock in the firm, had been a salaried employee all his life, at his death being worth only $200,000, which at the time could sustain a comfortable lifestyle, but by no means meant a millionaire lifestyle. Even if he was not extremely wealthy, Spaulding did have power within and outside of the company through his contacts with influential Whites. He was also extremely powerful in the realm of education, serving on the Boards of Trustees of Howard University and Shaw University, and campaigning to save financially-strapped Black colleges from extinction. In 1980, Spaulding became the first African-American to be inducted into the national Business Hall of Fame by *Fortune* magazine and Junior achievement.

In 1952, William Jesse Kennedy, Jr., who had been with the company since 1925, succeeded C.C. Spaulding as president. This event did not cause much turbulence for the company, for Kennedy had been running its day-to-day operations for the last three decades already. Kennedy, like C.C. Spaulding, was one of the most influential forces to lead North Carolina Mutual. He was born in Andersonville, Georgia on June 15, 1898, and as a young boy received a good formal education from the Americus Institute as well as taking up his family's carpentry trade. Following graduation, Kennedy worked as a carpenter and traveling salesman for several years until he moved to Savannah, where he started selling insurance for another Black-owned insurance company. In 1916, he came to the attention of Spaulding and his partners, who asked him to come on board as the manager of their Savannah office. Kennedy ran the Savannah office until 1919, where he increased revenues by 500 percent. Following John Merrick's death in 1919, the Durham office asked Kennedy to come to their headquarters and manage the Ordinary Department. A year later, Kennedy became part of the Board of Directors, and after the death of Dr. Moore in 1923, Kennedy became a powerful player alongside C.C. Spaulding and Asa T. Spaulding. During the 1920's, Kennedy served as assistant secretary and office manager under John Moses Avery, later gaining control of the company's entire operation. During the 1930's, Kennedy was corporate secretary of the company, in 1932 also being named Vice President. During the three decades that preceded his presidency of the company, Kennedy's role was of principal problem solver, generally managing the company during this time and helping the company survive the difficult Great Depression.

Kennedy served as President of North Carolina Mutual from 1952 to 1959, leading the company through continued growth, increasing its assets from $38 million at the time of C.C. Spaulding's death, to over $67 million by the end of his presidency. The company's insurance in force also saw a steep increase, rising from $179 million to $337 million in only seven years. In 1959, Kennedy ascended to becoming Chairman of the Board of Directors, which he served in for two years before becoming Honorary Chairman, always staying very active in the leadership of the company. In other ventures, Kennedy also served as Chairman of the Board of Mechanics and Farmers Bank and of the Mutual Savings and Loan Association. He was involved in various community issues outside of the company such as his membership of the North Carolina State Board of Higher Education and his role as trustee and treasurer of the White Rock Baptist Church. Kennedy was also one of the founders of the Durham NAACP, whom he was honored by at that organization's Freedom Fund Dinner in 1977. Kennedy remained involved in the workings of the company until his death in 1985.

Asa T. Spaulding succeeded Kennedy as president in 1959. Spaulding, C. C.'s second cousin, was born in rural North Carolina to Armstead and Annie Bell Spaulding on July 2, 1902. Spaulding's father was a farmer and businessman who, among other ventures, ran a general store. He received his formal education in a one-room school in his home community until, at age 17, Spaulding came to Durham and enrolled in the National Training School. Asa Spaulding was able to enroll in this private school through a tuition scholarship and with the help of North Carolina Mutual's Dr. Moore and his family, whom he stayed with during this time, doing odd jobs to earn room and board. Until his graduation in 1923, during his summers, Asa Spaulding worked for Moore's company, still unaware that his future would lie with the insurance company. Upon graduating, Spaulding returned to his hometown to teach at his old one-room school. By 1924, however, he was back working at North Carolina Mutual, later that year taking one semester off to attend Howard University, soon again to return to the company to work and save for his college education.

In 1927, his dream of completing his college education finally started to come into motion when he enrolled at New York University to study accounting. This was an impressive move for an African-American person in these times, given that there was only one Black CPA in the entire United States. While attending New York University, one of Spaulding's professors suggested he consider becoming an actuary given there was not a single Black actuary in the country at that time. North Carolina Mutual had been using external White actuaries to do their actuarial work at that time, which inspired Asa Spaulding to pursue the suggestion of his professor. After receiving his Bachelor's degree in accounting from New York University, he enrolled in graduate school at the University of Michigan to study actuarial science. After he received his Master's degree in 1932, Spaulding went on to first serve an apprenticeship at a renowned actuarial firm, and then with F. B. Dilts, an actuary of the White Home Security Life Insurance Company in Durham. In January 1933, Spaulding returned to North Carolina Mutual to establish, staff and supervise its actuarial department, making it unnecessary for the company to any longer out-source its actuarial work.

Asa Spaulding's first two years as actuary were met with such tremendous success that the company elected him Assistant Secretary, just one position under William J. Kennedy in the hierarchy of the company. In 1938, he became the youngest member of the Board of Directors, and in 1945 he became Controller of the company. When Kennedy succeeded C.C. Spaulding as President in 1952, Asa Spaulding was promoted to the position of Vice President. Finally, in 1959 came his promotion as successor to Kennedy as President of North Carolina Mutual. During Spaulding's presidency in the 1960's, despite the fact that the civil rights movement had brought about changes which had caused White insurance companies to hire more Blacks and to write more insurance for Blacks, North Carolina Mutual continued to grow substantially. The company's assets increased from $60 million in 1958 to $94 million in 1968, and its insurance in force grew from $255 million to $467 million in that same period of time. By 1968, North Carolina Mutual served around 800,000 policyholders and held thirty-six branch offices.

In 1966 Spaulding completed perhaps one of his greatest accomplishments while president of the company: a new, twelve-storied office building, at the time the largest private building ever constructed in Durham. [3] Spaulding retired in 1967 and lived another two and a half decades before passing away in 1990. After his retirement, Spaulding ran for the county commission seat, and was successful (unlike his first try in 1954), becoming the first African-American in history to be elected to this position. Like his second cousin, Spaulding had become involved in politics, unsuccessfully running for mayor in 1971. Some of Spaulding's other political achievements during his time with North Carolina Mutual include his vice chairmanship of the Durham Human Relations Committee from 1957 to 1964 (a position he took over from his second cousin, C.C. Spaulding, upon his death in 1957), and his chairmanship of the North Carolina Advisory Committee to the Commission on Civil Rights. Also, in the year of his retirement, Spaulding joined other wealthy African-American business leaders to from the National Negro and Professional Committee, an organization which tried to raise $1 million to finance NAACP lawsuits which concerned themselves with enforcing of civil rights legislation. Spaulding won an impressive number of awards during his lifetime, one of the most significant ones being Howard University (where he served on the Board of Trustees) renaming their insurance society the Asa T. Spaulding Insurance Society.

One of the main problems that confronted North Carolina Mutual during the 1960's was defining the extent to which it could still be considered a 'Black-owned' company. When Asa Spaulding retired in 1967, he was succeeded by John Goodloe, and soon after his coming to power, the company signed a number of large group insurance contracts with corporate giants such as IBM, General Motors, Chrysler, and Procter & Gamble. The signing of these large clients brought about the largest increase in insurance in force for the company, growing from $438 million in 1969 to over $1 billion in 1971, nearly half of this tremendous growth being due to these large contracts. Given that the company at this time possessed a large number of White policyholders, and in a mutual insurance company policyowners own part of the company as shareholders, technically North Carolina Mutual could not be considered 'Black-owned' any longer. The ownership now rested in the hands of these corporate giants.

The most significant source of African-American influence on the company remaining at this time, as well as the key to Black political power in Durham, was the Durham Committee on Negro Affairs, organized by C.C. Spaulding in 1935. Even after C. C.'s death, the committee had continued being dominated by North Carolina Mutual officials, which in turn did much to ensure that the committee remain focused on the problems of Durham's African-American population. (Incidentally, during the 1970's and 1980's, one of the major players on the Durham Committee on Negro Affairs was Kenneth Bridgeforth Spaulding, son of Asa).

John Goodloe, Asa Spaulding's successor, acted as president of the company for only five years, in 1972 passing the torch to William J. Kennedy III, son of North Carolina Mutual's own William J. Kennedy. Born in Durham on October 24, 1922, Kennedy received his formal education first in Durham and later graduated from Virginia State College in 1942 with a degree in business administration. After a limited tour in World War II, he attended the Wharton School at University of Pennsylvania, where he earned his MBA in 1946, two years later obtaining a second MBA from New York University. [4] After graduating from New York University, Kennedy joined his father at North Carolina Mutual, where, over the next decade, he worked in several of the company's departments. In 1959 he was named Controller, which he served as until he was named Vice President in 1970, and then finally achieved the position of President and Chairman of the Board in 1972, a position he held for almost two decades, until 1990, when he retired. [5]

Under Kennedy's leadership, North Carolina Mutual hired increased numbers of White insurance salespeople to service the increase in White clientele the company had experienced since the 1960's. [6] The company continued growing slowly but consistently. The company's slow growth during the 1980's prompted Kennedy to begin phasing out industrial insurance. Kennedy realized that what had been the staple of North Carolina Mutual for eighty years was beginning to pose a problem for the company, and so he began to phase it out and began diversifying the company's services. In 1986, he set up North Carolina Mutual Capital Management Group (NCM Capital), an investment advisory firm meant to aggressively pursue the huge $3 trillion pension and corporate fund management business. [7] By 1989, NCM Capital was overseeing "$500 million worth of assets for thirty clients, including Chrysler, IBM and the Chicago Transit Authority." [8]

In 1988, North Carolina Mutual bought Virginia Mutual Benefit Life Insurance Company, a Richmond-based company. The acquisition brought NCM some $250 million in insurance in force and close to $1 million in assets. [9] All these moves of the late 1980's proved successful, by 1989 the company reached a peak of $215.7 million in assets, an insurance in force of $7.9 billion, and a net investment income of just under $14 million, making it the largest Black-managed insurance company in the world. [10]

Upon Kennedy's retirement in 1990, Bert Collins took over the position of Chief Executive Officer, after twenty-three years with North Carolina Mutual. Collins started working for the company in 1967, when he was hired as resident CPA. Collins received his Bachelor's degree from Tillotson College in Austin, TX and then earned his MBA at the University of Detroit. Later, while at NCM, Collins attended North Carolina Central College where he obtained his law degree. At the time of Collins' succession to CEO, NCM was not faring very well. The economy was slow and the sales of insurance policies were not at their best, these factors and others causing NCM's operating income to be a negative $1.616 million, and the company's net income to be a negative $819,745 by the end of that year.

The first steps Collins took to stabilize the company's environment involved the decreasing of expenses. The sales force was decreased from 325 to 240, a move that led to a $2 million decrease in expenses and a $4 million decrease in commissions paid to salespeople. The only negative effect of this move was that the decrease of salespeople led to a decline in policies sold, and thus a decline in premium income was experienced. Collins also changed the company's focus back to the more basic insurance companies, moving away from the large diversification of policies that had taken place before he took over the helm of the company. Under his leadership, North Carolina Mutual began seeking growth by "capitalizing on such provinces as pension fund advisory services and real estate management." [11]

In 1991, still as part of Collins' "war on expenses", the four-year-old NCM Capital Management was sold. Maceo Sloan, the chief investment officer for NCM Life Insurance Co., led the management buy-out of NCM Capital Management, a subsidiary of the insurance firm, to form Sloan Financial Group Inc. The sale brought North Carolina Mutual a $1 million profit, money which it immediately invested in "a new training facility for new sales personnel and ... an on-line computer system linking the 26 district offices to 11 states and the District of Columbia". [12] The sale brought the company's net income up to $4 million, but was not able to keep up its sales for the following year, sales falling to $713,036 in 1992.

As of 1993, Collins' goals have been to create new markets and new insurance products. He would like to attract a whole new level of customer, a customer that does not fit NCM's traditional lower and working class strata. Through a new customer market and new products, Collins hopes to raise the company's earnings and create a sales staff which is more equipped to deal with today's computer technology. A one-week training session has been instituted for all NCM employees at the Durham headquarters for this very purpose. Also, Collins has instituted a sales plan that offers life insurance to staff, graduates and families of historically Black colleges and universities.

Today, under Collins' leadership it is still the number one insurance company listed on **BLACK ENTERPRISE**'s BE 100 list. Not only has North Carolina performed well above the expectations of many, it has also played a key role over the last century in the creation of a solid, Black middle class in the city of Durham and elsewhere, even while handling increasing amounts of White business.

CHAPTER TWELVE: CARVER FEDERAL SAVINGS BANK

Profile

* First Black-owned and operated federally-chartered savings and loan association in New York State.
* Chartered by the Federal Home Loan Bank Board on November 5, 1948, and in 1949 began business with one employee at 55 West 125th Street in Harlem, New York.
* Founded by a group of thirteen public-spirited Harlem businessmen and women for the purpose of improving the quality of life in their Harlem community.
* Headed by Joseph E. Davis, a former employee of Emigrant Savings Bank. The institution expanded to three offices under Davis' leadership until his death in 1968. From 1969 to 1995 was headed by Richard E. Green. Since Greene's retirement it has been under leadership of Thomas Clark, Jr.
* Has expanded continuously since its inception, currently consisting of eight branches and by 1993, holding over $300 million in revenues.
* Staple of the Black banking community, focusing on, but not limited to the Harlem community, providing banking services, employment, and loans.
* Carver Federal Savings Scholarship Program was established in 1986, and awarded nearly $200,000 in scholarships to 190 students in its first six years.
* Carver Bank went public with an initial offering of $22 million in October 1994, becoming the first Black bank to trade on NASDAQ and one of only eleven Black publicly traded companies.

Summary

The first efforts to build Carver Federal Savings and Loan Association took place in 1943, led by a group of concerned citizens who wanted to make mortgages available to working class African-American families. Their efforts, however, due to the lack of state-wide and federal interest, took six years to come to fruition. It was finally on January 5, 1949 that Carver opened its first office in Harlem, starting with assets of $225,000 pledged by 800 Harlemites. In honor of scientist and inventor George Washington Carver, whose birthdate was January 5, the founders named the association Carver Federal Savings and Loan Association. Carver came at a time when conditions for its success were ideal: post-World War II Blacks throughout the city of New York needed money to buy homes but were not being offered mortgage services by White-owned banks. Additionally, there were no other Black-owned banking institutions they could turn to.

The 50's and 60's proved to be extremely successful. Carver experienced a steady growth in assets, mortgage portfolios and customers. As time progressed, Carver expanded its office space and built new branches throughout the city. By cleverly positioning its branch offices, Carver managed to stay in step with the changing movements of populations in and around the city. By 1954, Carver's growth had surpassed 150 older associations of the state. By 1957 Carver's growth was such that the association was restructured to convert the officers of the Board of Directors into paid employees. An office in Brooklyn, their first branch outside of Harlem, was opened in 1961. By this point Carver had already risen in rank to 94th place among 233 savings and loan associations in New York State. Since many White banks continued redlining Black neighborhoods, Carver continued providing mortgages and savings for working class Black families.

In 1969, Carver Federal Savings and Loan Association's name was changed to Carver Federal Savings Bank by its new president, Richard T. Greene. Carver continued serving the Black banking community and continued expanding its banking services through the addition of branches throughout the city. The 1970's were marked by a decline in economic conditions in Harlem, which led Carver to more cautious investing, and brought its slowest growth since its inception. The bank, however, managed to stay profitable through the opening of more branches in the city and one in Long Island. Carver managed to rank in first place on the BE 100 list of Black businesses between 1974 and 1978. No matter how trying the times, as the seventies and late eighties proved themselves to be, Carver always proved itself to be a survivor. After hitting a low 0.28 percent return on assets between 1988 and 1990, Carver rebounded in 1991, its assets rising $20.8 million. By 1992, Carver was worth $321.7 million in assets and had 100 employees. Carver is the largest minority savings and loan association and is larger than any of the nation's Black-owned commercial banks.

Now known as Carver Bancorp Inc., it is currently listed as the number one Financial Company on **BLACK ENTERPRISE**'s Top 100 list, with a total of $415.8 million in assets and over $60 million in loans.

History

The first record of Carver's beginnings can be found in a letter written by Hawthorne E. Lee, an insurance executive, on March 1, 1943. The letter was addressed to the Secretary of State in Albany, New York, and requested the requirements for starting a Building and Loan Association in New York State. Lee's interest in loan associations had been sparked after speaking with a friend, John Sylvester Stewart, who was Secretary-Treasurer of a Loan Association in North Carolina. Lee subsequently spoke to Mabel E. Beaud'Huy, a real estate insurance broker, and James Felt, then president of the Urban League. As a result of these and other conversations with various people, a group of interested citizens was invited to attend a meeting in the auditorium of the YMCA's Harlem Branch. Joseph E. Davis became Chairman of what would become Carver Federal Savings and Loan Association. During this meeting, a prospectus was drawn up and an application was made to the State of New York for permission to open a savings and loan association, and an interim Board of Directors was selected.

Under the leadership of co-chairs of this drive, Walter A. Miller and Clifford A. Daly, and the coordination and public relations efforts of Reverend M. Moran Weston, the movement to form Carver Savings and Loan Association quickly gained momentum. By July 1945 they had already passed the $200,000 in assets mark, and were quickly making their way to the $300,000 goal required by New York State to become a loan association. Despite this momentum, however, the next two years proved to be trying ones, the problem lying not with the organizers, but rather at the New York State level, where the project stalemated due to a lack of interest. Among those who were instrumental in providing help and encouragement were John R. Byers, a professor at City College and consultant to the New York State League of Savings and Associations, John S. Stewart, secretary-treasurer of the Mutual Building and Loans Association of

North Carolina, and John W. Harris, Jr., secretary-treasurer of the Savings and Loan Association of Philadelphia.

In order to move the project ahead, Byers put the group in touch with a savings and loan association lawyer, and suggested that they withdraw the state petition for a loan association and instead file an application with the Federal Home Loan Bank Board such that they could operate as a federal institution. This move proved to be just what the project needed. An application was submitted to the Federal Home Loan Bank Board in July of 1947, a hearing was held before the Board in February of 1948, and the application was finally approved in May of that same year. In November, a charter was granted, making Carver Federal Savings and Loan Association the first financial institution to be started, organized, and financed almost entirely by African-Americans in New York. In December the first organizational meeting was held at the United Mutual Auditorium, and all its officers were elected. On January 5, 1949 — George Washington Carver's birthdate— Carver Federal Savings and Loan Association celebrated its formal opening at its office on West 125th Street in Harlem, starting with assets of $225,000 pledged by 800 Harlemites. When Carver got its charter to open, the pledges were easily obtained since it was in response to a community's dire need that this association had been created. Post World War II Harlemites and Blacks throughout the city needed money to buy homes but were being barred from home financing at White-owned banks, and there were no other Black-owned banking institutions they could turn to. After six years of struggle, surveying, organizing, and convincing first state, then federal banking authorities that African-Americans wanted homes, could care for them, and were willing to pay for them, the savings and loan association finally came to full fruition.

By the end of 1949, their first year, there were two employees and Carver's assets already amounted to nearly $830,000, nearly $100,000 being invested in mortgages on Black-owned homes. Also, Washington Heights Federal Savings and Loan, in a gesture of support, sold a batch of their mortgages to Carver, providing the new bank with a six- percent return on its investment. 1950, their second year in business, was marked with high notes and low notes. Their departments experienced substantial growth, but in May, many customers and friends were saddened by the death of Walter A. Miller, the Association's first President. William R. Hudgins, then vice-president, became acting President and the following year was formally elected to that position. By the end of 1950, Carver Federal continued its steady growth, increasing its assets to a total of over $1.5 million, its mortgage portfolio increasing to $1.3 million, and the number of customers growing to over 3,500.

By 1951, Carver Federal Savings' growth called for a relocation. On January 12, 1952 its offices were moved to a new, two-story location in Harlem. By early 1952, assets had reached a new high total of over $2 million, a gain of over half a million over the previous year, home loans had increased to $1.8 million, and savers increased to a total of 5,390. By the end of 1952, its disclosed assets had increased an additional 48.6 percent to over $3 million, its personal savings had increased to $2.5 million and the total number of savers had risen to near 9,500. Carver Federal's growth was unstoppable, with all its departments growing and its mortgage portfolios and savings accounts constantly on the rise. By 1954, Carver's growth had surpassed 150 older associations of the state. With the resignation of James Felt and the election of George L. Jones to the Board of Directors in that year came an increase of twenty-three percent in total assets to an unprecedented $5 million.

A growth of at least twenty percent in total assets continued through the 1950's. By 1957, the growth of Carver Federal Savings was such that the Board of Directors, many of who also held titles as officers, decided a restructuring of their organization was necessary. They relinquished their titles on the board in order to fully perform the duties of their office as paid employees. Staff promotions and additions took place with this new policy, under which Carver continued growing and developing, showing a 19.3 percent increase in total savings that year. By the end of the 1950's, Carver was beginning to face increasingly intense competition, yet, despite this, managed to obtain substantial gains in assets, savings, home mortgages and reserves. By 1959, C.C. Gales had been elected to the Board of Directors as successor to the late Aldrich Turner, who had passed away a year prior, and an application was made to the Federal Home Loan Bank Board, requesting permission to open a branch office of the Association in Brooklyn.

With the new decade came the modernization and expansion in 1960 of their new headquarters into two adjacent buildings on West 125th Street, increasing the size of their banking facilities by almost three times its previous size. In August of that same year, permission was granted to Carver Federal Savings to open an office in Brooklyn, which opened in February 1961, in its own building on Fulton Street, with future president Richard T. Greene as the office manager. By the end of 1960, Carver had risen in rank to 94th place among 233 savings and loan associations operating in New York State. The first six months of 1961 set yet another record for Carver with an increase in assets of over $1.6 million dollars, the highest gain for any semi-annual period in the Association's history, and an increase for a six month period that almost equaled the gain for entire 1960. And so, with its twin goals of helping people by providing a safe depository for their money, and by supplying first mortgages to buy, build or refinance their homes on easy and liberal terms, Carver Federal Savings faced the remainder of 1961 with continuing high standards and steady growth.

Through the savvy positioning of its branch offices, Carver managed to stay in step with the changing movements of populations in and around the city, in the 1950's, for example, capitalizing on the transition of Harlem and Upper Manhattan from White to Black ownership. Carver challenged the downtown banking competition head-on with a branch in the opposition's own turf, becoming the first and only Black-owned financial institution in the city to make such a move. White banks, meanwhile, waited for Carver to fold up, but as Carver became progressively more successful, White banks began taking a new attitude toward the Black community, now as a possible investment. Pushed by Carver's example, competing institutions began to provide jobs and started offering mortgages to African-Americans. The White lending monopoly began to crack, and as many banks continued redlining Black neighborhoods, Carver continued providing more mortgages to working class African-American families. Through the years, Carver became a national leader in Black family financing, and while doing so helped pry open the gates of mainstream banking to Black New Yorkers. Carver brought about a monumental change in the nation's financial capital, expanding the availability of home mortgages for African-American working families, and breaking the lending monopoly previously held by the major banks.

Richard T. Greene was called to the Presidency in 1969 and changed the bank's name to Carver Federal Savings Bank. During Greene's presidency, Carver continued being a staple of the Black banking community, expanding continuously in its banking services and adding more branches. The investments made had a long-term and long-range impact that was felt for decades to come, marking the beginnings of a new class of Black homeowners. As a result of the declining economic conditions in Harlem, however, the 1970's proved to be a problematic decade for the bank. Carver continued to write home mortgages in Harlem, just moving more cautiously, shying away from properties located on abandoned blocks and limiting itself to mortgages on single family homes rather than large multiple family buildings. Also, by opening new branches in various other communities in New York City, as well as some of its northern suburbs of New York and Long Island, the bank remained profitable.

Despite it being a rough decade, between 1974 and 1978, Carver Federal Savings Bank still managed to rank in first place among savings and loan associations on **BLACK ENTERPRISE**'s list of top Black businesses (BE 100). In 1979, it slipped to second place on the BE 100, nevertheless managing to remain the leader in loans outstanding, at about $66 million. Carver marked this year with more than $78 million in assets and $69 million in deposits. Carver's slip to second place was due primarily to its minimal growth during 1978, given the high pressure of unemployment among its primary constituency and the generally poor economic conditions of the community. Also, some of those majority institutions which had previously redlined Black communities had become Carver's toughest competitors, in large part competing for the sons and daughters of those Black families whom Carver helped achieve home ownership in the 50's and 60's.

The late 1980's again proved to be a trying time after Carver averaged a meager 0.28 percent return on assets between 1988 and 1990. By 1991, however, Carver rebounded earning $1.7 million, more than it had earned in the three previous years combined and showed a 0.6 percent return on its assets. Carver's rebound began in the last few months of 1990, by November of that year having grown by almost thirty percent to $321.7 million in assets. Carver again proved itself to be a survivor.

In early 1991 the bank acquired a branch of the failed Nassau Savings and Loan Association in an attempt to turn it around. [1] That year, assets rose $20.8 million and Carver saw an increase of $44.1 million in mortgages and mortgage-backed securities.

By 1992, what had started as the first Black-owned and run financial institution, back in 1949 with only two employees, had grown to be an organization of 100 employees with $321.7 million in assets. What had started out of a "store front" on West 125th Street had grown to an institution with eight branches, seven in New York City (in Manhattan, Brooklyn, and Queens) and one in Roosevelt, Long Island. There is no other minority institution that either has or ever has had eight branches. Carver had become the largest minority savings and loans association, was larger than any of the nation's Black-owned commercial banks, and was the only remaining Black-owned bank in New York City, offering all types of services, from mortgage loans to automated teller machine cards. Even when it was hit by tragedy in 1992, with the burning down of its headquarters due to an electrical fire, Carver was able to survive without any major financial setbacks. Using insurance money and funds from its operating budget, Carver built a new $5 million four-storied office at its original location in Harlem.

In order to deal with the increasing competitiveness with other banks, whose branches are located in the same areas where Carver is located, Carver puts emphasis on doing things that its competition does not. One example is the accessibility Richard T. Green, Carver's president between 1969 and 1995, showed his customers. Most money-centered banks' CEOs cannot match this accomplishment. The bank's competitive advantage also comes from things like its strategic placement of its offices, which in part it acquired by buying out branches of majority-owned commercial banks that fled from minority neighborhoods. An example of this is its office near 23rd Street and Eighth Avenue, the center of the relatively affluent and integrated Chelsea neighborhood, a location not being served by any other Black-owned institution. Also, Carver has not let itself be limited by racial boundaries, developing and doing business wherever there is a need for mortgage and other bank services.

In the mid 1990's, with the company going public in 1994, Greene's retirement in 1995, and the hiring of his successor, Thomas Clark, Jr., came a change in mission for the bank. [2] The bank has now started to place greater emphasis on lending by creating a new mortgage center, which includes a small business division. Of its $363 million in assets, currently seventy percent of these are invested in mortgage loans. Greene's conservative approach to banking has been given up by Clark, a move which has proven itself successful, leading to and increase of over 100 percent in loans from $2 million in 1995 to $4.1 million for the first three months of 1996. When Clark first came to Carver, only about eleven percent of its assets were in direct loans, by early 1996 that amount had already gone up to twenty-one percent, Clark planning for it to reach thirty percent by the end of that year. Other benefits of Clark's presidency can be seen in the increase of Carver's mortgage portfolio of direct loans from $45 million to $80 million.

Other plans of Carver Federal Savings Bank, under the leadership of Clark, include a plan to work with the New York State Business Development Corporation and the New York State Small Business Development Centers in helping local entrepreneurs become stronger candidates for a loan. Also, Chemical and Chase Manhattan Bank have recently become partners with Carver Bank, a venture that should further increase its loan portfolio and restructure its balance sheet. In order to keep up with the changing times in the banking industry, Carver is offering many of the services of a commercial bank, including ATM cards, interest-bearing checking accounts and secured MasterCard and Visa credit cards. [3] This diversification of services, including Small Business Administration (SBA) loans, will enable it to compete better with other minority banks as well as with other savings and loans and commercial banks doing business in the inner-city. [4] Finally, Clark plans to further expand the range of the bank's offices by opening a branch in Mount Vernon, New York in 1996 and three others over the next four years.

Carver still considers itself a community development bank and is still the safest and best run Black-owned bank in the country. It rejected and survived a July 1996 hostile takeover attempt by Wall Streeter Joseph Curry. [5] In late July, corporate raider Curry sent a letter to Carver Federal asking that the bank postpone its 1996 annual meeting and consider his offer to purchase a thirty-five percent controlling stake in it. Curry proceeded to notify the media of his intention to buy a stake in the bank for up to $9.20 per share. Officials at the bank were upset about Curry's revelations to the media and questioned the legality of his takeover bid. The board officially rejected the takeover bid and in response reorganized such to strengthen their anti-takeover measures. [6 & 7]

Greene continues to sit on the bank's seven member Board of Directors, and since each board member is required to own at least one hundred shares, both Clark and Green own shares in the company. Carver's current $415 million in assets put it in the mid-size financial institution category, but Clark's plan is to grow its assets to $500 million and then take the bank into the new millennium as a billion dollar institution, putting it in the large-size category of financial institutions. Recently, Carver Federal Savings Bank moved from NASDAQ to AMEX, making it the only and first Black-owned firm on the American Stock Exchange (AMEX). This will probably prove to be a good move for Carver, given that the price of stocks sold on NASDAQ "generally exhibit higher volatility than those sold on AMEX". [8] When Carver first went public in 1994, its stock sold for about $10 a share. However, after only four months, their prices decreased to $7 a share. Since its move to AMEX, Carver's stock prices have been higher again, opening at $9.25 a share. Carver's President and CEO, Thomas Clark, Jr., not only sees this move as one that will hopefully increase their stock prices, but also sees AMEX as "a more efficient market" for Carver's stock and one that will "improve liquidity for stockholders and create greater visibility for the company." [9]

CHAPTER THIRTEEN: H. J. RUSSELL & COMPANY

Profile

- Herman J. Russell, who currently still owns and ran the company until December 1996, started his first business in 1952. Now, more than 40 years later, his company is the largest minority-owned general contractor in the country.
- H. J. Russell & Company is an umbrella company which was created in the 1980's to oversee the growing amount of companies Russell had created.
- Russell oversees some thirteen Atlanta-based companies that deal in contracting, publishing and television communications, property management, and food and beverage concessions and distribution.
- Among the more notorious projects taken on by H. J. Russell & Company are the Equitable Life Insurance Building, the Atlanta Stadium, the Martin Luther King, Jr. Community Center, parking decks at Atlanta's Hartsfield International Airport, and the Metro Atlanta Rapid Transit Authority (MARTA).
- H. J. Russell is the first African-American to ever have owned or been involved in ownership of either an NHL or NBA franchise.
- As of December 1996, the company's CEO and Vice Chairman has been R. K. Sehgal. Russell remains in the position of Chairman of the Board.
- Since 1990, the construction company has built or managed projects worth more than $2.4 billion. Contracts currently in the works exceed $600 million.

Summary

Herman J. Russell, President of H. J. Russell & Co., started his business ventures in his hometown of Atlanta at the age of fifteen, when he bought his first piece of land. Over the next three and a half decades, Herman established one of the largest Black-owned businesses in the nation and in the process built some of Atlanta's most impressive skyscrapers. Today, his mini- conglomerate does business nationally and Russell has built a $132 million empire.

Over the years, Russell has developed into a multi-faceted entrepreneur, creating businesses in contracting, publishing and television communications, property management, and food and beverage concessions and distribution. Russell is President and Chairman of some thirteen Atlanta-based companies, all under the huge umbrella of H. J. Russell & Company. Together the firms brought in $132 million in 1986, making the parent company the third-largest on the **BLACK ENTERPRISE** List of Top 100 Black businesses. In 1987, the estimated value of Russell's whole enterprise was said to be worth $118 million, and Russell's personal wealth has been estimated to be over $10 million. In 1989 H. J. Russell & Company held a staff of 1,500 across the United States. In 1994 it continued being a strong presence on **BLACK ENTERPRISE**'s Industrial/Service 100 list with $154 million in sales, and in 1996 staffed 1,200 people and was worth $172.8 million in sales.

Russell started his business life in construction, and it continues being the heart of Russell's diverse business empire. His construction division is comprised of five firms: **H. J. Russell Construction Co., Inc.**, **Interstate Construction Co., Inc.**, **Diversified Project Management Inc.** (DPM), **H. J. Russell Plastering Co.** and **Wet Walls Inc.** These firms undertake everything from construction of small and large-scale projects and plastering work to the management of other constructors' projects. In construction's related area of real estate, Russell owns three firms: **Gibraltar Land Inc.**, **Paradise Management Inc.** and **Tradeport Development Co., Inc.** These companies focus on real estate development and management of thirty-five apartment complexes that Russell owns throughout Georgia.

To buffer himself against setbacks, Russell ventured into some business areas unrelated to his trade, one area being the food-and-beverage industry. **Concessions International Inc.**, a $10 million enterprise that operates eight snack bars, restaurants and bars at major airports throughout the country, employs about 200 people at its locations in the Los Angeles, Chicago, Dallas/Fort Worth, Atlanta, Louisville, Hartford and Seattle airports. Russell's beverage division, **City Beverage Co.**, distributes such brands of beer as Strohs, Coors and Beck's to stores throughout the southern metropolitan Atlanta area. City Beverage alone accounted for $20 million in sales in 1995. Russell also owns a liquor store that one of his brothers runs, and two grocery stores. Finally, Russell also owns and is Chairman of the Board of **Russell-Rowe Communications Inc.**, which owns and operates WGXA-TV, an ABC affiliate in Macon, Ga., and he is part owner of a weekly newspaper, *The Atlanta Inquirer*.

History

Herman J. Russell was born on December 23, 1930, the youngest of eight children, in Atlanta, Georgia. Russell grew up on the streets of Summerhill, a working-class community near downtown Atlanta. His father worked as a plasterer, teaching Russell his trade at a young age. He first went to work with his father at age ten, working as a plasterer and laborer among other jobs. Having grown up in a family that stressed the importance of hard work, it did not take long before Russell decided to start his first own business venture. He was only a fifteen year-old sophomore at David T. Howard High School when he cut his first deal, paying $250 for a modest strip of land near his South Side Atlanta home. [1] Russell spent his spare time and three subsequent summers, as a high school student and later while a student of building construction at the Tuskegee Institute in Alabama, building a duplex on that property with the help of some friends. Russell had arrived at Tuskegee with only $250, enough to cover his first quarter in tuition. Russell rented the completed duplex property out, and using that money, as well as his earnings from an after-school plastering job, was able to finance his college education. [2] In the nearly five decades since that venture, the young deal maker has established the fourth-largest Black business in the nation, has constructed some of Atlanta's most impressive skyscrapers, and has fashioned a multifaceted business empire that stretches from the East Coast to the West.

In 1953, after completing his college degree in building construction, Russell returned to Atlanta with the intent of creating his own construction business. Russell found himself with only a limited amount of start-up capital, and was only able to buy himself an old pick up truck for $150 and hire one worker. [3] Using the company name H. J. Russell Plastering Company, Russell offered services in plastering and repairing buildings. It did not take long before Russell started taking on larger projects such as the building of new homes, bidding on construction contracts, and buying land. This increased opportunity allowed him to expand his business and hire a total of twenty-five employees and buy three pickup trucks.

In 1957, upon his father's death, Russell took over his family's modest business, Russell Plastering Co. Historically, opportunities for Blacks in the construction industry had been limited primarily to small-scale residential development, but Herman Russell was soon to set out and change history. When Russell first took the helm of his father's business, he immediately set out to expand its estimated $15,000 value. [4] Given the success of his previous ventures, Russell had been able to obtain a good credit rating, thus making him eligible for financing from commercial banks. With this added capital, Russell, who had started off focusing on the construction of duplexes, was able to quickly move up to building four-unit and eight-unit apartments. It was only in a small matter of time that he was building 400- and 500-unit complexes. In need of a company which would supervise these large units as well as other types of property management, and before apartment management was big business, Russell created a new division to his company in 1959: Paradise Management Inc., an apartment management firm. Yet again Russell had shown his keen business insight! Russell now owns an estimated 3,500 rental units in about eighteen cities in Georgia.

All throughout the expansion of his work, Russell continued focusing on building housing for low-and middle-income families, and, unlike others, after he did the construction he retained the ownership, while others in the business sold their developments. His focus on low-income housing made him eligible for various HUD (Department of Housing and Urban Development) programs, which financed the construction of many of Russell's endeavors. By 1978, Russell had completed more than 4,000 units and had $12 million worth of HUD work under his belt.

Russell's company met the 1960's with rapid growth. The city's and the federal government's expansion of financial aid for residential construction opened doors for Russell to find capital for his development projects. Government projects such as those implemented during the Nixon administration gave hundreds of millions of dollars in loans, grants, and contracts primarily to Southern firms run by Blacks, Russell being one of those African-American business owners to benefit from these programs. Furthermore, as his reputation spread, he got increasingly more construction contracts and more notoriety throughout the area. In December 1962, Russell was invited to join the Atlanta Chamber of Commerce. This invitation really came by mistake for the organization had not yet opened its doors to African-American members. He accepted the invitation and became the first Black member of the Atlanta Chamber of Commerce. [5] The late 1960's brought about a real turning point for Russell when he landed work on large commercial projects. His first large project was a $1 million subcontract on construction of the thirty-four story Equitable Life Insurance Building, still one of the tallest structures in downtown Atlanta, and work on the Atlanta Stadium. [6]

By the early 1970's, Russell was bidding on, and winning, major projects, including the Martin Luther King, Jr. Community Center, his first major public project. His expansion from private to public construction was boosted by the 1973 election of Atlanta's first Black mayor: Maynard Jackson. When Jackson introduced mandatory affirmative action programs during the 1970's, issuing a bold new policy requiring contractors doing business with the city to hire minority-owned companies as subcontractors or develop joint partnerships with minority businesses, Russell and other struggling Black-owned firms benefited substantially. Other projects Russell accomplished during this time were: the Metro Atlanta Rapid Transit Authority (MARTA) train station, the $18 million construction project of the parking decks at the Hartsfield International Airport and the $115 million Georgia Pacific Corporation office tower, then the largest office building in the Southeast and Atlanta's second tallest building. Russell's personal worth in 1972 was estimated to be some $10 million. [7] By 1974 Russell was said to be owner of or partner in fifteen firms and represented about $30 million worth of business in four Southeastern States. [8] Additional business ventures included a twelve percent stock ownership (he is the largest stock holder) of Citizens Trust Company, Atlanta's only African-American-owned bank. [9]

It is important to keep in mind, however, that although Russell benefited from affirmative action programs implemented by Maynard Jackson, he was already successful before their implementation. This success is reflected in the 1972 invitation he received to join the Omni Group, a group of investors who had bought the St. Louis Blues, a National Hockey League (NHL) franchise that eventually became the Atlanta Flames. Russell also bought the management rights to the new Omni, a sports convention center complex and bought ownership of the Atlanta Hawks, a National Basketball Association (NBA) team. Russell became the first African-American to ever own or be involved in ownership of either an NHL or NBA franchise.

The growth of the company continued with the 1976 creation of DDR International, Inc., a project management division. It operated under this name until 1984, when it was reorganized and renamed Diversified Project Management (DPM). The newly organized DPM functioned as a consulting firm of professional architects, engineers, and contractors who coordinated and managed information services to organizations involved in capital improvement programs. In the 1980's many of his projects included such notable ones as the Robert Woodruff Library at the Atlanta University Center, the Carter Presidential Center, and the Atlanta City Hall Complex. Projects such as these, among others, contributed to the more than $103.8 million in sales the company achieved in the 1980's. Russell's company had not experienced a single losing year since its inception in the 1950's — three decades of profit!

Given the rapid growth of his company, as well as its expansion well beyond the borders of Georgia, into the Carolinas, Massachusetts, and Colorado, in 1985 Russell created H. J. Russell and Company, an umbrella organization to oversee all of his firms, of which he is Chairman and until 1996 was Chief Executive Officer. In that same year, in order to gain better control of all aspects of the development process, Russell created his real estate division Gibraltar Land Inc. This division was meant to oversee activities in the areas of housing, office, and industrial park development. Recently, through Gibraltar, Russell built and opened 330 McGill Place, a $16 million luxury condominium complex near downtown Atlanta, one of the fastest-selling in the Southeast. Four other major development projects launched by Gibraltar have been a $100 million international business park near the airport, an $11 million apartment complex and a $5 million medical building. By 1994, this branch alone was experiencing over $20 million in revenues. By the mid 1980's, all of the company's divisions, including Russell's four construction operations (H. J. Russell Construction Company, Interstate Construction, H. J. Russell Plastering, and Wet and Dry Walls), were in full swing. The only significant challenge Russell has had to face over the years in the construction business has been to combat White majority partners' tendency to use Black-owned firms to get government contracts, then relegate those firms to backseat status once the project begins. Otherwise, H. J. Russell & Company has not experienced any major setbacks since his first business started in 1953.

Perhaps the single characteristic that most distinguishes Russell from his business peers is his raw entrepreneurial savvy. He has diversified over the years, reaching outside of the construction and real estate business into communications and foods and beverage distribution. He owns Russell-Rowe Communications, which operates WGXA-TV, an ABC affiliate in Macon, Georgia, owns a beverage distribution firm, City Beverage Company, which distributes various brands of beer throughout southern Atlanta, and finally, owns Concessions International Corporation, a $10 million company which manages food concessions in major airports across the United States. In addition to all divisions of his company, he has dabbled in a number of other business ventures. These include a grocery store, a liquor store, an insurance firm, a partnership in two nursing homes and his part ownership of two of Atlanta's professional sports teams, the NBA Hawks and the now-defunct NHL Flames. Russell also served on the advisory board of the Atlanta Olympic Organizing Committee that landed the bid of hosting the 1996 Summer Olympics in his hometown and was involved in a joint-venture that built the Georgia Dome, a site which held various Olympic events. [10]

Russell has been one of Atlanta's most philanthropic businessmen. He sees his businesses as a vehicle for creating institutions that are sorely lacking in the African-American community. He remains committed to inner-city development. Unlike most large Atlanta businesses, which locate downtown or on the mostly White North Side, Russell's headquarters are on the predominantly Black South Side, where development is needed most. Russell also sponsors Little League athletic teams in public housing projects, donates land to Black churches and contributes to schools and participates in fund-raising geared at youth programs, as well as many other charitable causes.

A prime example of Russell's commitment to the African-American community came during the civil right era, in the *Atlanta Inquirer*, a weekly paper

Russell helped create in the 1960's to give civil rights movement's crusaders a place to express their philosophies, frustrations and criticisms. Russell's home served as a retreat for Martin Luther King, Jr. during the civil rights movement, and still is a meeting place for Atlanta's Black power elite and political strategy sessions. Other projects which illustrate Russell's commitment to his community are the construction of the Maggie Russell Tower, a senior citizens' residence named in the memory of his mother, the General Daniel "Chappie" James Center for Aerospace Science and Health Education at Tuskegee University (his alma mater), and the renovation and expansion of Grady Memorial Hospital, Russell's birthplace.

Russell is also a devoted family man. He and his wife, Otelia, have three children. Their only daughter, Donata Major is executive vice president of Concessions International. Herman Jerome is executive vice president of City Beverage Co., and Michael is a graduate of the University of Virginia. Russell continues being active in all his businesses, is a founding member of the Atlanta Forum, an influential group of Atlanta's business elite, and is a member of Atlanta's Chamber of Commerce, where he acted as President in 1981 (and was the second-ever African-American to hold that position). He sits on the board of various civic and public bodies such as the Fulton-DeKalb Hospital Authority, Metropolitan Atlanta Community Chest, the YMCA and YWCA, the Boy Scouts and the General Advisory Committee for Vocational Education for the Atlanta and Fulton County school systems. [11] Russell has been recognized various times for all of his achievements. In 1986 the Atlanta Business League voted him CEO of the Year, and in 1987 **BLACK ENTERPRISE** cited H. J. Russell and Company as their "Company of the Year". Also in 1987, Russell was honored during Black History Month by Atlanta's nineteen-member city council. He sits on the Board of Directors of numerous organizations, both purely business-oriented companies as well as those with public welfare as a priority, and has been a life-long member of the NAACP. Russell made headlines again in October of 1997, when First Southern Bank in Lithonia, Georgia announced its merger with Atlanta's Citizens Trust Bank, of which Russell is the Chairman. This merger created the fifth largest Black-owned financial institution in the country, with combined assets approaching $197 million. The new entity retained the name Citizens Trust, is headed by First Southern President James E. Young, and continues having Russell as its Chairman.

Russell's future plans are simple—to continue making money and building institutions. If there is any single issue on which Russell lacks resolve, it is plans for his true retirement. He occasionally speaks of completely passing the mantle, and indeed has taken some steps in that direction. The first step Russell has taken toward passing the mantle was the December 1996 naming of R. K. Sehgal as Vice Chairman and Chief Executive Officer. Russell has retained his post as Chairman of the Board, and some of his staff doubt that Herman Russell, as long as he lays claim to sound mind and judgment, will ever completely release the reins.

CHAPTER FOURTEEN: VIEW TO THE FUTURE

Our mission in writing this book was to increase the readers' knowledge base on African-American-owned businesses and to influence what they feel can be achieved. Too many times in the course of our education, the story of African-American-owned businesses has been forgotten. Their stories are important for they re-affirm the possibility of the American dream for all citizens.

We set out to create the type of conversation that you would ask of a parent or confidant if they were scholars on the subject of African-American business. Reading this book should leave you confident that you could discuss African-American-owned businesses with anyone, anywhere, with intelligence and insight. As a result, you will be able to further the necessary American discourse on African-American-owned businesses.

Although this book focuses on African-American businesses, all American businesses have been affected by the same forces of demand, strategy, barriers to entry, regional clusters and social discourse. Certainly, women, Asian, Latino and other minority-owned businesses have grown tremendously over the past thirty years due to these macroeconomic forces. The case of the African-American, however, is unique in that the laws, Slavery, our economic system, and focused violence against African-Americans have isolated their businesses like no other. Simply put, there can be no market when there are no civil rights. Yet, interestingly enough, some African-American businesses have always existed. Now, a new America that includes women, Latinos, Asians, and other minorities, as well as African-American entrepreneurs is imperative for its competitiveness in the twenty-first century. The success of minority-owned businesses serves as an important barometer of American economic opportunity and dynamism.

The History of Black Business set out to change what is possible for millions of Americans. The business cases in this book present new possibilities for anyone who has had a desire to influence society in positive ways. These African-American business cases have hopefully awakened the desire of many who would have never thought of the possibility of owning a business, being one of the 400 richest Americans, or buying a billion dollar company. As the individuals highlighted in this book show us, these things are possible.

The greatest opportunities for African-American entrepreneurs are beginning now. The last thirty years of increasing opportunity for African-Americans are unparalleled. Surely, America has many problems. Race and economic class are among them, however, America has opportunities unlike anywhere else in the world. The purchasing power of African-Americans alone surpasses all but the top economies in the world. Along side African-Americans, women, Asians, Latinos, and other "minorities" are also emerging as business owners and employers as never before in the history of human affairs.

Benefiting from these new opportunities, however, requires vision: vision to see the opportunity and desire to obtain it regardless of the negative influence of those without our vision. We need to understand that it is easier now than ever to obtain an education, a professional position, or a business in America, regardless of how hard it seems. This is what each of the entrepreneurs in this book has done, just as other African-American scholars, Civil Rights leaders, musicians, athletes, and business executives have done in the past.

Lessons Learned

The three most important messages in this book are:

(1) There have always been African-American entrepreneurs.

(2) The forces aligned against them in the past were great.

(3) The opportunities that exist today are unparalleled.

There have always been African-American-owned businesses: ever since the birth of this nation and enterprising men such as Paul Cuffe in 1776 to Madam C. J. Walker's appearance at Booker T. Washington's National Business League in 1912 to Reginald Lewis in 1987. This should not be new to anyone, but more than likely, it is. Just as the fact that thousands of free African-Americans fought in the Revolutionary, Civil, and Spanish-American Wars is for the most part not taught, the knowledge of African-American entrepreneurs is also forgotten. In this book, we have showcased some of these early businesses that were created by adventurers, inventors, financiers, and insurance providers so that their contributions can be brought to the forefront.

The Census tells us that there were over 17,000 business in 1893 and over 70,000 in 1926, but there were undoubtedly many more that were not counted. We have seen slaves who conducted business to buy their freedom, free African-Americans who served White clientele during Slavery, and free men and women who built Black towns in America that could support African-American entrepreneurship. These men and women should inspire those entrepreneurs of today who have more protected rights and better opportunities to achieve.

The forces aligned against African-American-owned businesses in the past were great. Black businesses existed in the face of a nation that created Slavery, Jim Crow Laws, Grandfather clauses, Redlining, and the Ku Klux Klan. The histories of civil rights, Slavery, Jim Crow Laws, the Klan, and African-American business are all linked. Economic pursuits by the first free Black explorers, enslaved Africans, freed slaves, African-Americans under Jim Crow, and African-American entrepreneurs of today, have all experienced the forces that cloud the free market system like racism, discrimination, exclusionary practices, and violence. During a large part of our history, our government may have been the largest single negative force on Black business as it upheld unjust statutes and failed to provide equal protection and economic treatment under the law. Only since the 1960s have America and the government begun retarding some of the forces that in the past dulled the entrepreneurial potential of African-Americans.

Three decades after the Civil Rights era, and only steps away from the twenty-first century, the opportunities for African-American-owned businesses are greater than ever. From this continuum of African-American entrepreneurship, new African-American businesses have begun to emerge seeking the promise of American capitalism. This trend will continue to grow for African-Americans, as it will for all minority-owned businesses that have traditionally been locked out of our capitalist society. African-American businesses, like other minority-owned businesses in America will continue to grow at a rapid rate into the new millenium.

The old critical success factors such as low capital intensity, focus on a niche market neglected by the majority, or finding coping mechanisms to conduct business across state lines are rapidly being supplanted by access to venture or LBO capital, diversified industries where the quality of management can decide who will own assets, and new industries that promise a wide open field to compete. These are the "New Rules" that face any business regardless of race or gender, but, for the largest African-American business these "New Rules" are sharply different from the past:

Factor	Old Rules	New Rules
Entrepreneurs' relationship to company	Founder of Business	Value Added Equity Stake
Education	Informal Education	Formal Education and Networks
Business partnerships	Limited Cluster	Global Clusters
Use of capital	Low Capital Intensity (Mom & Pop)	LBO/ Buyout, Multi-Million Dollar Deals
Number of investors or stakeholders	Sole Proprietorship	Above 35 shareholders
Market focus	Niche Market	Any Market where Competitive Advantage can be Gained
Technology use	Low Tech	High Tech

Today the most successful entrepreneurs will be more connected, educated, experienced, and have greater access to capital than in the past. Some businesses will be inherited, such as C.H. James & Company which will be handed over to the third generation of James's, or TLC Beatrice Holdings, Inc. which Reginald Lewis left to his wife and children. New businesses will continue to be bought and sold. Companies like FEDCO, Motown, Johnson Products, McCall, and Soft Sheen on the BE100 list all have used acquisitions to grow or have profited from being sold. It is likely that within the next fifteen years, Reginald Lewis's foray into billion dollar acquisitions will be surpassed by other African-Americans.

New Opportunities in America

In a world where over half the Fortune 400 are self-made millionaires, minorities should see the next twenty years as an opportunity to take part in America's creation of new products and industries. Oprah Winfrey has done this. John Johnson has done this. The Lewis household is likely to continue to do this. The fact that over twenty percent of the Fortune 400 made their money in ways that did not exist twenty years ago such as computer software, wireless communications, and the internet means that it is possible.

The opportunity to earn a way into the Forbes 400 is growing as entrepreneurs create new markets and new fortunes. African-Americans will take part in this creation as they continue to find unique ways to meet the needs of African-Americans through business; but, more importantly, they will find unique ways to meet the needs of all Americans. We have seen Berry Gordy, Johnson Publishing, Johnson Products, and Madame CJ Walker uniquely meet the needs of African-Americans. In the future we will see more Oprah Winfreys, and Reginald Lewises who will uniquely meet the needs of all Americans.

The Entrepreneur's Purpose

The value of African-American entrepreneurs can be seen in our music, our TV, and our sports. Without companies like Motown, perhaps many of the legends of music would never have gotten a chance to sing. Perhaps without entrepreneurs like Madame

C.J. Walker or John Johnson, there would be fewer hair care products geared toward African-American women. Perhaps without a company like BET, we would have seen less African-Americans on TV. Without entrepreneurs/artists like Spike Lee, perhaps, advances on the silver screen would have been slower. Perhaps without Oprah Winfrey, we might never have seen "The Color Purple". Perhaps if the Negro Leagues did not exist, then many Baseball greats such as Jackie Robinson may never had been given a chance, and so on. These forces and many others businesses mattered to America because they added something new.

The entrepreneurs of tomorrow will add tremendous value in areas that may not exist today. While in our society many kids dream to have fame and fortune, too few realize that 85% of all millionaires own businesses. Education and the ability to think creatively in a timely and relevant way are the prerequisites for the successful entrepreneur. If this realization gives our children one more reason to stay in school, stay off drugs, and stay in healthier relationships then so be it. The entrepreneurs in this book should be added to the names of abolitionists, civil rights activists, athletes, and entertainer role models, which the media shows us today.

The Possibilities are Boundless

The intention of this book was to increase the knowledge of African-Americans who have played a role in making America a better place to live. These business stories, which are often left untold, are important testaments on America's history that is told so often without their mention. These African-American entrepreneurs have added to their communities and to their obligation to hold "America" to the true meaning of its creed.

The entrepreneurs in this book had visions for the future. Visions which made it easier for others to see a new vision and possibility for themselves. Those that think in the past only are stuck in the past and those that think in only the present are not prepared for tomorrow. These examples of these entrepreneurs have challenged us to see a new future that belongs to those who think and plan in the future while understanding our past. We have seen African-Americans own airlines, oil fields, technology companies, food chains, envirotech companies, and other businesses, in hostile environments designed to exclude them. The entrepreneurs of tomorrow will create new industries and new markets, play on more level playing fields, and make America more competitive than ever. We hope this book has set out to inspire one of those entrepreneurs to begin preparing today.

Martin K. Hunt

Jacqueline E. Hunt

Appendix

A. Selected Contextual Milestones in Black Business History
B. Number of Black Businesses, 1863-1998
C. Glossary
D. Publicly-Owned African-American-owned businesses
E. Top Commercial and Industrial Companies in 1997
F. Top Auto Dealerships in 1997
G. Top Banks in 1997
H. Top Insurance Companies in 1997
I. Top Investment Banks in 1997
J. Leading Black Entrepreneurs 1820-1865

A.
Selected Contextual Milestones in Black Business History

Year	Important Information
300's - 1591 AD	Three wealthy empires in Western Africa, Ghana, Mali, and Songhai, (an area known as the Western Sudan) thrive with a strong economy based on farming, gold, and trade with North Africa. Most African-Americans are decendants from these three wealthy empires.
1500's - 1800s	Europeans begin slave trade to their colonies in the Americas. About 10 million Blacks are enslaved during this time, 6% of them are brought to North America. (Haiti and Jamaica received greater numbers of enslaved Africans than the U.S.) In 1619, 20 African laborers are brought in and sold by captain of a Dutch ship. Laborers are purchased to help relieve Jamestown's labor shortage. In this same year, 100 Englishmen are brought to the new English colony for the same purpose. (These people were indentured servants, not slaves, so were freed following an agreed-upon number of years of labor). In 1641, Massachusetts becomes the first colony to legalize slavery. In 1644, 11 Blacks petition for freedom in New York, the first legal Black protest in America. In 1651, Anthony Johnson imports 5 servants, thus allowing him to receive a 200-acre land grant in Northhampton County, Virginia. In 1652, John Johnson obtains 550 acres in Northhampton County, VA. Other Blacks join Johnson and attempt to launch an independent Black community. In 1688, Mennonites and **Quakers** in Germantown, PA issue the first group of protests against Slavery in America. The enslaved African-American population increases rapidly as newly established colonies in the South create a greater demand for plantation workers.

By 1750	About 200,000 enslaved African-Americans live in the colonies (most of them in the South). Only 12% of slave owners operate plantations with over 20 enslaved African-Americans. By 1770, There are 40,000 or more free Blacks in American colonies.
1770	Crispus Attucks is first of five to die in the Boston Massacre of 1770.
1773	Phyllis Wheatley's *Poems on Various Subjects, Religious and Moral,* is published in England, becoming the first book published by a African-American author.
1775	The first abolitionist society in the U. S. is organized in Philadelphia.
1775 - 1783	**Revolutionary War** Blacks fight at Lexington and Concord, the first battles of the American Revolution. By the time the war begins, slave population in the South exceeds the free population in many areas. (Ex: In South Carolina, slaves made up 65% of the total population). In 1775, The Royal Governor of Virginia issues an invitation to Blacks to join the British Army. 5,000 American Blacks escape to the British lines. In 1775, The Continental Congress approves an order from General Washington that allows free African-Americans to enlist in the army. The colonies, however, overlook the ruling and draft slaves in order to meet their quotas. After the war, numerous free African-Americans find jobs in factories and mills, on ships, in carpentry and on railroads. In 1777, Vermont becomes the first American colony to abolish slavery. In 1780, Paul Cuffee and other Black taxpayers of Massachusetts protest to the Revolutionary government against "taxation without representation". As a result, three years later, in 1783, a MA court rules that African-Americans do have the right to vote if they pay taxes. In 1780, **The Treaty of Paris** ends the Revolutionary War. The treaty provides that escaped and captured slaves be returned to their owners. By the early 1800's most Northern states have taken steps to end Slavery. More than 700,000 enslaved African-Americans live in the South and make up 1/3 of the region's people (in some states enslaved African-Americans are the majority).

1783	Slavery in the Commonwealth is abolished by the Massachusetts Supreme Court. Virginia grants freedom to all enslaved African-Americans who fought in the Continental Army during the Revolutionary War.
1787	The Continental Congress excludes Slavery from the newly established Northwest Territory (Michigan, Illinois, Indiana, and Wisconsin) but allows for Slavery in the original 13 states.
1790	**Freeman and African-American, Jean Baptiste Point Du Sable** establishes a trading settlement that later becomes the city of Chicago.
1793	Congress enacts the first **fugitive slave law**.
1793	Eli Whitney of Massachusetts invents the cotton gin, a machine which removes seeds from cotton as fast as 50 workers. Farmers can now better meet the demand for cotton and the cotton industry expands in response. Large increase in the slave population takes place (from less than a million in 1793 to 4 million just before the Civil War.) The price of slaves rises from $200 to $2,000 each.
1787	Sept. 17, 1787, the **U.S. Constitution is adopted.** In order to keep loyalty of slaveholders and slavetraders in the North and South, they agree to protect slave property in three separate sections of the Constitution: 1. African slave trade is given 20 more years (until 1808) in which to cease operations. 2. It is provided that all runaway slaves be returned to their owners. 3. Because slaveowners were to be taxed for their slaves, as property, they are allowed three votes for every five slaves owned.
1788	**U.S. Constitution is ratified.**
1790	Census shows 59,000 free Blacks (27,000 of which are in the North).
1793 - 1803	Only successful slave revolt in human history takes place in Haiti. Led by **Toussaint L'Ouverture**, half a million African slaves, joined by thousands of free Blacks who live on the island, rise against their French masters. After its success in delivering freedom to Haiti's Africans, the French capture L'Ouverture and take him to France where he dies of starvation in prison.
1798	**James Forten**, **Sr**., a Philadelphian veteran of the U.S. Navy, establishes the first major Black-owned sail making company. He becomes wealthy and uses the money earned to further the abolitionist cause.
1800	The Ohio legislature passes the first of a succession of Northern Black Laws which restrict the rights and movements of **free African-Americans** in the North. Free Blacks in Philadelphia petition the U. S. Congress to end Slavery gradually. Congress rejects the petition by a vote of 85-1.
1803	**U.S. buys Louisiana from France for $15 million, resulting in the doubling of the country's size.**

1808	Transatlantic slave trade is banned. Legally, slaveowners can now only obtain slaves from the already present pool in the U.S. Regardless, the Slave trade continues until the **Civil War**.
1810	**The African Insurance Company** of Philadelphia is established and becomes the first known African-American-owned insurance company (it was not incorporated, but did have capital stock).
1812	At least 1/6 of the U.S. Navy is Black by the end of the **War of 1812**.
1816	**The African Methodist Episcopal Church** (AME Church), the first Black denomination in the country, is set up by Richard Allen, a Black Philadelphia minister.
1817 - 1818	Led by Abraham, an escaped Slave, Seminole Indians fight U.S. Troops during the **First Seminole War**. Seminoles are now an "Afro-Indian" tribe, with African members from the Ibo, Egba, Senegalese, and Ashanti tribes. By 1818, there are 11 states that permit enslavement and 11 free states that do not.
1820	**The Missouri Compromise**–Allows Missouri's entry into the Union as a slave state and the entry of Maine as a free state.
1827	First Black newspaper, **Freedom's Journal**, is started by Samuel Cornish and John Russwurm.
1829	A delegation of **Cincinnati** Blacks, seeking refuge after being driven from the town by Whites, request the assistance of Sir James Colebrook, Governor of Upper Canada. He answers their plea by offering them freedom and the same privileges entitled to other Canadians. A significant number of African-Americans migrate to Canada at this time and form the settlement of Wilburforce.
1829 - 1841	During their terms, 7th and 8th Presidents **Jackson** and **Van Buren** both **oppose voting rights for free African-Americans**. In the 1830s, Abolitionists begin to spring up in the North. Ex.: William Lloyd Garrison, Lewis Tappan, Lucretia Mott, and Theodore Dwight Weld. By 1830 there are already 50 anti-Slavery groups in Northern cities and towns. That same year, African-American leaders from several states meet in a first convention to discuss problems of Slavery and discrimination.
1831	**Nat Turner**, an enslaved African and preacher, leads the most famous Slave revolt of the over 200 U.S. Slave revolts attempted until that time. Rebels and about 60 Whites are killed before Turner is captured.
1833	David Ruggles becomes the first known **Black bookseller**. He was burned out of business by a White mob in 1835.
1835	**Second Seminole War** – Over 500 escaped slaves are recaptured.

1838	**Frederick Douglass** escapes from Slavery and flees to Baltimore, then New York.
1846	**William Alexander Leidesdorff**, a Black man, becomes the first person of any race to open a hotel in San Francisco. One year later, Leidesdorff is elected an acting city official in San Francisco, becoming the first African-American to be elected on the continent.
1847	**Liberia** becomes the first self-governing Black republic in Africa. By 1855 only 12,000 Blacks have settled in Liberia. **Frederick Douglass,** the most influential Black leader of the time, starts an abolitionist newspaper, **North Star**.
1849	**Congressman Abraham Lincoln** introduces a bill calling for the gradual end of Slavery.
1850	**Compromise of 1850** signed (led by Henry Clay). Allows slavery to continue but prohibits Slave trade in Washington DC.
1852	**James Beckwourth** establishes hotel and trading post in **Beckwourth Valley, CA**. (Beckwourth, an ex-slave from Missouri, was taken in by the Crow Tribe in 1819 and soon became their chief. He also disco-vered a pass through the Sierra Nevadas that became an important getaway to CA during the Gold Rush).
1854	**Kansas-Nebraska Act** passed. Law creates 2 federal territories and provides that people of each territory decide whether to permit slavery or not. Nebraska opposes Slavery; Kansas, after many bloody and bitter conflicts joins the Union as a free state in 1861. **Lincoln University**, the first historically African-American University, is founded.
1857	**Dred Scott v. Stanford** Court case declares that no African-American, free or enslaved, can be an U.S. citizen and states that Congress has no power to ban the spread of Slavery.
1860	By 1860, there are 4 million enslaved African-Americans in the South. **Nation has about 490,000 free Blacks (250,000 of those live in the South).** Less than 5% of Southerners own enslaved African-Americans. 2% of slaveowners have more than 5 enslaved African-Americans.
1861 - 1865	**Civil War** 11 Southern states secede from the Union and become the Confederate States of America. Lincoln forbids Blacks to fight in the war in order to keep the few slaves states that were still part of the Union loyal to the Union cause. Does not allow Blacks to fight in the war until he realizes that he cannot win the war without their military power (less than 100 Blacks become officers).

1862 -1863	In April 1862, President Lincoln approves legislation that ends slavery in Washington DC and provides funds for any freed slaves who wish to move to Haiti or Liberia. In June 1862, Lincoln signs bill that ends Slavery in all federal territories. In July 1862, the **Militia Act of 1862** authorizes the enlistment of Black troops. Blacks are accepted in the Union army. 200,000 African-Americans fight on the side of the Union. 29 Blacks win medals of honor for their service in the war. In September 1862, preliminary order is issued to emancipate enslaved African-Americans. Order states that all enslaved African-Americans in areas of rebellion against the U.S. are to be forever free on January 1, 1863. The order excludes areas loyal to the Union. **In 1863, Emancipation Proclamation** Enslaved African-Americans are freed in areas of rebellion against the union, as per agreement of September 1862. The Emancipation Proclamation opens the U.S. armed forces to African-Americans, free and enslaved.
1865	**In 1865, the Civil War ends.** Main Southern army surrenders in December. **13th Amendment to the U.S. Constitution** officially ends Slavery throughout the nation. There are now **4 million freedmen**. **Ku Klux Klan** is organized in Pulaski, TN. Over 5,000 Blacks murdered; extreme organized violence against African-Americans. On March 3, Lincoln signs a **Reconstruction post-Civil War Congressional Act** that creates the **Freedmen's Savings and Trust**. This organization supposedly serves as a place where African-Americans can safely put their money without harassment. In 1874 **Freedmen's Savings and Trust** goes bankrupt due to irregular loans to White-owned companies. Over 60,000 newly freed Blacks lose their life savings and their trust in White-owned banking institutions. 100,000 of the 120,000 skilled artisans in the South are African-American. Excluded by discrimination, African-American artisans are nearly extinct 25 years later.
1865-1869	President Andrew **Johnson** makes it clear that he opposes any federal laws to protect freedmen, and leaves the matter up to the individual states. He opposes any idea that African-Americans have a "natural" right to vote.

1865-1869	Johnson denies federal protection to Blacks, thus encouraging those in the South to continue with their oppression. Johnson pardons many Confederate leaders and returns their land to them (**much of which had been sold to Freedmen by the U.S. Army**). A battle over Reconstruction results in the unsuccessful attempts to remove Johnson from office. By a single Senate vote, Johnson keeps the presidency until 1869.
1866	**Civil Rights Act of 1866** passed by Congress. Gives Blacks rights and privileges of full citizenship.
1868	**14th Amendment to the U.S. Constitution** Further guarantees citizenship of Blacks and protects their right to own property.
1870	**15th Amendment to the U.S. Constitution** Protects African-Americans' right to vote. **Hiram R. Revels** becomes America's first Black Senator.
1870-1901	Between 1870 and 1871 **Enforcement Acts** are passed by Congress. Laws are passed that authorize the use of federal troops to enforce voting rights of Blacks. In 1871 Congress passes a law to end the KKK menace, but other organizations spring up at once to take the Klan's place; the Klan nonetheless continues its terrorism. Between 1870 and 1901, **22 Blacks serve their states as Congressmen**. Southern Blacks sit in every Congress from the 41st to the 56th, with only one exception.
1872	**Elijah McCoy**, the son of runaway slaves, invents a lubricating cup that feeds oil to parts of a machine while it is in operation. McCoy, a mechanical engineer educated in Scotland, comes to play a prominent role in the development of transportation and factory machinery and receives more than 75 patents for his inventions.
1873	Depression in the South drives a rapid decline in the **price of cotton**. By 1868 the price had already fallen from $1 a pound to $0.25. By 1894 the price is down to $0.05.
1876	A special "deal" grants the Presidential election to Rutherford B. Hayes. (Although while campaigning Hayes had commented on caring for the "poor colored man of the South", a deal is made with him that if he backs down on his cause for helping Blacks, he could gain the Presidency). Hayes (who before the Civil War had served as a volunteer lawyer for runaway slaves) as President orders that the last federal troops, which had been sent there to protect African-American voting and other rights, be withdrawn from the South.

1881	Tennessee legislature passes law that segregates train passengers.
1883	**The Supreme Court declares the Civil Rights Act of 1875 to be unconstitutional.** This Act had been the last of the civil rights laws remaining. All other Acts had already been struck down by Congress after the Civil War. Black conventions are held in Kentucky, Arkansas, South Carolina, and Texas to protest against this denial of civil rights.
1888	**The True Reformers' Bank of Richmond, VA and the Capital Savings Bank of DC** become the first banks created and run by Blacks.
1893	The **North Carolina Life Mutual Company** is formed.
1894 - early 1900s	In 1894, a section of **the Emancipation Act** dealing with the rights of Blacks to vote, is repealed. **1896-Plessy v. Ferguson-**Supreme Court declares segregation on trains constitutional. Supreme Court argues for "separate but equal" doctrine. In Louisiana, in 1898, the first **"Grandfather Clause"** enables poor Whites to qualify to vote and curtails Black voter registration. More than 3,000 Blacks are lynched. Laws prohibit African-Americans from owning saloons, teaching, and entering certain other businesses and professions. **Many states outlaw Black-owned businesses.**
1900	The **National Negro Business League** is founded by Booker T. Washington.
1903	**Maggie Lena Walker** becomes the first woman, regardless of race, to found a bank (The Saint Luke Penny Savings Bank – saving bank for Blacks in Richmond, VA).
1905	**Niagara Movement-W.E.B. Du Bois** and other critics of Booker T. Washington meet in Niagara Falls, Canada and organize a campaign to protest racial discrimination.
1905	The first issue of the *Chicago Defender* is published.
By 1907	**Every Southern state requires racial segregation on trains, in churches, schools, hotels, restaurants, theaters, and other public facilities.**
1909	**National Association for the Advancement of Colored People,** led by Ida B. Wells, is formed. A number of white Northerners join some of the Blacks involved in the Niagara movement to form the **NAACP.**
1910	By 1910, every Southern state has taken away or begun to take away the right of Blacks to vote. **Madame C. J. Walker** becomes one of the first Black women entrepreneurs (**Annie Turbo Malone**, who Walker once worked for, is said to have become a millionaire in the same time period.)

1913	Presenting plan for his "New Freedom" for America, Woodrow Wilson is elected President. New Freedom proves empty with Wilson's restoration of segregation of government employees. Blacks who had voted for him lose faith.
1915	The boll weevil beetle devastates the cotton crop throughout the South, leading to economic chaos and massed migrations to the North.
1914 - 1918	**World War I** 100,000's of Southern Blacks migrate to the North to seek jobs in defense plants and other factories. Over 360,000 Blacks serve in the armed forces during the war, all in all-Black units.
1910 - 1930	About 1 million Southern Blacks migrate to the North.
1915	The **new Ku Klux Klan** is chartered in Fulton County, Georgia. Peak membership rises to 4 million.
By 1919	25 race riots have broken out across the country in response to growing tensions and hostility between African-Americans and European-Americans.
Mid 1920's	Marcus Garvey, who founded his **Universal Negro Improvement Association** in Jamaica in 1917, brings his movement to Harlem. More than 700 branches are established in 38 states.
By the mid 1920s	There are 25 Black-owned insurance companies carrying policies amounting to $2 million. By 1928 Blacks also own 50 banks.
1928	**Oscar de Priest** of Illinois becomes the first Black congressman from the North.
1929	**Great Depression** Many African-Americans lose their jobs ("last hired and first fired"). Black Banks are crushed.
1930	A Chicago Black newspaper, the **Whip** leads a boycott of stores that do not hire Blacks. By the end of its fifth month, the boycott leads to the hiring of 1,000 Blacks.
1936	**Franklin D. Roosevelt** wins reelection for president. Roosevelt forms the "**Black cabinet**", a group of African-Americans meant to advise him on race problems in America.
1939 - 1945	**World War II** Nearly 1 million Blacks serve in the U.S. Armed Forces during the war. The desegregation of the armed forces begins on a trial basis during the war. Many Southern Blacks move to seek jobs in Northern industrial cities.
By 1939	**Roosevelt** administration orders the creation of a civil rights section in the Department of Justice. It receives 8,000 to 14,000 complaints each year of his presidency but few actions are taken.
1941	**U.S. Supreme Court** rules that separate facilities for White and Black train passengers must be significantly equal.

1941	F.D. **Roosevelt** issues executive order forbidding racial discrimination in defense industries.
	The first U. S. Army flying school for Black cadets (the 'Tuskegee Airmen') is dedicated at the Tuskegee Institute in Alabama.
1944	Court declares that the "White Primary', which excluded Blacks from voting in the only meaningful elections in the South, was unconstitutional.
	The **United Negro College Fund** is incorporated.
1947	The **NAACP** reports that during 1946, killings, eyegouging and lynchings showed an increase over previous years.
	Jackie Robinson becomes the first African-American player in modern major league baseball (Nearly a dozen African-Americans played in the major leagues in the late 1900s.) This marks the beginning of the end for the emerging **Negro Baseball League**.
1948	**Executive Order 9981** After pressure from Black civilian groups, President Truman issues an executive order for the desegregation of the armed forces.
	Shelley vs. Kraemer The Supreme Court rules that federal and state courts can not enforce restrictive covenants which bar persons from owning or occupying property because of race.
1949	**Truman** establishes the President's Committee on Civil Rights to study the problem of race and issue recommendations for progress.
1948-1951	Several Supreme Court decisions rule that separate higher education facilities for Blacks must be equal to those for Whites.
1950	**Korean War** begins. 1000's of African-Americans serve in the U. S. Armed Forces during the war. The all-Black 24th Infantry Regiment re-captures city of Yech'on, the first American victory in the Korean War.
1952	Tuskegee Institute reports that no lynchings have occurred during that whole year, the first such year in the 71 years that Tuskegee had been keeping track of such information.
1954	**Brown v. Board of Education of Topeka**-On May 17 the U.S. Supreme Court rules that segregation in public schools is in itself unequal and therefore unconstitutional.
1955	On November 25, the **Interstate Commerce Commission** bans segregation in buses, in waiting rooms and in travel coaches involved in interstate travel.
	Montgomery bus boycott-Rosa Park's Dec. 5 arrest for not giving up her seat on the city bus spawns a 382-day protest, which leads to a change in the bus-seating law.

1956	On June 5, Federal Court rules that racial segregation on Montgomery city buses violates the Constitution. On December 21, at two mass meetings, Montgomery Blacks call off a year-long boycott. Buses are integrated on that day with Martin Luther King, Jr. riding the first one.
1957	On August 29, Congress passes the **Civil Rights Act of 1957**, the first civil rights legislation since 1875.
1959	**Berry Gordy** establishes **Motown Records**.
1960's	**The Civil Rights Movement** Combined efforts of various civil rights groups end segregation in many public places.
1960	In the **Eisenhower Committee's** final report to the president, Vice President Nixon urges the incoming administration of President John F. Kennedy to require federal contractors to use something stronger than passive nondiscrimination to achieve equal employment opportunities. In May, President Eisenhower signs the **Civil Rights Act of 1960**.
1961	**President Kennedy** orders federal contractors to stop discriminating in the workplace and to use affirmative action to ensure employment without regard to race, creed, color and national origin. **Adam Clayton Powell** becomes chairman of the Education and Labor Committee of the House of Representatives.
1962	President **Kennedy** issues an Executive Order barring racial and religious bias in federally-financed housing.
1963	**March on Washington-**In August 1962, more than 200,000 attend the rally led by Dr. King.
1964	Lyndon B. Johnson passes JFK's proposed laws in the **Civil Rights Act of 1964**. Civil Rights Act prohibits racial discrimination in pubic places and calls for equal opportunity in employment and education. Act bars workplace discrimination.
Mid 1960's	Major riots take place throughout the nation. Ex: Harlem riots in 1964; Riots in Watts (Los Angeles, CA) in 1965.
1965	LBJ calls for ending *de facto*, not only *de jure* (by law) segregation. Calls for **affirmative action** programs in businesses and schools. This creates new educational and economic opportunities for Blacks.
1965	**Voting Rights Act of 1965** passed by Congress. Act bans the use of the poll tax as a requirement to vote and forbids major changes in Southern voting laws without the approval of the Department of Justice. Act leads to increase in voting by Blacks and to an increase in the number of Black elected officials. President Johnson signs **Executive Order 11246**. Order requires employers who receive federal funds to establish minority hiring goals – but not quotas.

1965	February 21, 1965, **Malcolm X is assassinated in New York.** President Johnson signs the **Voting Rights Bill**, which authorizes the suspension of literacy tests and the sending of federal examiners into the South.
1966	**Black Panther** Party founded by Huey P. Newton and Bobby Seale. **Edward W. Brooke** (R-MA) is elected U.S. Senator, the first Black senator since **Reconstruction**.
1967	**August 30, 1967, Thurgood Marshall** becomes the first African-American justice on the U.S. Supreme Court. LBJ names Walter E. Washington as commissioner and "unofficial" mayor of Washington, DC; Washington becomes the first African-American to head the government of a major U.S. city.
1967-1968	LBJ establishes commission to study the cause of riots: **Kerner Commission**. Study puts blame on racial prejudice of Whites and recommends programs to improve ghetto conditions.
By 1968	Race riots have broken out in at least 100 communities across the nation.
April 4, 1968	**Martin Luther King, Jr. assassinated in Memphis, TN.**
1968	**Civil Rights Act of 1968** passed by Congress. Also known in part as the **Fair Housing Act of 1968**. Act prohibits racial discrimination in the sale and rental of most of the housing in the nation. LBJ signs a bill that makes it a crime to interfere with civil rights workers and to cross state lines to incite a riot. **U.S. Small Business Administration** begins its redistricted-competition **8 (a)** set-asides program to aid minority businesses in their pursuit of government contracts.
1969	**Nixon administration** issues the **Philadelphia Plan**. Forces federal contractors to set forth plans for increasing the number of minorities in construction jobs.
1969	President Nixon signs **Executive Order 11458**. Order directs secretary of commerce to coordinate the federal government's efforts to promote minority enterprise. Leads to the establishment of the **Office of Minority Business Enterprise** (now the **Minority Business Development Agency**).
1970-1980	College enrollments among Blacks rise from about 600,000 in 1970 to 1.3 million in 1980. Number of Black-owned businesses in the U.S. increase from 190,000 to 425,000.

1970	Formation of first **MESBICs** (Minority Enterprise Small Business Investment Corps.) **Johnson Products Co.** becomes the first Black firm to be traded on a major stock exchange (American Stock Exchange). **Parks Sausage Co.** debuts on the **NASDAQ** exchange.
1971	**American Association of MESBICs** is established in Washington, DC to provide venture capital to minority start-up companies. Association now known as the National Association of Investment Companies (NAIC). **Daniels and Bell** becomes the first Black-owned investment bank to become a member of the **New York Stock Exchange (NYSE).** **Rev. Jesse Jackson** announces the formation of Operation PUSH, a national political and economic development organization. The U. S. Supreme Court rules unanimously that busing is a constitutionally acceptable way of integrating public schools. Eleven years later, in 1982, the U. S. Senate votes 75-37 to eliminate busing.
1972	**National Black MBA Association** is founded. Purpose is to help African-Americans enter and progress in the business world. **Johnson Publishing** headquarters open in Chicago, IL. Its headquarters become the first building constructed downtown by a Black-owned contracting company.
1973	**Bert Mitchell and Robert Titus form Mitchell, Titus, & Co.** By 1994 becomes the largest minority-owned certified public accounting firm and the 37th largest in the nation with $17 million in assets. **Thomas Bradley** is elected 1st Black mayor of Los Angeles. **Maynard Jackson** is elected first Black mayor of a major Southern city (Atlanta). **Coleman Young** is elected mayor of Detroit. These and other Black mayors institute policies that create business and political opportunities for African-Americans.
1978	**Regents of University of California v. Bakke** The Supreme Court strikes down a university program that set aside 16 of 100 openings for minorities. The court suggests for less formal race-conscious solutions. **CEO's of 130 Black-owned businesses** meet with President Carter at the White House. It is the first time a group of Black business leaders gains an audience with a U.S. President.

1978	**Bell Telephone System** challenges the legality of racial quotas in hiring and promotions. The U.S. Supreme Court rules that racial quotas are constitutional and a viable means of ending discrimination.
1979	A study compiled by the Anti-Defamation League of B'nai B'rith indicates a sharp rise in **KKK** activity.
1980	**Fullilove v. Kultznick** The Supreme Court allows for a federal public works program that sets aside 10% of grants to minority businesses. **Minority Business Enterprise Legal Defense and Education Fund** is launched in Washington DC Launched, after 9 years of championing the cause of Black business development in Congress, by Rep. Parren J. Mitchell (D-Md.)
1981	**Justice Department**, under **President Reagan**, announces it will no longer demand that employers maintain affirmative action programs or that they hire according to numerical racial goals. A successful national boycott against Coca-Cola, organized by **PUSH**, ends with the company's agreeing to invest $34 million in Black businesses and communities.
1982	President Reagan signs a 25-year extension of LBJ's Voting Rights Act of 1965.
1984	**TLC Group**, led by **Reginald Lewis**, acquires the **McCall Pattern Co.** for $25 million. In 1987, Lewis sells the firm for $90 million. **Edward Dugger III** builds an $18 million fund for **UNC Ventures** in Boston, making it the nation's largest privately run Black-owned venture capital firms.
1986	The Supreme Court, as remedy for on-job bias, upholds Affirmative Action. **Wygant v. Jackson Board of Education**-Supreme Court rules that "race conscious" hiring is permissible, but there must be convincing evidence of past discrimination. After much pressure from sensible electorate forces, Congress passes the **Anti-Apartheid Act** over the veto of President Reagan.
1987	**Stock Market crashes in October.** **Reginald F. Lewis** initiates the largest offshore leveraged buy-out in history with a $985 million acquisition of Beatrice International Foods.
1989	**Ronald H. Brown** is elected chairman of the Democratic National Committee, becoming the first African-American to head a major U.S. political party.

1989	U.S. Army **General Colin L. Powell** becomes the first Black chairman of the **Joint Chiefs of Staff**. **L. Douglas Wilder** is elected Governor of Virginia, becoming the first Black elected state governor in U.S. history. **Croson v. The City of Richmond** U.S. Supreme Court's decision wipes out the city's 30% set-aside program for minorities. It rules that past discrimination in the letting of contracts must be documented. Ruling threatens minority set-aside laws in other cities.
1990	**Brimmer-Marshall Report** drafted. Provides evidentiary basis for Maynard Jackson's establishment of Atlanta's **Equal Business Opportunity Program** in 1991, which sets a 30% contract participation goal for African-Americans. **President Bush vetoes a Civil Right Bill** on grounds that it imposes quota systems.
1991	**Thurgood Marshall** retires from the U.S. Supreme Court after 24 years and is replaced by Republican conservative Clarence Thomas. **BET Holdings, Inc.** becomes the first Black company traded on the New York State Exchange. The offering raises $72.3 million. President Bush signs the **Civil Rights Act of 1991**.
1992	Former **Democratic National Convention Chairman Ronald H. Brown** is appointed U.S. Secretary of Commerce. **Carol Moseley-Braun** (D – IL) becomes the first Black woman elected to the U.S. Senate. She is only the second African-American to be elected to the Senate since Reconstruction (the first was Republican Senator Edward M. Brooke, who was elected from Massachusetts in 1966).
By 1994	**EEOC** (Equal Employment Opportunity Commission) has a backlog of 96,945 cases, more than double its 1990 complaints, and only 732 investigators and a $230 million budget to deal with them.
1995	In October, **Oprah Winfrey** is listed for first time on list of Forbes 400. With 1995 earnings estimated at $415 million, she becomes first African-American woman to make the list. She is estimated to be worth around $1 billion by the year 2000. **Robert Holland** is recruited to Ben & Jerry's Homemade Inc. as CEO and President. He is the first African-American to be CEO of a major public U.S. company.

1995	The U.S. Supreme Court backs Federal Affirmative Action plan.
1996	**April 2, 1996, Ron Brown** is killed in a plane crash in Croatia.
1997	**Kenneth Chenault** is named president and CEO of American Express Company.
1998	Fannie Mae's **Franklin D. Raines** becomes the first African-American CEO of a FORTUNE 500 company.
1999	The Knowledge Express Company publishes the **History of Black Business: the Coming of America's Largest African-American-owned Businesses** to bring the history of black business ownership to your homes, schools, and libraries.

B.

Number of Black Businesses, 1863-1998

1863	1873	1883	1903	1913	1920
2,288	4,904	9,054	25,000	40,000	70,000

Source: The Negro Year Book

1969	1982	1987	1992	1998
163,000	308,260	424,165	620,912	970,000

Source: U.S. Census, 1998 Estimated by the Knowledge Express Company.

Distribution of Black Businesses, 1982-1992

Type of Business	1982	1987	1992
Automotive Dealers and Service Stations	3,448	3,690	4,040
Miscellaneous Retail	53,981	34,870	49,381
Food Stores	9,187	8,952	8,466
Eating and Drinking Places	11, 629	11,834	13,832
Health Services	17,195	30,026	43,860
Special Trade Contractors	18,399	29,631	36,057
Personal Services	40,394	56,772	76,988
Wholesale Trade (Non-DurableGoods)	2,441	2,727	3,461
Trucking and Warehousing	13,029	19,663	25,756
Business Services	NITT	59,177	80,330
Wholesales Trade (Durable goods)	1,210	2,792 (NITT)	4,088
Grand Total	**308,260**	**424,165**	**620,912**

Source: 1982, 1987, 1992 Economic Census, "Survey of Minority-owned Business Enterprises",

U.S. Department of commerce, Economics and Statistics Administration, BUREAU OF THE CENSUS.

Top 10 Standard Metropolitan Areas of Businesses 1982 - 1992

City	1982	1987	1992
New York	20,520	28,063	39,404
Los Angeles	23,520	23,932	32,645
Washington, DC	18,805	23,046	37,988
Chicago	13,660	15, 374	24,644
Houston	12,206	12,989	18,840
Atlanta	7,077	11,084	23,488
Philadelphia	8,581	10,249	13,956
Detroit	8731	9,852	13,910
Baltimore	N/A	8,593	12,492
Dallas	7,825	7,857	11,395
San Francisco	9,388	3,131	3,779

Source: 1982, 1987, 1992 Economic Census, "Survey of Minority-owned Business Enterprises", U.S.
Department of commerce, Economics and Statistics Administration, BUREAU OF THE CENSUS

C.
Glossary

Word	Definition
BE 100	BLACK ENTERPRISE magazine's yearly list of the hundred largest auto dealerships and commercial and industrial Black-owned firms.
Black Codes	Laws passed to restrict the Civil Rights of African-Americans. Many of these laws were used to end the guarantees of Reconstruction and to preserve the Slave Society power structure developed in the South.
CEO	Chief Executive Officer
CFO	Chief Financial Officer
De Jure	"by law", as opposed to 'de facto',or in fact/in actuality.
Indentured servant	A person who works for no wages but is guaranteed freedom after having served for a determined number of years.
IPO	Initial Public Offering; process by which a private firm sells its ownership in the form of shares in a public stock market. Money gained from this sale can be used by the pre-IPO owners to grow the business or to be used as profit.
Jim Crow Laws	Laws designed to separate and exclude African-Americans from the Civil and economic freedoms necessary to acquire wealth and develop structures that ensure the freedom's guaranteed under the Constitution.
Klux Klux Klan	Terrorist, White supremacist organization responsible for tens of thousands of murders from the end of Slavery until present.
Lasting	The act of shaping or repairing shoes or boots on a wooden or metal form in the shape of the human foot.

LBO	Leveraged Buy-Out. A technique used by entrepreneurs to buy the equity (ownership) of a firm.
Majority-owned	Owned by Whites, non-minorities.
MBO	Management Buy-Out. When the managers of a firm buy the equity of the firm such that they become the owners.
MESBICS	Minority Enterprise Small Investment Companies – venture capital firms formed by corporations which operate under the supervision of the U.S. Small Business Administration.
Octoroon	Someone considered to have 1/8 (one-eighth) African ancestry.
Poll Tax	Tax levied on African-Americans to exclude them from voting.
Private	A company owned by a private group of individuals, and not traded on a stock exchange is said to be a private company.
Public	A company traded on the stock market is said to be publicly-owned.
Quadroon	Someone considered to have 1/4 (one-fourth) African ancestry.
Redlining	Technique used by banks and realtors to exclude African-Americans from living in certain neighborhoods. Includes the denying of mortage loans, refusal to show African-Americans homes in the area, and misleading African-Americans about home availability.
Slave Codes	Laws used to restict the freedom, movement, and ability for legal protection by enslaved individuals.
Stock Market	NYSE – New York Stock Exchange; AMSE – American Stock Exchange; NASDAQ—National Association of Securities Dealers and Quotations
Venture Capital	Capital (money) invested in innovative and start-up companies for a percentage ownership of the firm.
Venture Capitalist	A person involved in providing capital for a start-up or promising projects that generally cannot get money from traditional sources.

D.   Publicly-Owned African-American-owned businesses

Company	Symbol : Exchange
American Shared Hospital Services	AMS : AMEX
Ault Inc.	AULT : NASDAQ
BET Holdings (went private 1998)	BTV : NYSE
Broadway Financial Corp.	BYFC : NASDAQ
Caraco Pharmaceutical Labs	CARA : OTCBB
Carson Inc.	CIC : NYSE
Carver Bancorp	CNY : AMEX
Chapman Holdings	CMAN: NASDAQ
Envirotest Systems	ENR : NASDAQ
Granite Broadcasting	GBTVK: NASDAQ
Carver Bancorp	CNY : AMEX
Pyrocap International	PYOC : OTCBB
United American Healthcare	UAH : NYSE

Source: **BLACK ENTERPRISE,** "B.E. Black Stock Index". July 1998, pg. 46.

E.
Top Commercial and Industrial Companies in 1997
(Top 25 - Sales in millions of dollars, rounded to the nearest million)

1997	Company	Chief Executive	Sales
1	TLC Beatrice International Holdings Inc.	Loida N. Lewis	$1,400
2	Johnson Publishing Co. Inc.	John H. Johnson	$361
3	Philadelphia Coca-Cola Bottling Co. Inc.	J. Bruce Lewellyn	$357
4	Active Transportation	Charlie W. Johnson	$250
5	The Bing Group	Dave Bing	$183
6	Granite Broadcasting Corp.	W. D on Cornwell	$181
7	BET Holdings Inc.	Robert L. Johnson	$170
8	H. J. Russell & Co.	Herman J. Russell	$155
9	Pulsar Data Systems Inc.	William W. Davis Sr.	$151
10	Anderson-Dubose Co.	Warren E. Anderson	$139
11	World Wide Technology Inc.	David L. Steward	$135
12	Mays Chemical Co. Inc.	William G. Mays	$123
13	Midwest Stamping Inc.	Ronald L. Thompson	$121
14	Barden Companies Inc.	Don H. Barden	$110
15	Simeus Foods International	Dumas M. Simeus	$105
16	Essence Communications Inc.	Edward T. Lewis	$105
17	Spiral Inc.	Reggie Fowler	$100
18	Soft Sheen Products Inc.	Terri L. Gardner	$95
18	Wesley International Inc.	Delbert W. Mullens	$95
20	Thomas Madison Inc.	Geralda Dodd	$90
21	Digital Systems International Corp.	Willie E. Woods	$89
22	Fuci Metals USA Inc.	A. Demetrius Brown	$87
22	Stop Shop Save Food Markets	Henry T. Baines Sr.	$87
24	La-Van Hawkins Urban City Food Markets	La-Van Hawkins	$86
25	Calhoun Enterprises	Gregory Calhoun	$80

Source of this and all of the following B.E. lists: BLACK ENTERPRISE, June 1998.

F.

Top Auto Dealerships in 1997
(Top 25 - Sales in millions of dollars, rounded to the nearest million)

1997	Company	Chief Executive	Sales
1	Mel Farr Automotive Group	Mel Farr Sr.	$573
2	Chicago Truck Center Inc.	Robert L. Hatcher	$223
3	S & J Enterprises	Sam Johnson	$158
4	Martin Automotive Group	Cornelius A. Martin	$138
5	Warner Robins Oldsmobile Cadillac Pontiac GMC-Truck	Jesse A. Moore	$137
6	Southgate Automotive Group	Fred. J. Poe	$125
7	Hubbard Investments LLC.	Reginald T. Hubbard	$121
8	Avis Ford	Walter E. Douglas Sr.	$113
9	Armstrong Enteprises	William Armstrong	$111
10	32 Ford Lincoln-Mercury	Clarence F. Warren	$110
11	Ray Wilkinson Buick Cadillac Inc.	Raymond M. Wilkinson Jr.	$108
12	Brandon Dodge Inc.	Sanford L. Woods	$98
13	Simi Valley Pontiac GMC Buick Inc.	Frank E. Marley Jr.	$95
14	B&G Associates	Franklin D. Greene	$91
15	Board Ford Inc.	Raymond Dixon	$90
16	Heritage Automotive Group	Ernest M. Hodge	$80
17	Prestige Automotive Group	Gregory Jackson	$74
18	Tropical Ford Inc.	Hamilton W. Massey	$73
19	Bob Johnson Auto Group	Robert Johnson	$72
20	University Automotive Group	Ronald L. Hill	$7
21	Village Ford of Lewisville	Charles E. Bankston	$68
22	Baranco Automotive Group	Gregory Baranco	$68
23	Bob Ross Buick Inc.	Norma J. Ross	$67
24	Davis Automotive Inc.	Richard O. Davis	$64
25	Spalding Automotive Group	Alan Reeves	$63

Source: BLACK ENTERPRISE, June 1998.

G.
Top Banks in 1997
(Top 25 - Assets in millions of dollars, rounded to the nearest million)

1997	Company	Chief Executive	Assets
1	Carver Bancorp Inc.	Thomas L. Clark Jr.	$416
2	Independence Federal Savings Bank	William B. Fitzgerald	$270
3	Industrial Bank N. A.	B. Doyle Mitchell Jr.	$251
4	Highland Community Bank	George R. Brokenmond	$247
5	Seaway National Bank of Chicago	Walter E. Grady	$246
6	Citizens Trust Bank of Atlanta	James E. Young	$185
7	Family Savings Bank FSB	Wayne-Kent A. Bradshaw	$175
8	Liberty Bank and Trust Co.	Alden J. Mcdonald Jr.	$148
9	City National Bank of New Jersey	Louis E. Prezeau	$139
10	The Harbor Bank of Maryland	Joseph Haskins Jr.	$136
11	Mechanics and Farmers Bank	Julia W. Taylor	$131
12	Broadway Federal Bank, FSB	Paul C. Hudson	$125
13	Consolidated Bank and Trust Company	Vernard W. Henley	$110
14	Illinois Service Federal S&L Assoc.	Thelma J. Smith	$110
15	United Bank of Philadelphia	Dr. Emma C. Chappell	$109
16	Founders National Bank of Los Angeles	Carlton J. Jenkins	$100
17	First Independence National Bank	Donald Davis	$100
18	Tri-State Bank of Memphis	Jesse H. Turner Jr.	$98
19	Citizens Federal Savings Bank	Bunny Stokes Jr.	$94
20	Dryades Savings Bank, FSB	Virgil Robinson Jr.	$76

21	**Boston Bank of Commerce**	Kevin Cohee	$74
22	**Douglass National Bank**	Ronald Wiley	$68
23	**Mutual Community Savings Bank Inc. SSB**	George K. Quick	$59
24	**First Tuskegee Bank**	James W. Wright	$54
25	**Peoples National Bank of Commerce**	Rachel Reeves	$53

Source: BLACK ENTERPRISE, June 1998.

H.

Top Insurance Companies in 1997

(Top 10 - Assets in millions of dollars, rounded to the nearest million)

1997	Company/ Location	Chief Executive	Assets
1	**North Carolina Mutual Insurance Co./** Durham, North Carolina	Bert Collins	$215
2	**Atlanta Life Insurance Co./** Atlanta, Georgia	Charles H. Cornelius	$202
3	**Golden State Mutual Life Insurance Co./** Los Angeles, California	Larkin Teasley	$103
4	**Universal Life Insurance Co./** Memphis, Tennessee	Eldredge M. Williams	$60
5	**Booker T. Washington Insurance Co./** Birmingham, Alabama	Kirkwood R. Balton	$58
6	**Protective Industrial Ins. Co./** Birmingham, Alabama	James C. Harrison	$18
7	**Winnfield Life Insurance Co./** Natchitoches, Louisiana	Ben D. Johnson	$11
8	**Williams-Progressive Life & Accident Ins. Co./** Opelousas, Louisiana	Randolph J. Donatto	$8
9	**Golden Circle Life Insurance Co./** Brownsville, Tennessee	Cynthia Rawls Bond	$7
10	**Reliable Life Insurance Co./** Monroe, Louisiana	Joseph H. Miller Jr.	$6

Source: BLACK ENTERPRISE, June 1998.

I.

Top Investment Banks in 1997

1998	Company	Chief Executive	Senior-Managed Issues ($M)	Co-Managed Issues ($B)
1	Utendahl Capital Partners L.P.	John O. Utendahl	$2,100	$4.6
2	Jackson Securities Inc.	Maynard H. Jackson	$1,100	$5
3	The Williams Capital Group L.P.	Christopher J. Williams	$755	$0.304
4	First Commonwealth Securities Corp.	Norbert A. Simmons	$650	$0.450
5	Apex Securities Inc.	Rodney Ellis	$507.750	$4.255
6	Siebert Branford Shank & Co. L.L.C.	Napoleon Branford III & Suzanne F. Shank	$345.040	$16.9
7	M. R. Beal & Co.	Bernard B. Beal	$150	$26.150
8	Blaylock & Partners L.P.	Ronald E. Blaylock	$150	$11.282
9	SBK-Brooks Investment Corp.	Eric L. Small	$115	$2.666
10	Powell Capital Markets Inc.	Arthur F. Powell	$82.659	$2.892
11	Gilchrist & Co. Inc.	Harold Gilchrist	$72	$0.555
12	The Chapman Co.	Nathan A. Chapman Jr.	$50	$2.7
13	Pryor McClendon Counts & Co. Inc.	Malcolmn D. Pryor	$36.710	$33.766
14	Doley Securities Inc.	Harold E. Doley Jr.	N/A	$3.505
15	Rideau Lyons & Co.	Lamar A. Lyons	N/A	$1.4

Source: BLACK ENTERPRISE, June 1998.

J.
Leading Black Entrepreneurs 1820-1865

Name	Location	Business Activity	Accumulated Wealth
Leidersdorff, William	San Francisco	Merchandising, real estate	$1,500,000
Smith, Stephen	Columbia, PA; Philadelphia	Lumber merchant, real estate	$500,000
Soulie, Albin & Bernard	New Orleans	Merchant broker, capitalists	$500,000
Lacroix, Francois	New Orleans	Tailor, real estate	$300,000
Lacroix, Julien	New Orleans	Grocer, real estate	$250,000
Ricaud, widow & son Pierre	Iberville Parish	Sugar planters	$221,500
Du Buclet, August	Iberville Parish	Sugar planter	$206,400
Pottier, Honore	New Orleans	Commission broker, in cotton	$200,000
Du Puy, Edmond	New Orleans	Capitalist	$171,000
Reggio, Auguste and Octave	Plaquemines Parish	Sugar planter, overseer	$160,000
McCarty, Cecee	New Orleans	Merchandising, money broker	$155,000
DeCuir, Antoine	Pointe Cupee Parish	Sugar planter	$151,000
Logoaster, Erasme	New Orleans	Landlord	$150,000
Colvis, Julien and Dumas, Joseph	New Orleans	Tailors	$150,000
Metoyer, Augustin	Natchitoches Parish	Cotton planter	$140,958
Durnford, Thomas	Plaquemines Parish	Sugar planter	$115,000
Metoyer, Jean Baptiste	Natchitoches Parish	Cotton planter	$112,761
Casenave, Pierre A. D.	New Orleans	Commission broker, undertaker	$100,000
Donato, Martin	St. Landry Parish	Cotton planter	$100,000
Forten, James	Philadelphia, PA	Sailmaker	$100,000
Spraulding, Washington	Louisville, KY	Barber, real estate	$100,000

Source: Walker, Juliet E.K., "Racism, Slavery, and Free Enterprise: Black Entrepreneurship in the United States before the Civil War." *Business History Review*, Autumn 1986: 343-382.

CHAPTER ONE
Endnotes

(1) James, Portia P., The Real McCoy (Washington DC: Smithsonian Institution, 1989), 30.

(2) James, Portia P., The Real McCoy (Washington DC: Smithsonian Institution, 1989), 30.

(3) Oak, Vishnu V., The Negro's Adventure in General Business. 1949. (Westport, Negro Universities, 1971), 48.

(4) Low, W. Augustus and Virgil A. Clift, Encyclopedia of Black America. (New York: Da Capo, 1971), 82-83.

(5) Bennet, Lerone Jr., "Money, Mechants, Markets: The Quest for Economic Security," Ebony, February 1974: 67.

(6) Two sources were used for this section.
Empak Black History Publication Series. Historic Black Pioneers (Chicago: Empak Publishing, 1990), 14.
Empak Black History Publication Series. A Salute to Black Pioneers (Chicago: Empak Publishing, 1986), 15.

(7) Three sources were used for this section.
Empak Black History Publication Series. Historic Black Pioneers (Chicago: Empak Publishing, 1990), 8.
Empak Black History Publication Series. A Salute to Black Pioneers (Chicago: Empak Publishing, 1986), 11.
Ingham, John N. and Lynne Feldman, African-American Business Leaders – A Biographical Dictionary (Westport: Greenwood, 1994), 597.

(8) Two sources were used for this section.
Empak Black History Publication Series. Historic Black Pioneers (Chicago: Empak Publishing, 1990), 14.
Empak Black History Publication Series. A Salute to Black Pioneers (Chicago: Empak Publishing, 1986), 15.

(9) Estimated as a relative percent of per capita income from 1899 compared to per capita income in 1995; National Income in the United States 1799-1938, Robert F. Martin, National Industrial Conference Board Inc. and the U.S. Statistical Abstract 1997.

(10) Three sources were used for this section.
Empak Black History Publication Series. <u>Historic Black Pioneers</u> (Chicago: Empak Publishing, 1990), 26.
Empak Black History Publication Series. <u>A Salute to Black Pioneers</u> (Chicago: Empak Publishing, 1986), 24.
Ingham, John N. and Lynne Feldman, <u>African-American Business Leaders – A Biographical Dictionary</u> (Westport: Greenwood, 1994), 597.

(11) Two sources were used for this section.
Empak Black History Publication Series. <u>Historic Black Pioneers</u> (Chicago: Empak Publishing, 1990), 14.
Empak Black History Publication Series. <u>A Salute to Black Pioneers</u> (Chicago: Empak Publishing, 1986), 15.

(12) James, Portia P., <u>The Real McCoy</u> (Washington DC: Smithsonian Institution, 1989), 85-86.

(13) Papanek, John L., ed., <u>Voices of Triumph: Leadership</u> (Alexandria: Time-Life, 1993), 81.

(14) Shapiro, Barbara and Arthur M. Johnson, <u>The Second Bank of the United States (Abridged)</u>. Harvard Business School Case 9-391-262. Boston: Harvard Business School, 1991.

(15) Shapiro, Barbara and Arthur M. Johnson, <u>The Second Bank of the United States (Abridged)</u>. Harvard Business School Case 9-391-262. Boston: Harvard Business School, 1991.

(16) Ingham, John N. and Lynne Feldman, <u>African-American Business Leaders – A Biographical Dictionary</u> (Westport: Greenwood, 1994), 597.

(17) Salzman, Jack and David Lionel Smith and Cornet West, eds., <u>Encyclopedia of African-American Culture and History</u> (New York: Simon & Schuster MacMillan, 1996), 246.

(18) Salzman, Jack and David Lionel Smith and Cornet West, eds., <u>Encyclopedia of African-American Culture and History</u> (New York: Simon & Schuster MacMillan, 1996), 247.

CHAPTER ONE
Bibliography

Asante, Molefi K., and Mark T. Mattson, *Historical and Cultural Atlas of African Americans*. New York City: Macmillan, 1991.

Bailey, Ronald W., ed., *Black Business Enterprise: Historical and Contemporary Perspectives*. New York: Basic Books, 1971.

Bennett, Lerone Jr., *Before the Mayflower: A History of Black America, The Classic Account of the Struggles and Triumphs of Black Americans*. New York City: Penguin, 1962.

Bennett, Lerone Jr., "Money, Merchants, Markets: The Quest for Economic Security." *Ebony*. February 1974: 66-78.

Blasisingame, John W., *Black New Orleans* . 1860. Chicago: University of Chicago, 1973.

Bolster, W. Jeffrey, *Black Jacks*. Cambridge: Harvard University, 1997.

Bundles. A'Leila Perry, *Madam C.J. Walker*. New York: Chelsea House, 1991.

Burt, McKinley, Jr., *Black Inventors of America*. Portland: National Book Company, 1969.

Chappell, Kevin, "How Black Inventors Changed America." *Ebony*. February 1, 1997: 40.

Collins, Charles M., and David Cohen, eds. *The African Americans*. New York City: Penguin, 1993.

Dabney, Wendell Phillips, *Cincinnati's Colored Citizens; Historical, Sociological and Biographical*. New York City: Negro Universities: 1970.

Delaney, Martin Robison, *The Condition, Elevation, Emigration, and Destiny of the Colored People of the United States*. Philadelphia: Delaney, 1852.

Du Boise, W.E.B., *The Negro in Business*. 1899. New York: AMS, 1971.

Gibson, John William, *Progress of a Race*. Naperville: J. L. Nichols & Co., 1929.

Green, Richard L., ed., *A Gift to Heritage: Historic Black Pioneers*. Chicago: Empak, 1990.

Green, Richard L., ed., *A Salute to Historic Black Abolitionists*. 1988. Chicago: Empak, 1993.

Green, Richard L., ed., *A Salute to Historic Black Women*. Chicago: Empak, 1984.

Green, Richard L., ed., *A Salute to Black Pioneers* . Chicago: Empak, 1986.

Green, Richard L., ed., *A Salute to Black Scientists and Inventors*. Chicago: Empak, 1985.

Green, Shelley, and Paul Pryde, *Black Entrepreneurship in America*. New Brunswick: Transaction, 1990.

Green, Shelley, and Paul Pryde, *Black Entrepreneurship in America*. New Brunswick: Transaction, 1990.

Harris, Abram L., *A Black Classic: The Negro as Capitalist—A Study of Banking and Business Among American Negroes*. Chicago: Urban Research, 1992.

Harris, Abram L., *The Negro Capitalist*. New York: Negro Universities, 1969.

Ingham, John N. and Lynne B. Feldman, *African-American Business Leaders - A Biographical Dictionary*. Westport: Greenwood, 1994.

Jones, Edwards H., *Blacks in Business*. New York: Grosset & Dunlap, 1971.

Katz, William Loren, *Black People Who Made the West*. Trenton: Ethrac, 1992.

Kennedy, William J., Jr., *The North Carolina Mutual Life Insurance Company*. Durham: North Carolina Mutual Insurance Company, 1970.

Kinzer, Robert H., and Edward Sagarin, *The Negro in Business*. New York: Greenberg, 1950.

Kunjufu, Jawanza, *Black Economics*. Chicago: African American Images, 1991.

Logan, Rayford W. and Michael R. Winston, eds., *Dictionary of American Negro Biography*. New York: W.W. Norton & Co., 1982.

Low, W. Augustus and Virgil A. Clift, *Encyclopedia of Black America*. New York: Da Capo, 1981.

McCoy, Frank, "The African Presence in the West." *Black Enterprise*. February 1990: 21.

McCraw, Thomas K., Slavery. Harvard Business School Case N9-792-001.
    Boston: Harvard Business School, 1991.

Mott, A., *Biographical Sketches and Interesting Anecdotes of Persons of Color*.
    New York: Lindley Murray, 1839.

Oak, Vishnu V., *The Negro's Adventure in General Business*. 1949. Westport:
    Negro Universities, 1971.

Papanek, John L., ed., *African Americans: Voices of Triumph: Leadership*.
    Alexandria: Time-Life, 1993.

Pierce, Joseph Alphonso, *Negro Business and Business Education*. New York:
    Harper & Brothers, 1947.

Ploski, Harry A. and Ernest Kaiser, *The Negro Almanac - A Reference Work on the
    African American*. New York: Bellwether, 1971.

Puth, Robert C., "Supereme Life: The History of a Negro Life Insurance Company."
    Business History Review. Spring 1969: 1-20.

Quarles, Benjamin, *The Negro in the Making of America*. 1964. New York:
    Collier, 1987.

Salzman, Jack, David Lionel Smith and Cornel West, eds., *Encyclopedia of African-
    American Culture and History*. New York: Simon & Schuster MacMillan, 1996.

Smith, Jessie Carney, *Black Firsts*. Detroit: Visible Ink, 1994.

Spear, Allan H., *Black Chicago: The Making of a Negro Ghetto, 1890-1920*. Chicago:
    University of Chicago Spear, 1967.

Walker, Juliet E.K., "Racism, Slavery, and Free Enterprise: Black Entrepreneurship
    in the United States before the Civil War." *Business History Review*, Autumn
    1986: 343-382.

Washington, Booker T. *The Negro in Business*. 1907. Boston: AMS, 1971.

Winch, Julie, *Philadelphia's Black Elite: Activism, Accommodation, and the Struggle
    for Autonomy, 1787-1848*. Philadelphia: Temple University, 1988.

Winston, Michael R. and Rayford W. Logan, eds., *Dictionary of American Negro
    Biography*. New York: W. W. Norton, 1982.

CHAPTER TWO

Endnotes

(1) Analysis of: Porter, Michael, <u>The Competitive Advantage of Nations</u> (New York City: Macmillan, 1990).

(2) Gaiter. Dorothy G., "Black Entrepreneurship – Short Term Despair, Long Term Promise." <u>Wall Street Journal</u> April 3, 1992: R1.

(3) <u>Banking on Black Enterprise</u>, Joint Center for Political and Economic Studies.

(4) Brown, Carolyn M., "Coming Through in the Clutch." <u>Black Enterprise</u> June 1994: 114.

(5) Brown, Carolyn M., "Coming Through in the Clutch." <u>Black Enterprise</u> June 1994: 116.

(6) Brown, Carolyn M., "Coming Through in the Clutch." <u>Black Enterprise</u> June 1994: 116.

(7) Brown, Carolyn M., "Coming Through in the Clutch." <u>Black Enterprise</u> June 1994: 122.

(8) Enrico, Dottie, "Spike Lee Ad Agency to Target Urban Market." <u>USA Today</u> December 5, 1996: 1B.

(9) Newton, Edmund, "Countdown to Takeoff – Inner City Broadcasting is Assembling the Components That Will Make It One of the World's Top Telecommunications Companies." <u>Black Enterprise</u> June 1982: 132.

(10) Edmond Jr., Alfred, "It's Showtime! – The Suttons Are A Family Act That's Tough to Follow. They've Made IBC Corp. the Hardest Working Media Company in Show Business." <u>Black Enterprise</u> April 1989: 50.

(11) Newton, Edmund, "Countdown to Takeoff – Inner City Broadcasting is Assembling the Components That Will Make It One of the World's Top Telecommunications Companies." <u>Black Enterprise</u> June 1982: 130.

(12) Editors, "Inside Inner City Broadcasting." <u>Broadcasting</u> January 8, 1990: 104.

(13) Smith, Eric L., "Now Serving South Africa – Investment Team Lands Domino's Master Franchise Agreement." <u>Black Enterprise</u> February 1996: 17.

CHAPTER TWO
Bibliography

Ahiarah, Sol. "Black Americans' Business Ownership Factors: A Theoretical Perspective." *The Review of Black Political Economy*. Fall 1993: 15-36.

Anderson, Bernard E., "A Tale of Two Decades." *Black Enterprise* June 1992: 207-216.

Ando, Faith H., "An Analysis of the Formation and Failure Rates of Minority-Owned Firms. " *The Review of Black Political Economy*. Fall 1986: 51-71.

Bailey, Ronald W., ed. *Black Business Enterprise: Historical and Contemporary Perspectives*. New York City: Basic Books, 1971.

Benjaman, Peter, *The Story of Motown*. New York City: Grove Press, 1979.

Bennett, Lerone Jr., "Money, Merchants, Markets: The Quest for Economic Security." *Ebony*. February 1974: 66-78.

Brimmer, Andrew F., "The Future of Black Business: Short-Run Problems Will Not Halt an Upward Trend." *Black Enterprise*. June 1974: 27-30.

Brown, Carolyn M., " Coming Through in the Clutch." *Black Enterprise*. June 1994: 108-122.

Brown, Carolyn M., ed., "The Hottest Industries for New Business Opportunities." *Black Enterprise*. March 1995: 65-73.

Ebony Success Library, Vols. 1 and 2. Chicago: Johnson Publishing Company, 1973.

Editors, <u>African Americans- Voices of Triumph: Perseverance</u>. Alexandria: Time-Life, 1993.

Editors, "20 Years of Black Business Leadership, Overview: A Tale of 2 Decades." *Black Enterprise*. June 1992: 207-216.

Editors, "B.E. 100 Overview: Building a New Tradition." *Black Enterprise*. June 1983: 68-74.

Editors, "B.E. 100 Overview: Maintaining the Bottom Line." *Black Enterprise*. June 1985: 87-94.

Edmond, Alfred, Jr., "BE 100s Overview: Coming on Strong." *Black Enterprise*.
     June 1994: 75- 84.

Editors, "Inside Inner City Broadcasting." *Broadcasting*. January 8, 1990: 104-105.

Editors, 1982 Survey of Minority-Owned Business Enterprises: Black 1982
     Economic Census. Washington D.C.: U.S. Department of Commerce, 1982.

Editors, "The Magic and the Money." *Forbes* December 16, 1996: 264.

Editors, Survey of Minority-Owned Business Enterprises: Black. 1987 Economic
     Census. Washington D.C.: U.S. Department of Commerce, 1987.

Editors, "Thriving Under Pressure." *Black Enterprise* June 1992: 99-112.

Editors, "B.E. 100s Overview: Thriving Under Pressure." *Black Enterprise*.
     June 1992: 99-113.

Edmond, Jr., Alfred A., "Should Black Businesses Be Sold to Whites? Sure - If the
     Price is Right. How Else Can Black Entrepreneurs Raise the Capital to Finance
     Expansions and Acquisitions?" *Black Enterprise*. November 1993: 45-51.

Edmond, Jr., Alfred, "It's Showtime! – The Suttons Are A Family Act That's Tough To
     Follow. They've Made IBC Corp. the Hardest Working Media Company in
     Show Business." *Black Enterprise*. April 1989: 46-54.

Elias, Marylyn, "Race Bias Mars Mortgage Gains." USA Today February 13, 1997: 2B.

Gaiter, Dorothy G., "Black Entrepreneurship – Short-Term Despair, Long Term
     Promise." Wall Street Journal April 3, 1992: R1.

Gordy, Berry, *To Be Loved: The Music, the Magic, the Memories of Motown*.
     New York: Warner, 1994.

Green, Shelley, and Paul Pryde, *Black Entrepreneurship in America*. New Brunswick:
     Transaction Publishers, 1990.

Harris, Abram L., *The Negro as Capitalist*. 1936. New York City: Negro
     Universities Press, 1969.

Hoover, Gary, Alta Campbell and Patrick J. Spain, eds., *Hoover's Handbook of
     American Business 1993, Profiles of 500 Major Companies*. Austin: The
     Reference Press, 1993.

Hope, John, "Black & Green - The Untold Story of the African-American Entrepreneur." *Ebony*. February 1996: 36-37, 170-172.

Hutchinson, Earl Ofari, "The Continuing Black Myth of Black Capitalism." The Black Scholar. Vol. 23, No. 1: 16.

Ingham, John N., *Biographical Dictionary of American Business Leaders*. Westport: Greenwood, 1983.

Jones, Edwards H., *Blacks in Business*. New York City: Grosset & Dunlap, 1971.

Karr, Albert R. "Federal Drive to Curb Mortgage Loan Bias Stirs Strong Backlash." The Wall Street Journal February 7, 1995: A1.

Kennedy, William J., Jr., *The North Carolina Mutual Life Insurance Company*. Durham: North Carolina Mutual Insurance Company, 1970.

Kinzer, Robert H., and Edward Sagarin, *The Negro in Business*. New York City: Greenberg, 1950.

Kunjufu, Jawanza, *Black Economics*. Chicago: African American Images, 1991.

Lesly, Elizabeth and Maria Mallory, "Inside the Black Business Network - A Far-Flung Web of Entrepreneurs is Driving African American Economic Growth." *Business Week*. November 29, 1993: 70-81.

Lewis, Reginald F., and Blair S. Walker, *"Why Should White Guys Have All the Fun?": How Reginald Lewis Created a Billion-Dollar Business Empire*. New York City: John Wiley and Sons, 1995.

Maguire, Jack, and Tom Cowan, Ph.D., *Timelines of African-American History: 500 Years of Black Achievement*. New York: Pedigree, 1994.

Mast, Jennifer Arnold, *Ward's Private Company Profiles: Excerpts and Articles on Publicly Held US Companies*. Volume 1. Washington D.C.: Gate Research Inc.,1994.

Newton, Edmund, "Countdown to Takeoff – Inner City Broadcasting is Assembling the Components That Will Make It One of the World's Top Telecommunications Companies." *Black Enterprise*. June 1982: 128-133.

Porter, Michael, *Competitive Advantage: Creating and Sustaining Superior Performance*. New York: Macmillan, 1985.

Porter, Michael, *The Competitive Advantage of Nations*. New York City: Macmillan, 1990.

Salley, Columbus, *The Black 100: A Ranking of the Most Influential African Americans, Past and Present*. New York City: Citadel, 1993.

Sitkoff, Harvard, *The Struggle for Black Equality: 1954-1980*. Toronto: Harper and Collins, 1981.

Smith, Eric L., "Now Serving South Africa – Investment Team Lands Domino's Master Franchise Agreement." *Black Enterprise*. February 1996: 17.

Thompson, Kevin D., " Special Report: Is the 8(a) Process Worth All the Trouble?" *Black Enterprise*. August 1992: 64-74.

Vann, Kimberly, "Black Business Pioneers: Profiles of Courage and Prosperity." *Dollars and Sense*. February 1996: 50-61.

Wilke, John R. "Race is a Factor in Some Loan Denials." The Wall Street Journal July 13, 1995: A2.

Winston, Michael R. and Rayford W. Logan, eds., *Dictionary of American Negro Biography*. New York: W. W. Norton, 1982.

CHAPTER THREE
End Notes

(1) Puth, Robert C., "Supreme Life: The History of a Negro Life Insurance Company." <u>Business History Review</u> Spring 1969: 2.

(2) Puth, Robert C., "Supreme Life: The History of a Negro Life Insurance Company." <u>Business History Review</u> Spring 1969: 3.

(3) Puth, Robert C., "Supreme Life: The History of a Negro Life InsuranceCompany." <u>Business History Review</u> Spring 1969: 3.

(4) Pointsett, Alex, "Unsung Black Business Giants," <u>Ebony</u> March 1990: 96.

(5) Pointsett, Alex, "Unsung Black Business Giants," <u>Ebony</u> March 1990: 96.

(6) Pointsett, Alex, "Unsung Black Business Giants," <u>Ebony</u> March 1990: 96.

(7) Puth, Robert C., "Supreme Life: The History of a Negro Life Insurance Company." <u>Business History Review</u> Spring 1969: 2.

CHAPTER THREE
Bibliography

Adler, Jane, "Polishing Bronzeville." *Chicago Tribune.* October 12, 1997: 1P.

Ingham, John N. and Lynne B. Feldman, *African-American Business Leaders - A Biographical Dictionary.* Westport: Greenwood, 1994.

Leipold, L. Edmond, Ph.D., *Famous American Negroes.* Minneapolis: T.S. Denison and Company, 1967.

Poinsett, Alex, "Unsung Black Business Giants." *Ebony.* March 1990: 96-100.

Puth, Robert C., "Supreme Life: The History of a Negro Life Insurance Company." *Business History Review.* Spring 1969: 1-20.

Spear, Allan H., *Black Chicago: The Making of a Negro Ghetto - 1890-1920.* Chicago: University of Chicago, 1967.

CHAPTER FOUR
Endnotes

(1) Puth, Robert C., "Supreme Life: The History of a Negro Life Insurance Company, 1919-1962," <u>Business History Review</u> Spring 1969: 2.

(2) Puth, Robert C., "Supreme Life: The History of a Negro Life Insurance Company, 1919-1962," <u>Business History Review</u> Spring 1969: 4.

(3) Puth, Robert C., "Supreme Life: The History of a Negro Life Insurance Company, 1919-1962," <u>Business History Review</u> Spring 1969: 5.

(4) Puth, Robert C., "Supreme Life: The History of a Negro Life Insurance Company, 1919-1962," <u>Business History Review</u> Spring 1969: 7.

(5) Pointsett, Alex, "Unsung Black Business Giants," <u>Ebony</u> March 1990: 98.

(6) Pointsett, Alex, "Unsung Black Business Giants," <u>Ebony</u> March 1990: 98.

(7) Puth, Robert C., "Supreme Life: The History of a Negro Life Insurance Company, 1919-1962," <u>Business History Review</u> Spring 1969: 9-10.

(8) Puth, Robert C., "Supreme Life: The History of a Negro Life InsuranceCompany, 1919-1962," <u>Business History Review</u> Spring 1969: 10.

(9) Puth, Robert C., "Supreme Life: The History of a Negro Life Insurance Company, 1919-1962," <u>Business History Review</u> Spring 1969: 11.

(10) Puth, Robert C., "Supreme Life: The History of a Negro Life Insurance Company, 1919-1962," <u>Business History Review</u> Spring 1969: 12.

(11) Puth, Robert C., "Supreme Life: The History of a Negro Life InsuranceCompany, 1919-1962," <u>Business History Review</u> Spring 1969: 12.

(12) Puth, Robert C., "Supreme Life: The History of a Negro Life Insurance Company, 1919-1962," <u>Business History Review</u> Spring 1969: 14.

(13) Editors, "The North's Largest Negro Business – Supreme Liberty Life Ins.Co.," <u>Ebony</u> November 1956: 67.

(14) Editors, "The North's Largest Negro Business – Supreme Liberty Life Ins.Co.," <u>Ebony</u> November 1956: 67.

(15) Puth, Robert C., "Supreme Life: The History of a Negro Life Insurance Company, 1919-1962," <u>Business History Review</u> Spring 1969: 16.

(16) Puth, Robert C., "Supreme Life: The History of a Negro Life Insurance Company, 1919-1962," <u>Business History Review</u> Spring 1969: 1,16.

CHAPTER FOUR
Bibliography

Bennett, Lerone Jr., "Money, Merchants, Markets: The Quest for Economic Security." *Ebony*. February 1974: 66-78.

Editors, "The Miracle at Supreme Life." *Ebony*. October 1973: 116-124.

Editors, "The North's Largest Negro Business – Supreme Liberty Life Ins. Co." *Ebony*. November 1956: 64-69.

Ingham, John L., and Lynne B. Feldman, *African-American Business Leaders - A Biographical Dictionary*. Westport: Greenwood, 1994.

Poinsett, Alex, "Unsung Black Business Giants." *Ebony*. March 1990: 96-100.

Puth, Robert C., "Supreme Life: The History of a Negro Life Insurance Company, 1919-1962." *Business History Review*. Spring 1969: 1-20.

CHAPTER FIVE

End Notes

(1) Salley, Columbus, <u>The Black 100: A Ranking of the Most Influential African-Americans: Past and Present</u> (New York: Carol, 1993), 169.

(2) Author, "From Negro Digest to Ebony, Jet, and EM," <u>Ebony</u>, November 1992: 50.

(3) Hoover, Gary, Alta Campbell and Patrick J. Spain, <u>Hoover's Handbook of American Business - Profiles of 500 Major U.S. Companies</u> (Austin: Reference, 1993), 350.

(4) Randle, Wilma. "Johnson Publishing Heads Illinois Slate of Top 100 Black-Owned Firms." <u>Chicago Tribune</u> May 13, 1993: N1.

(5) McCann, Herbert G. "Johnson Publishing Turns 50: Ebony Magazine Key to Family-Owned Firm's Success," <u>Chicago Tribune</u> November 22, 1992: C8.

(6) Salley, Columbus, <u>The Black 100: A Ranking of the Most Influential African-Americans: Past and Present</u> (New York: Citadel, 1993), 169-171.

CHAPTER FIVE
Bibliography

Anderson, Veronica, "If There's Kente, Will They Come?" *Crain's Chicago Business*. October 11, 1993: 15.

Bennett, Lerone Jr., "Money, Merchants, Markets: The Quest for Economic Security." *Ebony*. February 1974: 66-78.

Editors, "Backstage." *Ebony*. June 1993: 17.

Editors, "Backstage." *Ebony*. December 1992: 19.

Editors, "Backstage." *Ebony*. February 1992: 25.

Editors, "From Negro Digest to Ebony, Jet, and EM." *Ebony*. November 1992: 50.

Editors, "Interview with John H. Johnson." *Ebony*. November 1985: 45-58.

Editors, "Inventing the Black Consumer Market." *Ebony*. November 1992: 56.

Editors, "Johnson Publishing Co. and Spiegel Offer Customized Catalog for African-American Women." *Ebony*. September 1993: 132.

Editors, "The JPC Family." *Ebony*. November 1992: 92.

Editors, "JPC Publisher Succeeds Against Odds and Daughter Prepares For Next 50 Years." *Jet*. November 9, 1992: 6.

Editors, "The New Black Cosmetics Magnate." *Black Enterprise*. June 1973: 71.

Hoover, Gary, Alta Campbell, and Patrick J. Spain, eds., *Hoover's Handbook of American Business 1993, Profiles of 500 Major U.S. Companies*. Austin: Reference, 1993.

Ingham, John N., *Biographical Dictionary of American Business Leaders*. Westport: Greenwood,1983.

Ingham, John L., and Lynne B. Feldman, *African-American Business Leaders - A Biographical Dictionary*. Westport: Greenwood, 1994.

Johnson, John H., *Succeeding Against the Odds*. Chicago: Johnson Publishing, 1993.

Kennedy, Randy. "W. P. Grayson, 79, Retired Executive of Publishing Firm." The New York Times September 30, 1993: B12.

Mangelsdorf, Martha E., ed., "From the Trenches; Straight to the Top: John Johnson." *Inc.* October 1993: 58.

Mast, Jennifer Arnold, *Ward's Private Company Profiles: Excerpts and Articles on Publicly Held US Companies*. Volume 1. Washington D.C.: Gate Research, 1994.

McCann, Herbert G. "Johnson Publishing Turns 50: Ebony Magazine Key to Family-Owned Firm's Success." Chicago Tribune November 22, 1992: C8.

Phelps, Shirelle, ed., *Who's Who Among African-Americans – 1996-1997*. Detroit: Gale Research, 1996.

Randle, Wilma. "Johnson Publishing Heads Illinois Slate of Top 100 Black-Owned Firms." Chicago Tribune May 13, 1993: N1.

Salley, Columbus, *The Black 100: A Ranking of the Most Influential African-Americans: Past and Present*. New York City: Carol Publishing, 1993.

Scott, Matthew S., "Johnson Celebrates 50th." *Black Enterprise*. November, 1992: 26.

CHAPTER SIX
End Notes

(1) Hoover, Gary, Alta Campbell, and Patrick J. Spain, eds., <u>Hoover's Handbook of American Businesses</u> (Austin: Reference, 1993), 56.

(2) Hoover, Gary, Alta Campbell and Patrick J. Spain, eds., <u>Hoover's Handbook of American Businesses</u> (Austin: Reference, 1993), 55.

(3) Salley, Columbus, <u>The Black 100: A Ranking of the Most Influential African-Americans: Past and Present</u> (New York: Citadel, Year), 467.

(4) Edmond Jr., Alfred, ed., "Another Lewis Leads TLC," <u>Black Enterprise</u> March 1994: 13.

(5) Solomon, Julie, "Operation Rescue," <u>Working Woman</u> May 1996: 58.

(6) Smith, Eric L., "TLC Beatrice Sells Off Major Food Division," <u>Black Enterprise</u> December 1997: 19.

(7) Smith, Eric L., "TLC Beatrice Sells Off Major Food Division," <u>Black Enterprise</u> December 1997: 19.

CHAPTER SIX
Bibliography

Editors, *1993 TLC Beatrice International Holdings, Inc.* The Reference Press, 1993.

Edmond Jr., Alfred, "Business History Deferred: The TLC Beatrice IPO." *Black Enterprise*. February 1990: 23-24.

Edmond Jr., Alfred, "Drexel's Fall: The Price of Backing Blacks?" *Black Enterprise*. May 1990: 14.

Edmond Jr., Alfred, "Forward Spin: Another Lewis Leads TLC." *Black Enterprise*. March 1994: 13.

Fleming, James and William C. Matney, eds., *Who's Who Among Black Americans*. Lake Forest: Educational Communications, 1988.

Graves, Earl G., "Shaping a New Tradition." *Black Enterprise*. November 1987: 9.

Hoover, Gary, Alta Cambell, and Patrick J. Spain, eds., *Hoover's Handbook of American Business 1993, Profiles of 500 Major Companies*. Austin: The Reference Press, 1993.

Ingham, John N., *Biographical Dictionary of American Business Leaders*. Westport: Greenwood Press, 1983.

Ingham, John L., and Lynne B. Feldman, *African-American Business Leaders - A Biographical Dictionary*. Westport: Greenwood, 1994.

Kupfer, Andrew, "Reginald Lewis – The Newest Member of the LBO Club." *Fortune*. January 4, 1988: 32-33.

Kyle, Cynthia and Robert H. Bork, "When Wall Street Began to Take Black Seriously." *U.S. News & World Report*. August 31, 1987: 44.

Lewis, Reginald F. and Blair S. Walker, *Why Should White Guys Have All the Fun? - How Reginald Lewis Created a Billion Dollar Empire* . New York City: Wiley & Sons, 1995.

McCarroll, Thomas, "A Woman's Touch." *Time*. October 28, 1996: 60-62.

Most, Jennifer Arnold, *Ward's Private Company Profiles: Excerpt and Articles on Privately Held U.S. Companies,* Volume 1, Washington DC: Gate Research Inc., 401-406.

Papanek, John L., ed., *African Americans Voices of Triumph: Leadership*. Alexandria: Time-Life, 1993.

Perry, Nancy J., "Reg to Riches." *Fortune*. September 14, 1987: 122.

Salley, Columbus, *The Black 100: A Ranking of the Most Influential African-Americans: Past and Present*. New York City: Citadel, 1993.

Smith, Eric L., "TLC Beatrice Sells Off Major Food Division." *Black Enterprise*. December 1997: 19.

Solomon, Julie, "Operation Rescue." *Working Woman*. May 1996: 54-59.

Stuart, Toby and Dr. George Baker, Beatrice Company—1985. Harvard Business School Case 9-391-191. Boston: Harvard Business School, 1991.

Thompson, Kevin D., "TLC Deal Signals New Era for Black Business." *Black Enterprise*. October 1987: 21.

CHAPTER SEVEN
End Notes

(1) Poe, Janita, "Parting Ways." <u>Chicago Tribune</u> August 23, 1993: 5,1.

(2) Poe, Janita, "Parting Ways." <u>Chicago Tribune</u> August 23, 1993: 5,1.

(3) Poe, Janita, "Parting Ways." <u>Chicago Tribune</u> August 23, 1993: 5,1.

(4) Poe, Janita, "Parting Ways." <u>Chicago Tribune</u> August 23, 1993: 5,1

(5) Feder, Barnaby J., "A Leader in Black Business, Johnson Products to be Sold." <u>New York Times</u> June 15, 1993: D1.

(6) McCoy, Frank, " Johnson Products Company Regroups After Family Rule," <u>Black Enterprise</u> May 1992: 17.

(7) McCoy, Frank, " Johnson Products Company Regroups After Family Rule," <u>Black Enterprise</u> May 1992: 17.

(8) Feder, Barnaby J., "A Leader in Black Business, Johnson Products to be Sold." <u>New York Times</u> June 15, 1993: D1.

(9) McCoy, Frank, " Johnson Products Company Regroups After Family Rule," <u>Black Enterprise</u> May 1992: 17.

(10) Editors, "JP to Sell Company to Fla. Business Firm for $67 M," <u>Jet</u> June 28, 1993: 6.

(11) Crown, Judith, "Johnson Products Running," <u>Crain's Chicago Business</u> February 1, 1993: 38.

(12) Poe, Janita, "Parting Ways." <u>Chicago Tribune</u> August 23, 1993: 5,1.

(13) White, George, "Black-Owned Hair Care Firm Ok's Purchase." <u>The Los Angeles Times</u> June 15, 1993: D1.

(14) White, George, "Black-Owned Hair Care Firm Ok's Purchase." <u>The Los Angeles Times</u> June 15, 1993: D1.

(15) Poe, Janita, "Parting Ways." <u>Chicago Tribune</u> August 23, 1993: 5,1.

(16) Chandler, Susan, "The Split Ends for a Hair-Care Duo." <u>Business Week</u> April 24, 1995: 6.

CHAPTER SEVEN
Bibliography

Bennett, Lerone Jr., "Money, Merchants, Markets: The Quest for Economic Security." *Ebony*. February 1974: 66-78.

Burrell, Berkeley G. and John W. Seder, *Getting it Together – Black Businessmen in America*. New York: Harcourt Brace Jovanovich, 1971.

Chandler, Susan, "The Split Ends for a Hair-Care Duo." *Business Week*. April 24, 1995: 6.

Crown, Judith, "Johnson Products Running." *Crain's Chicago Business*. February 1, 1993: 38.

Editors, "JP to Sell Company to Fla. Business Firm for $67 M." *Jet*. June 28, 1993: 6.

Editors, "Making Black Beautiful." *Time*. December 7, 1970: 87-88.

Feder, Barnaby J. "A Leader in Black Business, Johnson Products to be Sold." New York Times June 15, 1993: D1.

Ingham, John L., and Lynne B. Feldman, *African-American Business Leaders - A Biographical Dictionary*. Westport: Greenwood, 1994.

McCoy, Frank, "Johnson Products Company Regroups After Family Rule." Black Enterprise. May 1992: 17.

Phelps, Shirelle, ed., *Who's Who Among African-Americans – 1996-1997*. Detroit: Gale Research, 1996.

Poe, Janita. "Parting Ways." Chicago Tribune August 23, 1993: 5,1.

White, George. "Black-Owned Hair Care Firm Oks Purchase." Los Angeles Times June 15, 1993: D1.

CHAPTER EIGHT
Endnotes

(1) Russell, Deborah, "It's Ready, Set, Action for BET," <u>Billboard</u> August 7, 1993: 34.

(2) Jeffrey, Don, "Subscriber, Ad Revenues Augment BET Sales, Profits," <u>Billboard</u> March 27, 1993: 4.

(3) Atwood, Brett, "BET to Launch All-Jazz Channel," <u>Billboard</u> October 14, 1995: 82.

(4) McConville, Jim, "Black Films the Focus of New Pay Channel – Black Entertainment Television and Encore Media Group Create BET Movies/Starz!3," <u>Broadcasting and Cable</u> September 30, 1996: 63.

(5) Times Staff Writers, "BET, Microsoft Form Joint Venture," <u>Los Angeles Times</u> February 18, 1997: D3.

(6) Hudson, Jill, "BET Enters the Next Stage," <u>Baltimore Sun</u> January 18, 1997: D1.

(7) Tenny, Lori, "Hilton, Black Entertainment Firm Mull Partnership," <u>Travel Weekly</u> January 6, 1997: 56.

(8) Singletary, Michelle, "BET Entering The Financial Services Market," <u>Washington Post</u> April 1, 1997: C1.

(9) Singletary, Michelle, "BET Entering The Financial Services Market," <u>Washington Post</u> April 1, 1997: C1.

CHAPTER EIGHT
Bibliography

Atwood, Brett, "BET to Launch All-Jazz Channel." *Billboard*. October 14, 1995: 82.

Bigelow, Barbara Carlisle. Contemporary Black Biography. Detroit: Gale Research, 1993.

Brown, Rich, "BET Buys 80% of Action PPV." *Broadcasting and Cable*. June 14, 1993: 24.

Carvell, Tim, "What About the Shareholders?" *Fortune*. October 13, 1997: 27.

Chapelle, Tony, "Entrepreneur Makes BET and Wins." *The Network Journal*. June 30, 1995: 8.

Coulton, Antoinette, "Chevy Chase Bank, Cable Network Target Black Customers With BET Card." *American Banker*. April 4, 1997: 14.

Editors, "BET in Britain." *Broadcasting and Cable*. May 3, 1993: 79.

Editors, "Lee Named BET President." *Broadcasting and Cable*. March 25, 1996: 61.

Hudson, Jill, "BET Enters the Next Stage; Restaurant: CEO Robert Johnson Puts Entertainment and Style on the Menu with Gala Opening of Soundstage, a High Tech Eatery Created with African-American in Mind." Baltimore Sun January 18, 1997: 1D.

Iverem, Esther, "A Big BET in P.G.; Robert Johnson's $6.5 Million Restaurant is All Glitz in Shades of Black." Washington Post January 17, 1997: D1.

Kaplan, Peter, "Bob Johnson BET Chief Puts Smart Moves Amove Popularity." Washington Times February 10, 1997: D16.

Jeffrey, Don, "Subscriber, Ad Revenues Augment BET Sales, Profits." *Billboard*. March 27, 1993: 4-5.

Lewyn, Mark, "The Very Picture of Success." *BusinessWeek*. May 24, 1993: 67.

McConville, Jim, "Black Films the Focus of New Pay Channel – Black Entertainment Television and Encore Media Group Create BET Movies/Starz!3." *Broadcasting and Cable*. September 30, 1996: 63.

McConville, Jim, "Curtis Symonds BETs on Affiliates." *Broadcasting and Cable*. March 4, 1996: 81.

Reina, Laura, "N.Y. Daily News Debuts Niche Product – New York Newspaper Publishes Caribbeat Monthly as Insert." *Editor & Publisher*. March 15, 1997: 18.

Roach, Kia, "Affluent African-American's Appetites Target Market for New BET Restaurants." <u>Baltimore Daily Record</u> January 25, 1997: A5.

Roberts, Johnnie L., "Trials of Black Mogul." *Newsweek*. April 1, 1996: 71-72.

Russell, Deborah, "It's Ready, Set, Action for BET." *Billboard*. August 7, 1993: 34.

Sanchez, Jesus, "Hilton, BET May Build a Casino Aimed at Blacks." <u>Los Angeles Times</u> November 15, 1996: D1.

Singletary, Michelle, "BET Entering the Financial Services Market – Black Entertainment Television's Venture with Chevy Chase Bank." <u>The Washington Post</u> April 1, 1997: C1.

Sturgie, Ingrid, "BET Expands into Pay-Per-View." *Black Enterprise*. September 1993: 15.

Templeton, John W., "Ad Spending Slights Black Consumers – Advertising Spending in African American Community to Exceed $1 Billion in 1997." *Advertising Age*. March 17, 1997: 28.

Trescott, Jacqueline, "Fifteen Years and Rising for BET's Star." *Emerge*. September 1995: 66-67.

Waxler, Caroline, "Bob Johnson's Brainchild." *Forbes*. April 22, 1996: 98-100.

CHAPTER NINE
Endnotes

(1) Mair, George, <u>Oprah Winfrey - The Real Story</u> (New York: Birch Lane, 1994), 33.

(2) Mair, George, <u>Oprah Winfrey - The Real Story</u> (New York: Birch Lane, 1994), 36.

(3) Mair, George, <u>Oprah Winfrey - The Real Story</u> (New York: Birch Lane, 1994), 39.

(4) Winfrey, Oprah, "What We All Can Do To Change TV." <u>TV Guide</u> November 11, 1995: 12.

(5) Mair, George, <u>Oprah Winfrey - The Real Story</u> (New York: Birch Lane, 1994), 74.

(6) Mair, George, <u>Oprah Winfrey - The Real Story</u> (New York: Birch Lane, 1994), 78.

(7) Mair, George, <u>Oprah Winfrey - The Real Story</u> (New York: Birch Lane, 1994), 88.

(8) Mair, George, <u>Oprah Winfrey - The Real Story</u> (New York: Birch Lane, 1994), 88.

(9) Mair, George, <u>Oprah Winfrey - The Real Story</u> (New York: Birch Lane, 1994), 101.

(10) Mair, George, <u>Oprah Winfrey - The Real Story</u> (New York: Birch Lane, 1994), 132.

(11) Freeman, Michael, "Oprah Winfrey's Harpo Inc. Extends Contract With King World Productions." <u>Mediaweek</u> March 21, 1994: 16.

(12) Lieberman, David, "King World Sees New Ventures in its Script." <u>USA Today</u> July 14, 1997: 3B.

(13) Nathan, Paul, "Two Black Novels – Harpo Optioned the Rights to Dorothy West's Book 'The Wedding' and HarperPerennial Paid $185,000 for A.J. Verdelle's Novel 'The Good Negress'." <u>Publisher's Weekly</u> April 10, 1995: 17.

(14) Editors, "Harpo Films, Oprah Winfrey's Production Division, Has Optioned the Rights to 'Keepers of the House'." <u>Broadcasting and Cable</u> August 14, 1995: 56.

(15) Editors, "Oprah Winfrey's Harpo Films Will Produce Six Made-For-TV Movies." <u>Broadcasting and Cable</u> May 29, 1995: 32.

(16) Coe, Steve, "Winfrey Signs Film Deal With Disney." <u>Broadcasting and Cable</u> November 6, 1995: 58.

CHAPTER NINE
Bibliography

Coe, Steve, "Winfrey Signs Film Deal with Disney." *Broadcasting and Cable*. November 6, 1995: 58.

Editors, "ABC and Harpo Films." *Mediaweek*. May 29, 1995: 9.

Editors, "The Forbes 400." *Forbes*. October 16, 1995: 272.

Editors, "The Forbes 400." *Forbes*. October 14, 1996: 295.

Editors, "Harpo Films, Oprah Winfrey's Production Division, Has Optioned the Rights to 'Keepers of the House'." *Broadcasting and Cable*. August 14, 1995: 56.

Editors, *Hoover's Guide to Media Companies*. New York: Hoovers Business Press, 1996.

Editors, "Oprah Winfrey's Harpo Films Will Produce Six Made-For-TV Movies – Contract With ABC-TV." *Broadcasting and Cable*. May 29, 1995: 32.

Flint, Joe, "Winfrey's Harpo, ABC Pact for 6 Pix – Capital Cities/ABC Signs Three-Year Contract With Oprah Winfrey's Harpo Entertainment Group to Produce Six Made-for-TV Movies." *Variety*. May 29, 1995: 23.

Freeman, Michael, "Oprah Winfrey's Harpo Inc. Extends Contract with King World Productions." *Mediaweek*. March 21, 1994: 16.

Jensen, Elizabeth, "Oprah Winfrey and Capital Cities Sign 4-Year Deal." Wall Street Journal October 19, 1995: B8.

Mair, George, *Oprah Winfrey - The Real Story*. New York: Birch Lane, 1994.

Nathan, Paul, "Two Black Novels – Harpo Films Optioned Rights to Dorothy West's Book 'The Wedding' and HarperPerennial paid $185,000 for A.J. Verdelle's Novel 'The Good Negress." *Publisher's Weekly*. April 10, 1995: 17.

Nicholson, Lois P., *Oprah Winfrey - Entertainer*. Danbury: Chelsea House, 1994.

Phelps, Shirelle, ed., *Who's Who Among African Americans – 1996-1997*. Detroit: Gale Research, 1996.

Winfrey, Oprah, "What We All Can Do To Change TV." *TV Guide*. November 11, 1995: 12.

CHAPTER TEN
Endnotes

(1) Gordy, Berry, <u>To Be Loved - The Music, The Magic, The Memories of Motown</u> (New York: Warner, 1994), 31.

(2) Gordy, Berry, <u>To Be Loved - The Music, The Magic, The Memories of Motown</u> (New York: Warner, 1994), 140.

(3) Gordy, Berry, <u>To Be Loved - The Music, The Magic, The Memories of Motown</u> (New York: Warner, 1994), 270.

(4) Gordy, Berry, <u>To Be Loved - The Music, The Magic, The Memories of Motown</u> (New York: Warner, 1994), 390.

(5) Editors, "Tomorrow, The World." <u>Black Enterprise</u> June 1989: 188.

(6) Alexander, Keith, "Motown's Founder Sells Stake in Tunes." <u>USA Today</u> July 2, 1997: 3B.

CHAPTER TEN
Bibliography

Alexander, Keith, "Motown's Founder Sells Stake in Tunes." <u>USA Today</u> July 2, 1997: 3B.

Barol, Barry and David Friendly, "Motown's 25 Years of Soul." *Newsweek.* May 23, 1983: 75-76.

Bianco, David, *Heat Wave: The Motown Fact Book.* Ann Arbor: Pierian, 1988.

Brown, Ann, "Soul for Sale." *Black Enterprise.* October 1997: 22.

Davis, Sharon, *Motown: The History.* New York: Guiness, 1988.

Editors, "No Town Like Motown." *Newsweek.* March 22, 1965: 92.

Editors, "Triumph of a Stay-at-Home." *Ebony.* February 1966: 32-39.

Editors, "Tomorrow, The World." *Black Enterprise* June 1989: 187-196.

Gordy, Berry, *To Be Loved - The Music, The Memories of Motown.* New York: Warner, 1994.

Johnson, Herschel, "Motown: The Sound of Success." *Black Enterprise.* June 1974: 71-80.

Nelson, George, *Where Did Our Love Go? : The Rise and Fall of the Motown Sound.* New York: St. Martin's Press, 1985.

Taraborelli, J. Randy, *Motown: Hot Wax, City Cool, and Solid Gold.* Garden City: Doubleday, 1986.

Waller, Don, *The Motown Story.* New York: C. Scribner, 1985.

Woods, Nadra, "How Motown Made Millions in Music." *Sepia.* July 1971: 34-37.

CHAPTER ELEVEN
Endnotes

(1) Alston, Roland, "North Carolina Mutual's Policy for Growth," <u>Black Enterprise</u> June 1990: 218.

(2) Porter, David and Rosalyn Gist, "North Carolina Mutual – Out in Front and Running," <u>Black Enterprise</u> June 1981: 167.

(3) Editors, "N.C. Mutual Reaches the Heights – Dedication of New 12-Story Home Office Building Marks Firm's 67th Year of Growth," <u>Ebony</u> June 1966: 155.

(4) Editors, "White Markets for a Black Insurer – Kennedy's N.C. Mutual Signs Up the Blue Chips. Seeking White Salesmen," <u>Business Week</u> November 11, 1972: 66.

(5) Porter, David and Rosalyn Gist, "North Carolina Mutual – Out in Front and Running," <u>Black Enterprise</u> June 1981: 167.

(6) Editors, "White Markets for a Black Insurer – Kennedy's N.C. Mutual Signs Up the Blue Chips. Seeking White Salesmen," <u>Business Week</u> November 11, 1972: 68.

(7) Alston, Roland, "North Carolina Mutual's Policy for Growth," <u>Black Enterprise</u> June 1990: 216.

(8) Alston, Roland, "North Carolina Mutual's Policy for Growth," <u>Black Enterprise</u> June 1990: 216.

(9) Alston, Roland, "North Carolina Mutual's Policy for Growth," <u>Black Enterprise</u> June 1990: 218.

(10) Alston, Roland, "North Carolina Mutual's Policy for Growth," <u>Black Enterprise</u> June 1990: 216.

(11) Alston, Roland, "North Carolina Mutual's Policy for Growth," <u>Black Enterprise</u> June 1990: 214.

(12) McCoy, Frank, "Crunch Time for Bert Collins - North Carolina Mutual's CEO is Shrewd. But Can He Inspire the Innovations Needed to Keep His Insurance Firm Competitive?," <u>Black Enterprise</u> November 1993: 90.

CHAPTER ELEVEN
Bibliography

Alston, Roland, "North Carolina Mutual's Policy for Growth." *Black Enterprise*. June 1990: 214-218.

Bennett, Lerone Jr., "Money, Merchants, Markets: The Quest for Economic Security." *Ebony*. February 1974: 66-78.

Editors, "World's Biggest Negro Business – With $50 Million in Assets, 654,000 Customers, North Carolina Mutual is Top U.S. Firm." *Ebony*. September 1955: 35-39.

Editors, "N.C. Mutual Reaches the Heights – Dedication of New 12-Story Home Office Building Marks Firm's 67th Year of Growth." *Ebony*. June 1966: 151-158.

Editors, "White Markets for a Black Insurer – Kennedy's N.C. Mutual Signs Up the Blue Chips. Seeking White Salesmen." *Business Week*. November 11, 1972: 66 -68.

Franklin, John Hope and August Meyer, eds., *Black Leaders of the Twentieth Century*. Urbana: University of Illinois, 1982.

Ingham, John N. and Lynn B. Feldman, *African-American Business Leaders - A Biographical Dictionary*. Westport: Greenwood, 1994.

Jacobs, Sylvia, *Dictionary of American Negro Biography*. New York: Norton, 1982.

Kennedy, William J. Jr., *The North Carolina Mutual Story: A Symbol of Progress, 1898-1970*. Durham: North Carolina Mutual, 1970.

McCoy, Frank, "Crunch Time for Bert Collins - North Carolina Mutual's CEO is shrewd. But can he inspire the innovations needed to keep his insurance firm competitive?" *Black Enterprise*. November 1993: 89-92.

Phelps, Shirelle, ed., *Who's Who Among African Americans: 1996-1997*. Detroit: Gale Research, 1996.

Porter, David and Rosalyn Gist, "North Carolina Mutual – Out in Front and Running." *Black Enterprise*. June 1981: 167-170.

Simmons, Judy, "North Carolina Mutual: How One Family Insured Its Place in the Business." *Black Enterprise*. December 1979: 57-58.

Weare, Walter B., *Black Business in the New South: A Social History of the North Carolina Mutual Life Insurance Company*. Urbana: University of Illinois, 1973.

CHAPTER TWELVE
Endnotes

(1) Chinyelu, Mamadou, "Carver Buys Bank Branch." <u>Black Enterprise</u> March 1991: 11.

(2) Smith, Franklin, "Carver Federal hires Thomas Clark, N. Y. Regulator, as Chief Executive." <u>American Banker</u> January 5, 1995: 7.

(3) Editors, "Carver Federal Offering Mastercard and Visa." <u>American Banker</u> April 2, 1996: 12.

(4) Amdorfer James B., "Carver Federal Offers SBA Lending Services." *American Banker*. September 16, 1996: 8.

(5) Wyatt, Edward, "Leading Bank in Harlem Faces Hostile Takeover; Group Seeks One-Third of Carver Federal." <u>New York Times</u> July 29, 1996: B3.

(8) O'Hara, Terence, "Carver's Board Officially Rejects Takeover Bid by Wall Streeter." <u>American Banker</u> August 23, 1996: 6.

(7) Wyatt, Edward, "Carver Bank Stockholders Approve Reorganization; Takeover Proponent is No-Show in Harlem." <u>New York Times</u> July 30, 1996: B3.

(8) Conrad, Cecilia, "Deciphering Wall Street's Alphabet Soup." <u>Black Enterprise</u> October 1997: 26.

(9) Conrad, Cecilia, "Deciphering Wall Street's Alphabet Soup." <u>Black Enterprise</u> October 1997: 26.

CHAPTER TWELVE
Bibliography

Arndorfer, James B., "Carver Federal Offers SBA Lending Services." *American Banker*. September 16, 1996: 8.

Atlas, Riva, "Bargain Thrifts – Long Island Bancorp, Community Savings FA, FSF Financial, and Carver Federal are Savings and Loan Stocks Recommended by Researcher Neil Godsey." *Forbes*. April 24, 1995: 406.

Chinyelu, Mamadou, "Carver Buys Bank Branch." *Black Enterprise*. March 1991: 11.

Conrad, Cecilia, "Deciphering Wall Street's Alphabet Soup." *Black Enterprise*. October 1997: 26.

Editors, "Carver Approves Plan for Holding Company." *American Banker*. April 3, 1996; 7.

Editors, "Carver Federal Offering MasterCard and Visa – Carver Federal Savings Bank Markets First Credit Cards." *American Banker*. April 2, 1996: 12.

Editors, "Carver Shareholders Back Reorganization." *American Banker*. August 8, 1996: 7.

Fairley, Juliette, "A New Lease on Banking - Under New Leadership, Carver Federal Savings Bank Digs in its Heels for the Long Tern by Opening a Mortgage and Small Business Lending Center." *Black Enterprise*. June 1996: 174-181.

Gabriel, Frederick, "Harlem Thrift Carving Small Business Niches." *Crain's New York Business*. October 30, 1995: 15.

Leuchter, Miriam, "Black S&L Endures, But Not By Lending." *Crain's New York Business*. April 19, 1993: 3-4.

Milne, Emile, "Thirty Years Financing the Family - Carver Federal Savings Still Strengthens the Black Family with Home Mortgages, but Caught up in a Changing Urban Scene, Now Competes Vigorously for General Market." *Black Enterprise*. June 1979: 187-193.

Norris, Floyd, "A Bank Sells Sotck and is Hit." <u>The New York Times</u> October 27, 1994: C4.

O'Hara, Terence, "Carver's Board Officially Rejects Takeover Bid by Wall Streeter," *American Banker*. August 23, 1996: 6.

O'Hara, Terence, "Corporate Raider Bidding for Control of Minority-Owned N.Y. Thrift – Joseph Curry Tries to Acquire 35% Stake of Carver Federal Savings Bank." *American Banker*. July 31, 1996: 14.

Smith, Franklin, "Carver Federal Earnings Drop in Quarter." *American Banker*. February 24, 1995: 7.

Smith, Franklin, "Carver Federal Hires Thomas Clark, N.Y. Regulator, as Chief Executive." *American Banker*. January 5, 1995: 7.

Smith, Franklin, "For Harlem Thrift, Housing Spells Success." *American Banker*. May 6, 1992: 1, 8-9.

Wyatt, Edward, "Carver Bank Stockholders Approve Reorganization; Takeover Proponent is No-Show in Harlem." The New York Times. July 30, 1996: B3.

Wyatt, Edward, "Leading Bank in Harlem Faces Hostile Takeover – Group Seeks One-Third of Carver Federal." The New York Times. July 29, 1996: B3.

CHAPTER THIRTEEN
Endnotes

(1) Poinsett, Alex, "From Plasterer to Plutocrat – Multi-Millionaire Herman J. Russell of Atlanta shows how the 'system can be had'." Ebony May 1973: 89.

(2) Poinsett, Alex, "From Plasterer to Plutocrat – Multi-Millionaire Herman J. Russell of Atlanta shows how the 'system can be had'." Ebony May 1973: 89.

(3) Poinsett, Alex, "From Plasterer to Plutocrat – Multi-Millionaire Herman J. Russell of Atlanta shows how the 'system can be had'." Ebony May 1973: 90.

(4) Poinsett, Alex, "From Plasterer to Plutocrat – Multi-Millionaire Herman J. Russell of Atlanta shows how the 'system can be had'." Ebony May 1973: 90.

(5) Editors, "The Quiet Giant – Little known despite his influence, Herman Russell is both Horatio Alger and *eminence noir* of Atlanta's black community." *Atlanta Magazine*. May 1974: 147.

(6) Editors, "The Quiet Giant – Little known despite his influence, Herman Russell is both Horatio Alger and *eminence noir* of Atlanta's black community." *Atlanta Magazine*. May 1974: 198.

(7) Poinsett, Alex, "From Plasterer to Plutocrat – Multi-Millionaire Herman J. Russell of Atlanta shows how the 'system can be had'." Ebony May 1973: 88.

(8) Editors, "The Quiet Giant – Little known despite his influence, Herman Russell is both Horatio Alger and *eminence noir* of Atlanta's black community." *Atlanta Magazine*. May 1974: 147.

(9) Editors, "The Quiet Giant – Little known despite his influence, Herman Russell is both Horatio Alger and *eminence noir* of Atlanta's black community." *Atlanta Magazine*. May 1974: 196.

(10) Edmond, Alfred, Jr., "The Making of an Olympic City." *Black Enterprise*. January 1991: 39.

(11) Editors, "The Quiet Giant – Little known despite his influence, Herman Russell is both Horatio Alger and *eminence noir* of Atlanta's black community." *Atlanta Magazine*. May 1974: 200.

CHAPTER THIRTEEN
Bibliography

Editors, "H. J. Russell & Company Names New Vice Chairman and CEO." *Jet*.
    December 23, 1996: 34.

Editors, "The Quiet Giant – Little known despite his influence, Herman Russell is both
    Horatio Alger and *eminence noir* of Atlanta's black community." *Atlanta Magazine*.
    May 1974: 146-147.

Edmond, Alfred, Jr., "The Making of an Olympic City." *Black Enterprise*. January
    1991: 37-42.

Ingham, John N., and Lynne B. Feldman, *African-American Business Leaders -
    A Biographical Dictionary*. Westport: Greenwood, 1994.

Low, Augustus and Virgil A. Clift, *Encyclopedia of Black America*. New York City:
    McGraw-Hill, 1981.

Phelps, Shirelle, ed., *Who's Who Among African-Americans – 1996-1997*. Detroit: Gale
    Research, 1996.

Poinsett, Alex, "From Plasterer to Plutocrat – Multi-Millionaire Herman J. Russell of
    Atlanta shows how the 'system can be had'." *Ebony*. May 1973: 85-96.

Smith, Eric L. and Paula M. White, "The Urge to Merge." *Black Enterprise*.
    October 1997: 19.